Explorations
in the
Biology of Language

EDWARD WALKER, Editor

The Massachusetts Institute of Technology
Work Group in the Biology of Language

Bradford Books, Publishers   Montgomery, Vermont   db

Printed in the United States of America
Library of Congress Catalog Card Number 78-18352
ISBN 0-89706-000-8

Library of Congress Cataloging in Publication Data
appear on the last printed page of this book

First Edition

Contents

Preface

The impetus for this book arose from a series of informal discussions held at MIT within a group that included linguists, psychologists, and biologists. The theme that brought this group together can be stated straightforwardly.

There exists in all normal human beings a cognitive structure that expresses itself in the performance of language, which is a form of behavior unique to human beings. Recent developments in linguistics and psycholinguistics indicate that all human languages have in common certain features that can be interpreted in terms of universal grammar. Furthermore, normal human beings acquire language at a very early age in a developmental sequence whose regularity suggests the unfolding of an internally specified program in interaction with environmentally available language stimuli. These properties of language suggest that human beings have a species-specific innate capacity for language. It is evident that, in biological terms, the concept of an innate capacity must be equated with that of a genetically programmed structure.

It is apparent that human cognition is dominated by language. Most conscious cognitive activities, whether active or passive, are translated by the adult human being into linguistic constructs. Conversely, language deprivation has devastatingly deleterious effects on all cognitive performance. Either human cognition is "filtered" through a linguistic channel or, more likely, the capacity for language is an intrinsic and probably dominant component of the cognitive apparatus of *Homo sapiens*. It may even be suggested that the biological invention of language and its genetic improvement have been the driving forces for the catastrophic growth of the human brain to its present size within a few million years.

These speculations, whose antecedents are embodied in Eric Lenneberg's book, *Biological Foundations of Language* (Wiley, 1967), led the group to consider how questions of the existence and structure of a biological language program could be approached scientifically. Ideally the approach should be that of developmental physiological genetics: description of the function of an organ, analysis of its development, and identification of the genetic determinants whose activity is specifically operative in the unfolding of the program.

It seemed that current linguistic theory provided a sufficiently rich and elaborated formal framework to make it possible to raise meaningful questions about the biological bases of the cognitive mechanisms involved in the acquisition and use of language. Such hypotheses can be developed only from a thorough understanding of the relevant advances not only in linguistics and psycholinguistics but also in neurology, neurobiology, and genetics. Thus we hoped to be able to determine the feasibility of a concerted effort in this domain and to begin to develop testable hypotheses within it.

The difficulties of such an inquiry are obvious, ranging from those which are common to all human genetics (in fact, behavioral genetics is at present one of the least advanced areas of biology) to others specifically related to psychological and neurological experimentation with human beings. It was the group's feeling that significant progress could be made at this time in understanding the biology of language by rethinking the body of accumulated information on this topic from the perspective of the latest advances in linguistic theory.

The requisites for formulating a plausible research program appeared to be, first, a careful critical survey of the relevant findings in the literature and, second, the generation of an interdisciplinary professionalism within a group of interested scientists. These requisites were put forward by several members of the informal MIT group at a workshop held at MIT's Endicott House early in 1975 under the aegis of the Royaumont Center for A Science of Man (Paris), created by the late Professor Jacques Monod. They were then incorporated into a proposal submitted by Carey, Chomsky and Luria to the Sloan Foundation. A grant from that foundation and one from the MIT Administration made it possible to establish, in July, 1975, the Working Group in the Biology of Language. The group met regularly during the following academic year. The initial manuscript was completed in 1976. It is now felt that the material, published in book form, will be of interest to a number of investigators in related fields.

Morris Halle
Salvador E. Luria

Participants
Susan Carey, Ph.D.; Massachusetts Institute of Technology
Noam Chomsky, Ph.D; Massachusetts Institute of Technology
Kenneth Forster, Ph.D; Monash University
Morris Halle, Ph.D; Massachusetts Institute of Technology
Mary-Louise Kean, Ph.D; University of California at Irvine
Barbara Von Eckardt Klein, Ph.D; Yale University
Salvador E. Luria, M.D.; Massachusetts Institute of Technology
David Rosenfield, M.D.; Baylor University Medical Center
Edward Walker, Ph.D; Massachusetts Institute of Technology

Introduction

What Is the Biology of Language?

BARBARA VON ECKARDT KLEIN

A Preliminary View

Although the view that language is, in some important sense, a biological phenomenon has a long history [see Marx (1967)], as a scientific discipline biology of language is in its infancy. The first systematic description of the field as we shall understand it did not appear until 1967 with the publication of Eric H. Lenneberg's book, *Biological Foundations of Language.* Since then several major conferences have been held (among them Origins and Evolution of Language, sponsored by the New York Academy of Science, Sept. 22-25, 1975; and Psychology and Biology of Language and Thought: A Symposium in Memory of Eric H. Lenneberg, sponsored by the Department of Psychology, Cornell University, May 20-23, 1976); a new journal, *Brain and Language* (ed. Harry A. Whitaker, Academic Press), has appeared; and in general, researchers with a variety of interests have begun to realize that they are working within a common framework.

What is this common framework? Like most scientific disciplines, biology of language was born out of curiosity over a set of observations, coupled with a theoretical commitment as to how that set of observations ought to be understood. For the most part the observations are ordinary ones; only one (the last)

1

is the product of systematic linguistic inquiry. They include the following:

1. Although many creatures communicate in various ways, only man appears to speak and understand language.
2. Children develop the ability to use language at a very young age with incredible ease and in very regular ways.
3. Despite their diversity, human languages have certain fundamental features in common.

Each of these observations raises a question or set of questions which can be addressed by a program of empirical research. We may ask, for example: Why is it that only man appears to speak and understand language? How is it that children acquire language with such ease? Why is the course of acquisition so regular, despite the radical variation in child-rearing practices, linguistic experience, and so forth? What accounts for the underlying uniformity of all human languages?

There is no *a priori* reason why the account we provide for any one of these observations should have anything to do with the account we provide for any other. It was precisely Lenneberg's vision [Lenneberg (1967)] that the answers to each of the above questions ought to be part of a common discipline, a discipline united by its basic commitment to man as a biological creature. He saw in each of the observations a case of uniformity despite diversity: uniformity in the course of language acquisition despite differences in the child's linguistic experience; uniformity in man's linguistic capacity despite vast individual variation; and uniformity in the structure of natural languages despite cultural and racial diversity. His basic insight was that in each of these cases, the uniformity was due to man's biological makeup and, ultimately, to his species-specific genetic endowment. In Lenneberg's view, what accounts for a man's ability to use language is that his mind is constituted in a certain way. What accounts for a child's rapid and systematic acquisition of language is that his mind develops and matures in a certain way. Finally, what accounts for the uniformity of natural languages is that the human mind imposes constraints on what can count as a possible language. All (normal) members of the human species possess similar linguistic ability, acquire language similarly, and speak languages with similar underlying structures for the same reason—because in the relevant respects the mind of one man is much like the mind of another. And this is because uniformities in human mental structure are ultimately controlled in the same way as uniformities in human bodily structure—by the unfolding of the human genetic program. Thus the various questions about human language are replaced by what is essentially one question: what is the genetic program underlying the uniformity in human language capacity, the course of language acquisition in children, and the apparent diversity of natural languages?

What must a discipline be like whose primary research aim is to address that question? Certainly its research program must be so structured that, given what we know about language, the mind, and human physiology and genetics, it becomes possible to address the question scientifically. Let us see what that implies. We know that the mechanisms of genetic control operate, roughly, at the level of cell physiology. We also know that what is causally responsible for complex cognitive behavior on the part of a human being is some sort of structure inside his head. In order not to beg questions about the appropriate level of description for this structure, we will give it a neutral name—the "language-responsible cognitive structure," or LRCS for short. Any detailed theory of the genetic regulation of LRCS must describe LRCS as a network of neurons with various cytoarchitectural properties. Thus a biology of language requires a neurological theory of LRCS.

That is not all that is required, however. Not only must our ultimate biological theory of language make contact with mechanisms of genetic regulation, it must also make contact with human behavior. This requires a theory of LRCS at a far more abstract level; not a detailed neuronal map but a theory of the functional organization of LRCS. The distinction is similar to the distinction between hardware and software in a computer. An artifactual computational device, like a computer, can be described both abstractly as an information-flow mechanism and physically as an electronic device made of circuit components. Human cognitive structures can also be described both functionally and in terms of the neural apparatus by which that functional description is realized. It is important to note that by a "functional description" we do not mean primarily a description of a system in terms of its purpose (e.g., the function of the heart is to pump blood) but rather a description of *how* the system functions. There are at least two reasons why a more abstract description of LRCS is necessary. First, people clearly differ in the details of their neural apparatus, just as they differ in the specific shape, size, and internal structure of other bodily parts. There are, however, important uniformities. In the case of the brain, it is likely that these uniformities will become apparent only at a functional level of description. Details of neuronal hookup may vary enormously from individual to individual; what will be constant is what the brain is capable of doing, how it does it, and roughly speaking, what anatomical part of the brain does what—in other words, the anatomical organization of its functions. Second, although a neural theory of LRCS may, in principle, be capable of explaining human language capacity, in some philosophical sense of "explaining" (for example, the relevant observations will be deducible from the theory), it will not "shed light" on the nature of human language capacity or lead to greater understanding of it. For such a theory will be far too complex.

An analogy may help. Let us say we wish to account for the behavior of a computer that plays chess. We are shown two descriptions (theories) of the computer's structure. One is a wiring diagram from which the machine could actually be constructed; the other is a description of its functional organization, referring to how it codes various chess moves, what computations it performs to decide which move to make, what the sequence of information flow is, and so on. If the question we are addressing is: how is it that this device can play chess? the wiring diagram is clearly of little use, whereas the functional characterization would be enormously illuminating.

A biology of language thus must encompass within its disciplinary boundaries not only a theory of genetic regulation but also a neurology and psychology of language. Although Lenneberg talked about the cognitive structure responsible for language, he had little to say about the sort of psychological theory most appropriate for biology of language. In our view, the best available theory of the human mind treats it as a computational device in which understanding language, producing language, thinking, remembering, deciding, judging, etc., are all regarded as computational processes over some sort of internal representation of a sentence, thought, idea, decision, or whatever. At the psychological level of description, a person's LRCS then consists of a representation of that person's knowledge of his language (which takes the form of a grammar, according to contemporary linguistic theory) and of the various processing mechanisms for utilizing that knowledge. It is the job of linguistic theory to provide us with a description of a person's knowledge of his language; it is the job of psycholinguistics to provide us with a description of the processing mechanisms by which that knowledge is put to use. Although neurological evidence may lead to insights as to the most appropriate functional theory and certainly must be consistent with such theories, in general, research must proceed from psychology to neurology. The reason is simple. We will not be in a position to discover how LRCS is realized neurologically until we know what is so realized. In other words, evidence of the neurological realization of LRCS cannot be properly evaluated except in the context of linguistic and psycholinguistic models of LRCS. This will be a constant theme in the explorations which follow.

Characterizing a Discipline

Implicit in our discussion thus far is the suggestion that the research program of a field is best defined in terms of the questions that this program addresses [see Bromberger (1963)]. We are interested in describing as precisely as we can a feasible research program for biology of language, as well as evaluating current progress in the field. Thus it is extremely important to delineate the research questions of biology of language with as much care as possible.

Questions in science do not occur in a conceptual vacuum. What they are about is always conceived against the background of a set of beliefs whose truth is taken for granted, at least for the purposes of the inquiry. Thus to understand the questions which constitute biology of language, we must understand something about its background assumptions and domain of investigation. By the domain of investigation, we mean, roughly, that aspect of reality chosen for investigation by practitioners of the discipline, that is, that aspect of reality which theories within the discipline are theories *of.* Such domains are never simply concrete slices of the world, for they involve abstraction and idealization in their specification. The rough outlines of this specification are laid down by the background assumptions of the field.

The background assumptions of a discipline are a set of empirical hypotheses which give rise to the questions central to that discipline. This relation of "giving-rise-to" is best illuminated by example. According to Luria [(1973), p. 34], the recognition that genes have an internal structure, and in particular a structure which can be rearranged by genetic recombination, was "a momentous advance in the history of genetics," marking the transition from classical to molecular genetics. Why should the introduction of a rather trivial-sounding assumption make such a difference? The reason is that before the introduction of this assumption the gene was viewed as a hypothetical construct posited in order to account for the laws of mendelian genetics. If we assume, however, that the gene has a structure, it is natural to raise the question: what is that structure? and more precisely: what is that structure in biochemical terms? It was the attempt to answer this question that led to the discovery of DNA and the double-helix structure as the biochemical basis for heredity.

While a discipline is under investigation, its background assumptions are often not known to be true, although investigators committed to the discipline presumably would wager in favor of their truth. Confirmation of such assumptions often can come only by way of finding answers to the questions to which they give rise. Having discovered what the chemical structure of the gene is, *that* the gene has a structure is thereby confirmed.

To be considered a background assumption of a field of investigation, an empirical hypothesis ought to satisfy the following desiderata: (1) expert practitioners of the field should subscribe to it; (2) it should give rise to reasonably precise research questions; and (3) if it proves to be false, the research program of the field should be seriously undermined. The reason for (3) is worth spelling out. A background assumption has the logical status of a presupposition of the questions to which it gives rise: if the assumption is false, the questions have no answer; hence, any research program dedicated to answering such questions cannot in principle be carried out. Let us suppose, for instance—to stay with our gene example—that the assumption that the gene had structure had been false. Then clearly any research program dedicated to determining that structure would have been doomed to failure.

It is worth noting that we have oversimplified the situation somewhat. A scientific discipline has more than one set of background assumptions. It has, in fact, a hierarchical structure of assumptions, questions, and research programs nested within each other. One basic assumption of biology of language is obviously that a language-responsible cognitive structure exists. To investigate what the structure of LRCS is at a psychological level, certain further assumptions must be made about LRCS which dictate the sort of psychological research we ought to undertake. One such assumption is that LRCS is a computational device. Within the framework of a program to characterize LRCS functionally as a computational device, we can make the additional assumption that this device contains a representation of a person's knowledge of his language. If any of these assumptions turn out to be false, the research program built on that assumption will be thereby undermined. The field itself is undermined only if the most basic background assumptions turn out to be false.

A More Precise Characterization

Formulating a set of background assumptions for biology of language poses a considerable challenge both because the field is undeveloped and because there is little evidence regarding the theoretical commitments of the few practitioners. We shall take our inspiration from Lenneberg's writings, but what follows is far more a rational reconstruction of his views than an exposition.

We suggest that the following hypotheses have the status of background assumptions for biology of language.

B(0): What accounts for a person's capacity for language is that he possesses a language-responsible cognitive structure. Although the structure of LRCS may vary somewhat from speaker to speaker, certain universal features are common to the LRCS of each normal individual.

If one did not subscribe to B(0), one might deny that a person's capacity for language is accounted for by his possession of any sort of structure at all. This, however, seems a very implausible view. A more reasonable position might be to deny that this language-responsible structure is appropriately characterized in cognitive terms, that is, in terms of such notions as information processing and representation. This is presumably the position that a behaviorist like B. F. Skinner would take [see Skinner (1950)]. Yet another view might deny simply the last part of the assumption, namely, that the LRCS of each normal individual is characterized by certain universal features. Since in this view, the LRCS of each individual would be idiosyncratic, a science proposing to discover the universal features of this structure would be impossible.

One of the commonest questions raised about LRCS is the extent to which it is language-specific. Lenneberg seems to have adopted various positions on this question. On the one hand, he argues strongly for the independence of LRCS from general intelligence [Lenneberg (1964), pp. 76-81]. On the other, he suggests that language capacity ought to be regarded as a manifestation of other more general cognitive abilities such as categorizing, problem solving, and forming generalizations [Lenneberg (1967), p. 372]. The latter view, in fact, is included in his discussion of the basic premises of biology of language. Note that the latter hypothesis is precisely the sort that ought not to be included as a background assumption of the field. For should it turn out to be false, that is, should it turn out that LRCS is language-specific, biology of language would certainly *not* become impossible. Like the nature-nurture controversy, the debate over the language specificity of LRCS will probably not be resolved entirely in favor of either opposing view. Although it is probable that language learning is not a simple manifestation of general learning and that, hence, the principles that govern the *development* of LRCS are domain-specific [Chomsky (1975)] insofar as LRCS includes the processing apparatus necessary for language behavior, it will include such non-domain-specific apparatus as memory buffers and accessing and retrieval mechanisms. The question of interest is not: is LRCS language-specific? but: which components of it are language-specific?

The assumption that there exists a cognitive structure responsible for a person's capacity for language gives rise to research questions of the form: what particular feature or component of a person's LRCS accounts for some aspect of human language capacity? How we specify the aspect under consideration is not determined *a priori* but is a problem to be solved by linguists and psycholinguists in the course of theory construction. Data that are relevant for one kind of theory are not necessarily relevant for another.

> B(1): Considerable uniformity exists in the onset time and course of language acquisition among normal individuals. These universal features of language acquisition are controlled to a significant extent by maturational changes in LRCS.

That a person's language-responsible cognitive structure develops as he undergoes the process of language acquisition seems relatively uncontroversial, since babies are not born knowing how to talk. What is peculiar to the approach taken by biology of language is the assumption that the developmental history is, to a significant extent, internally regulated. We can distinguish various developmental stages or states of a person's LRCS, starting with the state at the time of birth and terminating with a mature state. The assumption, then, is that the transition from one developmental state to the next is largely under internal control. (The developmental sequence need not be regarded as discontinuous, although there may be abrupt changes in the behavior of children as they mature.)

Lenneberg recognized that this assumption runs directly counter to the basic tenet of most behaviorist theories of language learning. Behaviorist theories hold that the developmental course of the structure responsible for language ability is determined (either primarily or completely) by the history of *inputs* to the organism, i.e., its experience. Our view is not that environmental inputs (what Chomsky calls "the primary linguistic data") have nothing to do with the eventual structure of a person's LRCS in its mature state. It is rather that the mature structure results from an *interaction* of the primary linguistic data and the internally specified genetic program, for after all a child does learn the language it hears. We take the nature of this interaction to be fundamentally the same as that which determines an organism's morphology and physiology. The form and functions of an organism ordinarily are not imposed from the outside; they develop from a combination of genetic regulation and environmental influence. Although the mechanism for such interaction is virtually unknown, animal studies have taught us various ways in which it can occur. Environmental stimuli can trigger genetically specified patterns of development, or they can play a more substantive role by determining the values for parameters left partially unspecified by the internal program.

B(1) gives rise to two questions. First, which features of language acquisition are shared by all normally developing individuals? And second, which sort of maturational changes in LRCS control the appearance of some particular characteristic of the child's linguistic ability at some particular time?

B(2): The physical realization of LRCS is a brain structure. This realization is sufficiently uniform among neurologically normal individuals that an (idealized) description of LRCS as a neural structure is possible.

At least five levels of description of LRCS are of central importance for biology of language. LRCS can be described in terms of

1. The information or knowledge stored in long-term memory required for a person to exercise his language capacity.
2. The sequence of computational operations performed on 1 when a person exercises any particular aspect of his language capacity (such as object naming); such a description is akin to a computer program for doing some particular task.
3. The functional components which permit execution of the programs described in 2; at this level, LRCS is decomposed into functional parts such as a short-term memory, a lexicon, a mechanism for lexical look-up, a grammar, or a syntactic analyzer.
4. The physical localization in the body of the various functional components described in 3; at this level, we are essentially concerned with identifying the functional components of LRCS with particular (anatomically specified) structures.
5. The mechanisms which allow the physical structures identified in 4 to perform the functions specified in 3.

The force of assumption B(2) is that the physical structures which constitute the functional components of LRCS are parts of the brain and that in each neurologically normal individual, brain structures of the same sort perform the same functions. Furthermore, it is assumed that the physiological mechanisms whereby these functions are performed are essentially similar. B(2) gives rise to questions of the following form: What is the neurological basis of some component of LRCS?

B(3): The possession of LRCS is a species-specific trait; that is, the universal features of LRCS (both structural and developmental) are controlled by genetic factors which are characteristic of every normal member of the human species.

The claim that language is species-specific is subject to two interpretations. The weak interpretation is that the genetic factors which control LRCS and, hence, the universal features of LRCS are characteristic of every normal member of the human species. In other words, no claim is made about any other species. The strong interpretation is that such factors and features characterize *only* members of the human species (i.e., not chimpanzees, birds, dolphins, bees, or any other likely candidate). There is no evidence that Lenneberg had the stronger claim in mind, and even if he had, there are good reasons not to make the stronger claim a background assumption of biology of language. Assigning it such a fundamental status would have two consequences. First, current studies on the "language" capacities of chimpanzees and other non-human animals would have to be considered outside the framework of biology of language, since their aim is to investigate whether or not the strong claim is true. Second, if the strong claim turned out to be false, biology of language as a field of investigation ought to become impossible. The latter consequence seems especially undesirable. The focus of investigation of biology of language is the study of the structure, developmental pattern, and genetic regulation of LRCS in human beings. The question whether LRCS has anything significant in common with cognitive or brain structures in other species is interesting but by no means central to the discipline.

The Research Program

We are now in a position to identify the basic research goals of biology of language:

R(0): To develop and confirm hypotheses regarding the functional organization of LRCS in its mature state, with particular attention to its universal features.

R(1): To develop and confirm hypotheses regarding the developmental course of LRCS from its initial to mature state.

R(2): To develop and confirm hypotheses regarding the neurological realization of LRCS at its various stages of development.

R(3): To develop and confirm hypotheses regarding the genetic control of various aspects of LRCS (both structural and developmental).

We believe that a research program predicated on these goals is feasible. That is, we believe that we have available adequate theoretical and methodological apparatus to pursue these goals, within the constraints of ethical human experimentation. Current work in linguistics and psycholinguistics provides us with a preliminary but well-articulated framework for engaging in fruitful research on the nature and development of LRCS as a cognitive structure, i.e., R(0) and R(1). The nature of this framework is sketched in the second part of this chapter.

Neurological techniques, especially those related to the study of individuals with neurologically based language disorders, have been used for some time to study the neurological realization of LRCS. What is required to pursue R(2) with success is both a thorough understanding of the logical relationship of linguistic and psychological theories to models of neural realization and the application of the best available cognitive hypotheses regarding LRCS to the analysis of data obtained by using such neurological techniques. The bulk of this report exemplifies the kind of work we believe needs to be done with respect to R(2). We focus, in particular, on a research paradigm central to the study of aphasia, the method of functional localization. In Chapter 2, the logic of the method is investigated in order to discover whether, and under what conditions, it can validly support theories of neural realization. It is argued that in order to develop adequate functional-localization hypotheses, an inter-disciplinary approach, involving linguistics and psycholoinguistics, is absolutely essential.

Chapters 3 and 4 adopt such an interdisciplinary approach with respect to two aphasic syndromes—Broca's aphasia and deficiencies in lexical access. In Chapter 3, it is argued that on both linguistic and psycholinguistic grounds, recent characterizations of Broca's aphasia as a language deficit involving the compromise of phonetic, phonological, syntactic, and semantic functions are untenable. It is claimed that, instead, the manifested linguistic deficits of Broca's aphasia are due to an interaction between an impaired phonological capacity and otherwise intact linguistic capacities.

In Chapter 4, a theory of the process of lexical access in normal speakers is applied to suggest functional characterizations of such aphasic deficiencies in lexical access as semantic confusions, object-naming deficits, and restricted classes of word-finding difficulties.

To illustrate further the general applicability of the framework of interdisciplinary research we develop here, Chapter 5 uses this framework to discuss a nonverbal cognitive capacity, face recognition.

Although the third goal of biology of language, R(3), is largely unattainable by present research methods, the use of behavioral genetic techniques in the domain of language deserves more attention than it has received to date. Even though we have been unable to explore the use of such studies, we believe that if they are carried out within the framework of sophisticated linguistic and psycholinguistic theories, they may shed considerable light on what aspects of LRCS are heritable.

Studying animal communication might be considered an important method for investigating the developmental, neurological, or genetic basis of language because it need not be constrained by the same kinds of ethical considerations as apply to human experimentation. Chapter 6 argues, however, that despite many claims to the contrary, studies of animal communication and attempts to teach chimpanzees to use symbol systems show little, if any, relation to research in the biology of language. The communication systems of other animals, whether they occur naturally or result from training, have only the most superficial similarities to language in their structure, use, and development; and there is little evidence that comparable cognitive structures or neural mechanisms are involved in language and in communication by other animals. Hence there is little reason to suppose that studies of such systems provide useful techniques for studying language.

Throughout the preceding discussion, we have emphasized that an essential feature of research in the biology of language is a formal characterization of the knowledge that a person's language capacity requires and the psychological processes which operate on putting that knowledge to use. In the following chapters, certain basic features of the knowledge represented in LRCS and the mechanisms employed in language behavior are assumed. The linguistic and psycholinguistic background on which these assumptions are based is described briefly in the second part of this chapter.

Introduction

The Linguistic and Psycholinguistic Background

NOAM CHOMSKY
EDWARD WALKER

The research goal R(0) defines a central part of linguistics. Without entering into details, we will sketch a general point of view concerning the nature of LRCS that has developed in modern linguistics and that we feel is not only well motivated empirically but also appropriate to the task at hand. In the course of so doing, we will introduce some concepts and terminology to be used in later exposition.

Consider the following three basic questions:

A (1) What does a person know when we say correctly that he knows a language?
   (2) How is a person able to acquire knowledge of a language?
   (3) How is knowledge of language put to use?

To these three questions we expect to find corresponding answers of the following general sort:

B (1) The person who knows a language L has developed a certain LRCS, which among other things assigns to each sentence of L a full characterization of its (linguistically determined) properties, including aspects of its sound and meaning. If this aspect of LRCS is called LRCS (L), the grammar of L, we can say that to know a language is to have developed a mental representation of its grammar.

15

(2) Like any complex structure, physical or cognitive, LRCS(L) results from an interaction of the natural endowment of the child with the environment in which it is nurtured. The child starts to acquire language in some initial cognitive state S_0 which is genetically determined and essentially invariant for the species. Some subsystem represented in S_0, call it $LRCS_0$, is the system responsible for language acquisition. $LRCS_0$ represents the contribution of "nature" to the growth of language in the individual. In acquiring knowledge of a language, the child passes through a sequence of cognitive states S_0, S_1,..., in which LRCS is correspondingly modified from $LRCS_0$ to the mature state LRCS(L).

(3) Each successive cognitive state S_i, (including in particular the cognitive state of the mature speaker) includes a performance system P (or perhaps several such systems) that incorporates LRCS(L) as one component which interacts with others. Thus putting language to use involves much more than knowing grammar.

To answer questions 1, 2, and 3 of (A) we must attempt to develop theories of LRCS(L), $LRCS_0$, and P, respectively. The following remarks elaborate these notions in turn.

We assume that LRCS(L), the grammar of the language L as represented in the mind of the person who knows L, is a system of rules and principles that *generate* the sentences of L and assign to each sentence its grammatical properties. In this sense the grammar of English generates the first sentence of this paragraph, assigning to it various properties—its phonetic structure, its analysis into words and phrases, the meanings of its subparts at various levels, the meaning of the entire expression, and so on. Actually, we assume that the properties that the grammar assigns to this sentence are abstract, in that it is an interaction of the grammar incorporated in the performance system P with other cognitive systems which determines the actual physical realization of the sentence and much of what we call its "meaning" in informal discourse.

In speaking of LRCS (English) [or of LRCS(L) for any

language L], we are already operating at a high level of abstraction and idealization. Real individuals command a variety of related linguistic systems, styles of speech used in a range of social situations. Individuals within a speech community may differ in these respects, and speech communities sometimes may vary quite widely in the systems represented within what is popularly called a single "language." In the present discussion, we abstract away from these variations and assume that the grammar of a particular language, e.g., LRCS (English), is uniformly represented as a single invariant system in the mind of each English speaker.

The grammar of a language as constructed by the linguist must be distinguished from the internally represented grammar LRCS(L). The former is a scientific theory that purports to set forth explicitly the principles of the grammar represented in the mind of the person who knows the language in question. The linguist's grammar is correct or incorrect insofar as it succeeds in capturing the properties of this internally represented grammar. Thus we say that the linguist's grammar attempts to characterize the (grammatical) *competence* of the person who knows the language. We note the important conceptual distinction between *competence*—the system of knowledge attained—and *performance*—the use of this knowledge (along with much else) in producing and understanding speech (or in reading and writing).

Here we are using the term "grammar" in a broad sense to incorporate the domains of phonetics and phonology, morphology and syntax, and such aspects of semantics as are properly assigned to the language faculty, independent of the contribution of other cognitive systems.

Turning to question A(2), we observe that language growth in individuals is marked by rapid qualitative transitions from $LRCS_0$, through a series of ever more elaborated structures, to the attainment of LRCS(L) at a relatively early age (before puberty, it appears). Following this rapid initial development, modifications of linguistic knowledge are marginal and relatively insubstantial—e.g., new vocabulary items are added throughout life. The timing and sequence of transitions from $LRCS_0$ to LRCS(L) form the subject matter of the research inquiry R(1), and it is quite probable that these transitions and their sequence are highly constrained by the genetic program of human beings.

As we have already noted, the status of $LRCS_0$ within the general initial cognitive state S_0 is an open and important question. The question is whether certain aspects of $LRCS_0$ are specific to language growth and structure or merely represent particular forms of general cognitive structures. We will assume tentatively that LRCS is a specific cognitive capacity and that it makes sense to abstract $LRCS_0$ from S_0, just as we abstract $LRCS(L)$ as a subsystem of the mature cognitive state of the individual, which must include other kinds of competencies possessed by mature individuals.

The genetically determined system $LRCS_0$ determines what counts as linguistic experience and which grammars the mind can construct based on that linguistic experience. In other words, $LRCS_0$ specifies the properties of language that are biologically necessary. These properties are to be distinguished from those that are logically necessary or accidental. For example, it is a logically necessary property of a grammar of English that its rules and principles actually generate sentences; if they did not, we would not call the system in question "a grammar of a language." It is an accidental property of the grammar of English that it generates "the horse is brown" meaning that the horse is brown; the grammar of French does not do so. It is a biologically necessary property of the grammar of English that the sentences generated and the rules that generate them must meet general conditions fixed by $LRCS_0$. It is these biologically necessary properties that are of primary interest to us. We would expect to find such properties in every domain of grammar. For example, on the level of sound structure, sentences must contain units of a narrowly circumscribed class; theories of phonetics and phonology attempt to discover which categories of sound are available for human language, the manner of organization of sound systems, and the general principles governing phonological rules. Similarly, a traditional concern of inquiry into meaning has been to discover basic semantic categories and the principles of their combination and organization. To cite a simple example of a governing principle, take the case of so-called "scattered individuals." We may conceive in our imagination of a single scattered entity consisting of all parts of horses and nothing else. Thus each horse is a part of this entity, as is each part of a horse, as is the entity consisting of the head of one horse and the tail of another, or the entity consisting of all heads of horses, etc. But natural languages do not tolerate names for such entities, even though there is no logical necessity for this to be the case, and artificial languages have been constructed that permit references to such entities freely. Natural languages use a very different principle; they resort to collective nouns, rather than to nouns designating scattered individuals. We speak of a herd of horses, but the herd is a collective with each horse as a member, not a single entity of which each horse, each limb, each combination of limbs of various horses, etc., is a part. If a horse loses a leg, we say that a member of the herd lost one of its limbs, not that the herd did so. Much current research in semantics is directed to pursuing the traditional program of determining what are sometimes called "semantic primitives," or basic semantic (thematic) relations, and the conditions they impose on the lexicon of a natural language. This too is an investigation of properties of language that are neither accidental nor logically necessary: biologically necessary properties of language.

The most far-reaching investigations of biologically necessary properties of language have no doubt been those concerned with higher levels of syntactic structure. Among these properties, if current theories of transformational grammar are near correct, are those which determine that sentences must be organized into words and phrases in a hierarchic fashion; that phrases belong to a limited class of syntactic categories (noun, verb, noun phrase, etc.), each with specific properties; and that grammatical rules fall into various fixed types (base rules determining an infinite class of abstract syntactic structures that we call "deep structures;" transformational rules applying to the deep structures in a cyclic order, from the smaller to successively larger phrases; and phonological and semantic rules that associate with the syntactic structures certain aspects of their sound and meaning, etc.).

A theory of linguistic structure will set forth explicit hypotheses with regard to the biologically necessary properties of language. Such a theory is sometimes called a theory of universal grammar or simply a "universal grammar." Thus universal grammar may be regarded as a partial theory of the initial state $LRCS_0$ which makes language acquisition possible.

The question, what are the biologically necessary properties of human language? is a typical question of science; it is, in fact, the question: what is $LRCS_0$? In contrast, the question, what is a logically necessary property of language? is a conceptual question of a different sort; it is the question: what kind of system would we call "a language"? Natural science will provide no answer to the latter question beyond determing the biologically necessary properties of human language, a task which falls within the range of natural science. The two questions are sometimes confused, leading to rather empty debates over whether one or another nonhuman or artificially constructed system (say, of communication) is or is not a "real language."

Returning to $LRCS_0$, there is good reason to suppose that its principles are highly restrictive. Obviously individuals within a given speech community acquire its language rapidly and uniformly, and the grammar acquired—i.e., $LRCS(L)$, for L, the language of this community (subject to the idealizations noted already)—is a rich and highly articulated structure, vastly underdetermined by the experience available to learners. No process of "induction," "habit formation," or "generalization" known to psychology or philosophy can relate the experience available and $LRCS(L)$. Rather, it seems that many of the specific properties of $LRCS(L)$ must be determined at $LRCS_0$, the task of the child being, in effect, to select a grammar consistent with experience and meeting the conditions of $LRCS_0$. If these conditions are restrictive and specific, it is possible for children equipped with $LRCS_0$ in their prelinguistic cognitive state to acquire a rich and complex system, and to do so uniformly, even on the basis of the limited experience available to them.

We may think of $LRCS_0$ as a function, in the mathematical sense, which maps experience onto $LRCS(L)$. It is a primary goal of linguistic research to replace a vague and metaphoric account such as the one given here with a detailed specification of the principles that constitute $LRCS_0$, thus specifying this function, at least abstractly. This enterprise is the topic of studies of universal grammar.

Turning to the final question, how is knowledge of language put to use? we note again that full competence in using language to achieve human ends involves much more than grammatical competence. Obviously, the ability to use language purposefully includes rules, principles, and conventions that determine how to convey information, how to establish social relations, how to express moods or thoughts, how to convince listeners, and so forth. We may assume that people who know a language fully have also developed a "pragmatic competence" governing its use in regard to such properties, which they use alongside the grammatical competence represented in LRCS(L). Besides this "pragmatic competence," normal speakers use a background of knowledge and beliefs about the nature of physical objects and their behavior, about human actions and their significance, and about social forms in producing and understanding sentences. And finally, the properties of memory, our emotional or physical state, our hearing, our ability to construct or analyze time-varying acoustic waves, and our concentration must affect any behavior we undertake. In short, the examples of language that we actually produce or perceive will result from an interaction of a number of cognitive systems and behavioral capacities, of which grammatical competence is only one.

However, the process of language use itself can be studied independently from its interaction with other cognitive systems in accomplishing some purpose. To do so, those psychological processes implicated in the act of using language per se must be distinguished from those implicated by the uses to which language can be put. That is to say, one must try to abstract a theory of P, a performance model, from the particular means or ends of using language which are employed in any particular instance, be it delivering a lecture, testifying in a trial, talking on the phone, or arguing with a neighbor. This is not to say that the consequences of such means or ends in language performance can be ignored or eliminated from examples of language use. In fact, the potential effects of these aspects of language use on the measures taken in an experiment or in finding examples of sentence types are just what psycholinguists or linguists "control for," informally or formally, in the conduct of their research. For example, in judging the grammaticality of (1), an experimental subject or a linguist (ideally) is not judging the truth of the sentence, its length, or the appeal of the thought expressed; nor is he offering his opinion of the sentence or its speaker. Rather he is judging whether the sentence is well or ill formed.

(1) Food production is humanity's most pressing problem.

Characterizing the ordinary process of using language certainly requires a theory of speech production and perception (or reading and writing); therefore, the linguistic aspects of visual or acoustic processing of sentences are a central concern of psycholinguistic research. However, much of the research directed at explaining the psychology of sentence comprehension and production is conducted under the assumption that at least some of the processes of normal language performance operate independently from input-output medium—as well as from the topic of discussion, the speaker's moods, etc.—to segment sentences into clauses, identify lexical items, and establish relations among the words in a sentence. For example, evidence that verbs like *know,* which can take complements, are psychologically more difficult than simple transitives like *met* comes from sources as diverse as the ease of solving written anagrams and the ability of subjects to understand time-compressed speech.

Undoubtedly there are aspects of written or spoken speech, such as intonation contour or punctuation marks, which could aid higher-level sentence processing. Obviously other cognitive capacities, particularly those involving one's knowledge of likely relationships among things in the world, *might* be implicated in such processes as well. For example, knowing the usual "spilling" relationships between "cooks" and "beans" could help in understanding (2)a to d, regardless of their superficial syntactic forms, by permitting the use of processing routines which either are independent of those for grammatical analysis or interact with grammatical analysis in some general sentence-perception process.

(2) a. The cook spilled the beans.
   b. The beans were spilled by the cook.
   c. It was the cook who spilled the beans.
   d. It was the beans that the cook spilled.

The use of such knowledge may provide the basis of everyday metaphorical extension, the resolution of ambiguity or vagueness, or the introduction of novel vocabulary items, word games, and so forth. (2)a and (2)c, taken to mean "the cook divulged a secret," are a now trite example. Unquestionably we can use such knowledge to "make sense of" strings that would be ill formed or nonsensical under an ordinary grammatical description, such as newspaper headlines, the speech of foreigners, or artfully deviant sentences like (3) and (4).

(3) 'Twas brillig, and the slithy toves did gyre and gimbal in the wabe.
(4) There's language in her eye, her cheek, her lip,
     Nay, her foot speaks; her wanton spirits look out
     At every joint and motive of her body.

But this apparent utility of background knowledge in understanding sentences contrasts with its corresponding disutility or irrelevance in understanding such sentences as (5) to (8).

(5) The man bit the dog.
(6) The doctor was treated by the patient.
(7) Martian rocks are not solid.
(8) The sparrow chased the swallow.

While knowing that the thoughts behind these examples are newsworthy may implicate knowing that dogs usually bite men, doctors usually treat patients, etc., knowing who did what to whom and thus *what* is news depends on grammatical analyses in which usual relationships of this kind are immaterial. The examples serve to demonstrate an obvious and uncontroversial point: knowledge of the world, or "context" as it is sometimes called, often gives only insufficient cues to the intrinsic formal

structure and meaning of lingustic expressions and cannot substitute in a principled way for grammatical analysis of the
relations among words in a sentence.

Furthermore, knowing what relationship must hold or is
likely to hold between words is not enough to predict the form
in which this relation will be expressed in any particular
sentence. Consequently, even a listener who assumes that the
normal "treating" relationship between a "patient" and a
"doctor" is unidirectional still will have to perceive the grammatical form in which such a relationship is expressed, both to
confirm his assumption and to understand the meaning of the
speaker's choice of form.

To construct a performance model P, we must abstract away
from the uses to which language can be put. Certainly much can
be discovered from a speaker's tone of voice, rate of speech, or
choice of words about the mood of a speaker, his intent, or his
state of mind, but a performance model attempts to make
explicit the fundamental principles and mechanisms that enter
into processing the linguistic aspects of the signal. A still richer
theory of human action might incorporate this theory of
linguistic performance, but that is another matter entirely.

What we observe in normal life and in experiments is performance. To say that grammatical competence is one component of a performance model is to say nothing more than
that a person makes use of his knowledge of language in
producing and perceiving sentences. The problem in modeling
performance is to say *how* this competence is used. Again, it is a
typical problem of science to attempt to determine, from investigation of performance, the nature and properties of the
various systems that interact in performance, in particular the
grammar. The investigation of grammatical or pragmatic
competence, then, necessarily begins with the study of
performance, and as performance models are developed and
improved, we can anticipate that this progress will lead to new
insight into the nature of both LRCS and the other systems that
enter into actual performance.

Correspondingly, any serious investigation of linguistic
performance is based on a (perhaps implicit) model of com-

petence. Thus, if all we knew about LRCS was that linguistic expressions consist of words in a sequence, each word with its phonetic and semantic properties, we would be limited to very superficial investigations of performance and highly unsatisfactory performance models. As insight into LRCS or other cognitive structures entering into language use increases, the study of performance models can become correspondingly richer and more significant.

In advance of inquiry, we cannot know what properties of actual linguistic performance are to be explained in terms of one or another of the systems that interact in ordinary language use. Rather, insight into such questions can come only as the result of investigation of various postulated cognitive structures and of performance models that incorporate and integrate them. In practice, inquiry concerned with a specific system such as grammar or universal grammar will attempt to devise situations in which the contribution of other components of mind to performance is controlled and can be essentially disregarded. Again, this is the normal and inescapable procedure of rational inquiry, and it has led to some success in determining properties of LRCS(L) for various languages L and, more deeply, for properties of universal grammar. An example might be the procedure of a linguist who assumes that a particular aspect of grammatical form varies significantly in the examples he has collected to illustrate the principles under discussion, rather than some other variable, such as word frequency, which would be significant under another description.

There are, of course, certain limits that cannot be transcended by the kind of investigation of grammatical competence pursued within linguistics proper. Pursuit of the research programs R(1), R(2), and R(3), for example, goes well beyond the methods of linguistics, strictly speaking, or even the domain of facts and observations characteristic of linguistic work, to include the issues of language use and of the neural mechanisms supporting language. Of course, such delimitation of intellectual domains is artificial, however useful it may be under given conditions; and it is to be hoped that an integrated study of language, its use and development, and its interaction with other cognitive systems will be able to produce richer and more adequate theories in each of the various domains that fall within this general inquiry.

1

Inferring Functional Localization from Neurological Evidence

BARBARA VON ECKARDT KLEIN

To date, the neural realization of the language-responsible cognitive structure in human beings has been studied almost exclusively by the deficit method of functional localization, utilizing evidence obtained primarily from the study of aphasic patients. Although such work has been carried on since the mid-nineteenth century, it has been subject to considerable controversy.

In this chapter, we investigate whether and under what conditions the deficit method of functional localization can validly support theories of neural realization. The deficit method of functional localization is characterized as a method for inferring localization of function in the normal human brain, based on two kinds of evidence from neurologically impaired patients: evidence of abnormal behavior in the patient and evidence concerning the site of brain damage. What is inferred as hypotheses of the form: the neural component which has function F is localized at such and such an anatomical site. Such hypotheses are inferred in two steps: first, a functional deficit in the patient is hypothesized from the kind of abnormal behavior which the patient exhibits; second, localization of function in the normal brain is inferred on the basis of the functional-deficit hypothesis, conjoined with evidence concerning the site of the brain damage.

Each of these steps is considered in some detail here. Determining the conditions under which the first step is justified requires consideration of what constitutes a function, what constitutes an explanation of a system's capacities, and what constitutes an explanation of a system's incapacities. It is concluded that, given a functional-deficit hypothesis H that some functional component F_c (i.e., the component with constituent capacity c) in an organism O is deficient, we are justified in regarding H as *established* on the basis of evidence of pathological behavior P just in case

(1) P is correctly interpreted as the failure to exercise some complex capacity C of the organism.
(2) There exists a functional analysis A of how it is that O normally has C which includes c as a constituent capacity.
(3) A provides the best available explanation of how O has C.
(4) Operation of the program described in A, minus the operation of F_c, results in P as an output.
(5) There is no better available explanation for the existence of P.

A case reported in Geschwind and Kaplan (1962), interpreted by Geschwind as an "associative disorder" rather than as an instance of classical agnosia, is discussed in light of (1) to (5). Determining the conditions under which the second localization step is justified involves a brief consideration of the localization/antilocalization controversy, as well as delineation of possible circumstances under which a functional-localization claim would not be warranted even where the correct functional-deficit analysis is at hand. Such results on the logic of functional localization have an important bearing on the conduct of research in the biology of language, for they suggest that in order to develop adequate functional-localization hypotheses, an interdisciplinary approach is absolutely essential.

Preliminary Remarks

A person's language-responsible cognitive structure is both a computational device and a neural structure. As such it is subject to various kinds and "levels" of description. We are beginning to gain some understanding of the character of LRCS both from the "top," as an abstract computational device, and from the "bottom," as a structure composed of single neural units. What remains a profound mystery is how neural action gets translated into computational processing relevant to human behavior.

It is one of the principal goals of a biological approach to language to bridge this gap by investigating the neural realization of LRCS viewed as a computational device.

To date, the neural realization of LRCS has been studied almost exclusively by the deficit method of functional localization, utilizing evidence obtained primarily from the study of aphasic patients. Although such work has been carried on since the mid-nineteenth century, it has been subject to considerable controversy and has yielded only limited insight into the functional organization of the brain.

We are interested in outlining a fruitful program of research into the neural realization of LRCS. Clearly, a prerequisite to making any such proposal for future research is a thorough understanding of current method. In this chapter we shall evaluate the deficit method of functional localization as a research tool for constructing adequate theories of the neural realization of LRCS. We shall start by providing a characterization and an example of the deficit method of functional localization. Then we shall attempt to characterize the sort of neural models to which this method of functional localization is intended to be relevant. Finally, we shall investigate whether and under what conditions this method of functional localization can validly support theories of neural realization.

Since the legitimacy of functional localization has been a controversial matter for many decades, a careful consideration of the deficit method of functional localization seems appropriate at this point in the history of neural-localization research.

We are engaged in the enterprise of making explicit certain features of scientific practice. The hope is that by reconstructing precisely *how* neurologists infer conclusions regarding functional localization, we can ascertain more clearly under what conditions such conclusions are legitimate, given the usual canons of rationality and scientific methodology.

We shall argue that the deficit method of functional localization is a valid method *only* if it is utilized in a research context in which neurology, linguistics, and psycholinguistics interact significantly.

The Deficit Method of Functional Localization

Functional localization is a method for inferring localization of function in the normal human brain, based on two kinds of evidence from neurologically impaired patients: evidence of abnormal behavior in the patient and evidence concerning the site of brain damage. What is inferred are, roughly, hypotheses of the form: the neural component which has function *F* is localized at such and such an anatomical site. Such hypotheses are inferred in two steps: first *functional deficits* in the patient is hypothesized from the kind of abnormal behavior which the patient exhibits; second *localization of function* in the normal brain is inferred on the basis of the functional-deficit hypothesis conjoined with evidence concerning the site of the brain damage.

Let us consider as an example Wernicke's (1908) use of the method to support his hypothesis that the first temporal convolution is the center for sound images.

Wernicke's paper aims to resolve many of the puzzles and contradictions which plagued the study of aphasia in the 1870s. Previously aphasiologists had assumed there was a single speech center. This assumption, however, squared poorly both with the lesion data which were available and with the various clinical pictures of aphasia which, according to Wernicke, "provided every new observer with new riddles to solve." Wernicke's solution was a simple though extremely important one. He realized that a complex capacity like language must result from interactions among subcomponents of a highly complex neural system. Thus he broke down the neural apparatus for language into different functional parts, assigning each to a different anatomical location. In this way different clinical pictures could be explained as deficits in different functional components. And the alternative lesion sites discovered in aphasics could then be identified as the sites of these various functional components.

On Wernicke's model, the neural apparatus of language consists of two basic centers, plus various pathways connecting these centers to each other and to other functional components of the brain. Both centers are, fundamentally, memory units. In one, sound images are stored; in the other, representations of articulatory movement. The sound-image memory (S) is connected anatomically to the auditory apparatus, the centers for the storage of visual and tactile images, and the center for articulatory-movement memory (M). M is connected anatomically to the articulatory muscles, other motor centers, and S. See Figure 1.

Both sound images and representations of movement are stored representations, which are coded neurophysiologically. These representations result from sensory experience, and their activa-

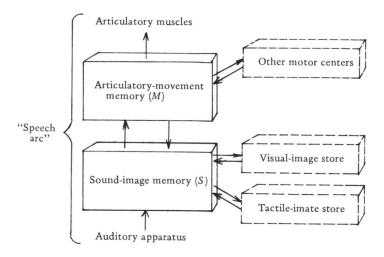

Three-dimensional boxes represent components of a system and two-dimensional boxes represent operations specified by a flowchart. Arrows in both cases indicate the direction of information flow.

Figure 1

tion in turn results in sensory experience. What makes a neuro-physiological "residue of past excitation" a certain sound image seems to be its causal relation to relevant experiences of sound.

As a result of language learning, individual sound images come to be linked associatively to individual representations of movement. These associative links presumably are realized neurologically by direct neuronal connections. For example, the sound image for "dog" comes to be linked to a representation of the articulatory movements involved in speaking the word "dog." Note that these movement representations are not, in Wernicke's view, what we now call "motor programs;" rather they are memory images of the kinesthetic sensations produced by the appropriate articulatory movements.

The functional role of the associative links is the transmission of activation from elements of one center to elements of another. Such associative links make it possible to analyze different language processes as involving different patterns of activation. For example, repeating a heard word can be analyzed as involving the entire "speech arc:" excitation travels from the ear via the acoustic pathway to S; there the appropriate sound image is activated, which in turn triggers activation in the appropriate representation of movement in M. The latter activates the articulatory muscles in such a way that the heard word is uttered. In contrast, understanding a word can be analyzed as involving only the initial segment of the arc. However, in addition to the sound image, relevant visual, tactile, and gustatory images may also be activated via S. The associative network connecting the sensory memory images in the various modalities for representing an object was considered by Wernicke to constitute the concept of an object. Understanding a word, then, involves activation of the concept subsequent to perceiving the word. Uttering a word also involves concept activation, but this time as the initiating force in the pattern of activation: the relevant concept activates the appropriate representation of movement, which in turn activates the appropriate articulatory muscles.

Wernicke realized that positing different functional deficits in the system permits the predicting of different patterns of abnormal speech behavior. Given a functional deficit in the *S* itself, for example, Wernicke predicts the following:

The sound images of the names of all possible objects will be extinguished from memory, although the concepts may still remain in their full clarity. For in most cases the sound image is of secondary importance for the concept of the object, whereas the somesthetic sense images are of critical importance for it. . . . It is clear that the preservation of the path [from S to M] has no value once the sound images have been lost. The words [e.g., representations of movement] are no longer innervated by the sound images. Furthermore, the path which connected the sound heard with the other sense images of the object . . . has also been interrupted. *The patient is thus capable neither of repeating a spoken word . . . nor of understanding the spoken word. . . .*

One pathway still remains by means of which representations of speech movements can be innervated. The patient with the characteristics just described has no disturbance of intelligence. Through his behavior and his comprehension of signs and gestures he makes it clear beyond a doubt that he is familiar with the sensory images of the concrete objects around him and thus with their concepts as well. Now the association of sound images with representations of movement essentially has its value in the fact that it makes it possible to learn language. Very soon after we have learned to speak a word, the intention of merely reproducing the sound disappears, making way for the intention of reproducing a specific meaning. The actual sensory images of an object, that is, are now able directly to innervate the representation of movement of a word directly. The capacity to speak is thus retained, but with a certain limitation. In normal speech the sound image always seems to be unconsciously innervated at the same time, as is easily understandable in terms of the genesis of language. The sound image seems simultaneously to be hallucinated, as it were, and thus exercises a continuous corrective function on the course of the representations of movement. . . .

Aside from his deficient comprehension, the patient has

*aphasic manifestations in speaking because of the absence of
the corrective function exercised unconsciously by the sound
images.* (pp. 50-52)

Wernicke described two patients whom he diagnoses as
sensory aphasics, that is, as aphasics with a functional deficit in
S. Unfortunately, neither taken singly presented him with a
complete set of data relevant to the support of his hypothesis.
In the first case, he has fairly detailed behavioral data but no
lesion information; in the second, he has lesion data but impoverished behavioral data. Since we are interested primarily in
the logic of functional localization at this point, the fact that he
presents us with a composite picture should not be disturbing.
Wernicke describes the patient for whom he had no lesion data
in part like this:

> She understands absolutely nothing that is said to her; but
> care must be taken not to betray one's meaning through
> gestures. When called, she answers 'yes' to her own as well as
> to any other name and turns around. To the superficial
> observer she gives the impression of confusion, because not
> only do her answers fail to correspond to the meaning of the
> questions put to her, but also because the sentences she
> utters are often themselves faulty in that they contain non-
> sensical or distorted words. Nevertheless the meaning of any
> of her sentences that one manages to understand at all is
> always reasonable. There is no trace of flight of ideas. . . .
> Very often, especially when emotionally aroused, she suc-
> ceeds in forming whole sentences which are completely cor-
> rect. . . . She knows how to use all objects, puts on her glasses
> correctly, etc. (p. 67)

The second patient is described thus:

> Her mental condition was regarded at the time as a con-
> fusional state associated with aphasia. She answered all
> questions directed at her in a completely confused way, and
> carried out commands either not at all or in a completely
> confused manner. . . . The attendants thought that she was
> deaf because of her lack of understanding of what was said to
> her. Furthermore, she paid little attention to her sur-

roundings, and in keeping with her severe malaise showed little urge to communicate. Her (spontaneously used) vocabulary thus seemed small in contrast to that of the case described above but was nevertheless large enough that motor aphasia [e.g., a functional deficit of M] could not be considered. The presence of aphasia could be recognized by her substitutions and distortions of words. (p. 71)

The autopsy of the second patient shows a "generalized convolutional atrophy" as well as softening of the left first temporal convolution. On the basis of previous experience in examining the brains of patients suffering from senile or alcoholic cerebral atrophy, Wernicke concluded that

We can thus assert with certainty that the softening of the left first temporal convolution in the case of [the second patient] . . . was the only brain lesion which could have caused the localized symptom of aphasia . . . and that the generalized convolutional atrophy was either the result of senescence or, which is considerably more probable, a consequence of the presence of a circumscribed focal lesion. (p. 73)

On the basis of such evidence Wernicke correlated the temporal-lobe lesion site with the pattern of deficits predicted from his model. He then utilized the correlation to infer that the anatomical site of speech center S was the first temporal convolution of the left hemisphere.

Functional-Component Models

Whether the method of functional localization is valuable to the biology of language depends on two things: (1) whether *what* we infer on the basis of the method is of interest to us, and (2) whether the inferences licensed by the method are warranted. In this section we shall explore the first question by attempting to answer the following:

(1) What is a functional-localization hypothesis?
(2) To what sort of neural model is it relevant?

(3) What is the relationship between a functional-localization hypothesis and such a neural model?

Functions as capacities   The use of the term "function" in attributions of functional localization seems to be related to its use in biology. The biological sciences treat living organisms as complex systems whose "cells and organs are more or less specialized in an efficient division of labor to perform each of the several functions that are essential for every sort of animal." [Griffin (1962), p. 3.] Typical biological functions are digestion, respiration, mobility, internal transport, regulation of chemical composition, reproduction, and regulation of function. In comparison, neurologists talk about such functions as representation of movement, representation of past sense impressions by memory images, and association of different sense impressions to form a concept [Wernicke (1908)]; or regulation of the level of excitation and tone of the cortex, coding and storage of information, and formation of intentions and programs of behavior [Luria (1970)].

Cummins (1975) has suggested that the biological notion of function can be explicated, in part, by the notion of capacity. For some component of a system or organism to have, say, digesting as one of its functions is for that component to be capable of digesting.

It might be argued that such an explication is not helpful because the notion of capacity is just as obscure as the notion of function. This is not correct, however. For while Cummins does not do so, the notion of a capacity can be precisely defined in terms of an input-output description of the organism having that capacity.

Let us assume that there exists an optimal description of the behavioral repertoire of a system $\mathscr{S}$ within a domain $\mathscr{Q}$ of the form

$$f: (S \times I) \to (S \times O)$$

i.e., as an input-output device, where S represents the set of relevant internal states of the system (i.e., those states that make a difference to the behavior), I of relevant inputs, and O

of relevant outputs. The function f is then a mapping from all possible state-input pairs into all state-output pairs.

Given such a description, we can define a *capacity* C of $\mathscr{S}$ in $\mathscr{A}$ as a subset of the set of all possible input-output pairs $I \times O$ which satisfies some naturalness condition. The point of the naturalness condition is that most subsets of $I \times O$ will not correspond to what we ordinarily think of as a capacity.

$\mathscr{S}$ then *has* C provided that for each input-output pair $\langle i,o \rangle$ where $\langle i,o \rangle \in C$ there exists an internal state s, where $s \epsilon S$ such that $f(s,i) = $ o.

But more is needed by way of definition, because not everything that a component of a system is capable of doing ought to count as one of its functions, as Cummins points out. The heart, for example, is capable of producing sound; yet we would not regard producing sound as one of the functions of the heart. It has frequently been noted that what distinguishes the capacities of system components that are *functions* of components from those that are not has something to do with the relationship of the component capacity to the functioning of the whole system or organism. Precisely what this relationship is has been a matter of philosophic controversy. [Cummins' account of functional explanation is by no means the classical account. For the classical account, see Hempel (1965). For an argument that the classical account is not correct, see Cummins (1975).] Cummins' view is that what is relevant is whether the component capacity figures in an *explanation* of some capacity of the entire organism.

Functional explanation   Presumably what we want to explain is how the organism is able to do something, for example, how Mr. Jones is able to name objects upon confrontation. Explaining this capacity is to be contrasted both with explaining why Mr. Jones engages in object naming upon some specific occasion (the psychologist asked him to) and explaining how Mr. Jones came to be able to have this capacity (his mother taught him). Cummins suggests that a system's or organism's capacity to do something can be explained by a *functional analysis* of that capacity. By a functional analysis of some capacity C, he means, roughly, a breakdown of the complex capacity into a set of constituent capacities $(c_1, c_2 \ldots c_n)$, with a specification of the sequence in which those constituent capacities must be exercised for the result to be a manifestation of the complex capacity.

Let us consider an example. A person's capacity to cook an omelet can be analyzed into a set of constituent capacities such as the capacity to break eggs into a bowl, the capacity to stir the eggs, or the capacity to pour the mixture into a pan. But simply possessing all the requisite skills will not do the trick. The order in which they are to be exercised must also be specified. Thus it is essential that one stir the eggs before pouring the mixture into the pan; otherwise the result will be scrambled eggs. In effect what is required is an algorithm or program for exercising C in terms of $c_1, c_2, \ldots c_n$. Such algorithms can be displayed graphically by a flowchart such as Figure 2. Note that a capacity like omelet making differs in one important respect from the sorts of capacities of concern to an aphasiologist. The constituent capacities of omelet making are normally exercised intentionally by a person. In contrast, the constituent capacities of, say, object naming, must be assigned to something inside the organism. Suppose that naming an object involves perceiving the object, computing a conceptual representation, looking up the appropriate lexical entry for that representation in some internal dictionary, and so forth. None of these are steps taken intentionally by the person naming the object in the same way that breaking eggs, stirring them, etc., are steps taken intentionally in making an omelet. This fact does not mean, however, that functional analysis is inappropriate to what we might call *basic* human capacities, i.e., those which cannot be broken down into steps under intentional control. One of the assumptions of cognitive psychology is precisely that functional analysis *is* appropriate in dealing with basic human capacities and that it makes sense to assign constituent capacities to subpersonal functional components.

Having clarified what Cummins means by "functional analysis," we must now ask: does a functional analysis of some capacity C provide us with an explanation of how an organism

O has capacity *C*, as Cummins claims? Certainly it provides us with an explanation of how some organism *might* have *C*. That is, it provides us with a *possible* explanation of how *O* has *C*. But it does not necessarily tell us how the organism under study has *C*. The reason is this: complex capacities may be broken

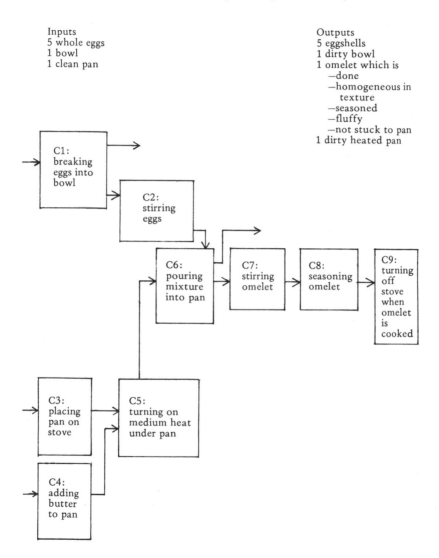

Figure 2   A Functional Analysis of Omelet Making

down into various constituent capacities. For example, there are
a variety of ways to design a calculator to do square roots. Any
one of the many possible functional analyses of the capacity to
do square roots explains how some device might have the
capacity to do square roots, but it does not necessarily explain
how the particular device in front of me has that capacity.
Hence a functional analysis of how O has capacity C will not
quite do as an explanation of how O has C in fact. It has been
suggested that the difficulty lies with the level of abstraction at
which most functional analyses are formulated. What is required, according to this view, is that the functional analysis be
pushed to a level where the capacities in question can be
subsumed under some general physical law governing the behavior of things. But while we surely want basic physical laws to
be somehow relevant to functional analysis, they do not in this
instance suffice to fill the explanatory gap. That the lowest-level
capacities adduced in our functional analysis turn out to be
manifestations of certain physical laws does not provide the
needed connection to the specific organism under study. In the
case of the calculating device, almost *any* functional analysis
which analyzes the capacity to do square roots in terms of
capacities to perform some set of basic arithmetic operations
will be physically realizable. This means that at some level of
description the mechanism performing the relevant arithmetic
operations will be doing so because it is operating according to
physical laws. Thus satisfaction of the physical-law requirement
does not help us pick from among the possible explanations the
one which corresponds to how the device under study actually
has the capacity. Cummins is correct in his intuition that in
principle we can explain how it is that an organism has a
capacity by showing that the organism has various constituent
capacities. But he fails to note precisely what is involved. To
explain how it is that a particular organism has capacity C, we
must show two things (1) that if *any* organism has the enumerated constituent capacities, it has C; and (2) that the
particular orgamism in question in fact has C in virtue of having
those constituent capacities. A functional analysis provides us
with only (1). Hence we have an explanatory gap.

To fill this gap we must supply (2), that is, we must tie the analysis to the organism under study. For reasons that will become clear shortly, we shall call a functional analysis for which (2) is the case a *structurally adequate functional analysis*. The notion of a structurally adequate functional analysis is important for the following reason: We have defined a function to be a constituent capacity which can figure in an explanation of a capacity of the system as a whole. But since only a structurally adequate functional analysis can explain how an organism has some capacity C, what counts as a function can be determined only relative to a structurally adequate functional analysis.

What is required for a functional analysis to be structurally adequate? A functional analysis A of how an organism O has capacity C is structurally adequate if there exists a *structural decomposition* of O into component (physical) parts such that

(1) Operation of those parts results in O's exercising C.
(2) For each constituent capacity of A, there exists at least one of those structural components which has that capacity.
(3) The order in which those component parts operate when O is exercising C mirrors the algorithm specified in A.

Condition (1) guarantees the existence of a physical mechanism underlying the capacity C. Condition (2) ensures that some part of the mechanism corresponds to each constituent capacity specified by the functional analysis. Condition (3) guarantees further that the sequence of operation of these physical parts corresponds to that specified by the functional analysis. Condition (1) alone will not ensure the structural adequacy of A because (1) alone is compatible with O's exercising C in a way which does not involve the exercise of any of the constituent capacities of A. Conditions (1) and (2) alone are not enough because they are compatible with O's exercising C by exercising the constituent capacities in a sequence different from that specified by the functional analysis.

Consider now a model which describes a possible structural decomposition of O such that if it were true of O, conditions (1) to (3) would be met. We shall call such a model a *functional component model of how O has C*. Such a model *incorporates* A.

To give an example, a functional-component model incorporating our functional analysis for making omelets might consist of a component for cracking, a component for stirring, a component for adding ingredients to a pan, a heating unit, a heat switch, and so forth. In other words, it would be a description of an omelet-making machine in terms of parts which can exercise the constituent capacities specified in the analysis.

It is important to realize that for any given functional analysis of some capacity C, more than one functional component model incorporating A is possible. Suppose, for example, that capacity C is analyzed as involving steps P and Q, and these in turn, are analyzed into the primitive operations s, t, and u as shown in Figure 3.
At least two structural decompositions of a system which has C are possible: one which maps capacities onto structural components only at the level of primitive operations (model 1), and one which reflects the hierarchy of capacity analysis and hence includes a device corresponding to each intermediate capacity P and Q (Model 2). See Figure 4.

The existence of a functional-component model incorporating a functional analysis of how O has C does not yet suffice to bestow structural adequacy on the analysis. For just as a functional analysis provides a description only of how the organism *might* exercise C, so a functional-component model provides a description only of a *possible* structural decomposition of O. Imagine, for example, that a system exists for making omelets by piercing the eggs, blowing the insides out of the shell, whipping the batter in a blender, and then pouring the batter into an appropriately shaped heated slot much like that in a toaster. Neither the functional analysis we described nor the functional-component model we sketched would be true of this system. Hence neither would provide an explanation for

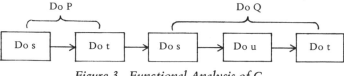

Figure 3   Functional Analysis of C

how this system makes omelets. What is required for there to be an explanation is that the functional-component model be *true*. We shall say that such a model is true of an organism just in case there exists a part of the organism which is the physical realization of each functional component specified by the model and these parts are connected in such a way as to constitute the input-output network described by the model.

The conditions of structural adequacy for a functional analysis can now be restated. A functional analysis A of how O has C *is structurally adequate if there exists a functional-component model which both incorporates A and is true of O.*

We can now use the account we have developed to make Cummins' suggestion about what a function is more precise. Recall that Cummins suggested that a function of some part of an organism is a capacity of that part if that capacity figures in an explanation of how the organism as a whole has some complex capacity. To be more precise:

> F is a *function* of some part of O, where O has capacity C, just in case

(i) There exists a functional analysis A of how O has C in terms of constituent capacities $c_1, c_2, \ldots, c_n$.

(ii) A is structurally adequate.

(iii) $F = c_i$, where $1 \langle i \langle n$.

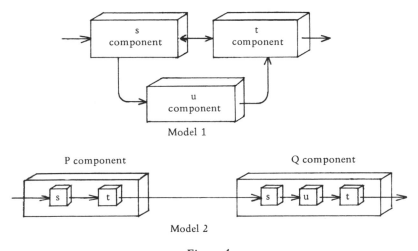

Model 1

Model 2

Figure 4

We introduced the notion of a functional-component model in order to satisfy the requirement that the functional analysis of how O has C counts as an explanation of how O has C. Note that such a model is important for another reason. Without a functional-component model, we have no way of determining which particular parts of the organism have the functions in question. While attributing a function like pumping blood to the organism as a whole seems legitimate, it is hardly illuminating. The value of functional analysis derives from the value of understanding properties of a whole in terms of properties of its parts. To do so, it is essential to be able to identify the relevant parts.

Let us now return to the three questions posed earlier, viz., What is a functional-localization hypothesis? To what sort of neural model is it relevant? What is the relationship between functional-localization hypotheses and such neural models?

A functional-localization hypothesis is a hypothesis of the form: brain structure S in O has constituent capacity c, where c is a function of some part of O. The sort of neural model to which such a hypothesis is relevant is a functional-component model. The functional-localization hypothesis specifies one aspect of the structural realization of the functional-component model. Thus it is not itself part of a functional-component model; rather it is part of the determination that such a model is true of O, in other words, part of a theory of neural realization for the model.

Validity of the Method

We can now investigate whether and under what conditions the deficit method of functional localization is a valid method for supporting theories of the neural realization of LRCS. Breaking the problem into parts corresponding to the two inferential steps of the method, we shall ask: under what conditions are we justified in inferring a functional-deficit hypothesis from behavioral data? and then: under what conditions can localization of (normal) function be inferred, given a functional-deficit hypothesis plus lesion data?

The functional-deficit hypothesis Confronted with two patients exhibiting a certain pattern of symptoms (they could not understand spoken language, they could produce meaningful sentences, they could handle objects correctly, etc.), Wernicke inferred that both suffered from a deficit in the sound-image center. Based on the text cited, it seems plausible to reconstruct his reasoning thus:

> Given my model of the neural components relevant for language capacity, positing a deficit in the speech center allows us to *explain* the kinds of symptoms manifested by my two patients. Hence, given the existence of such symptomatology, it is reasonable to infer the existence of such a deficit.

I would like to suggest that the pattern of reasoning attributed here to Wernicke is typical of that employed to infer a functional-deficit hypothesis from behavioral data. In fact, it is an instance of a rather widespread species of scientific reasoning that philosophers have called "inference to the best explanation." The general form of the inference is this: we are warranted in inferring some proposition T on the basis of some proposition U if the truth of T provides us with the best available explanation for the truth of U. In the aphasic case, inferring the existence of a functional deficit on the basis of some behavioral pathology is justified *if* positing the existence of that functional deficit provides us with the best available explanation for the existence of the aphasic symptoms.

To see how positing the existence of a functional deficit can provide such an explanation, we must extend the account of functional explanation, which we developed in the context of normal behavior. We have seen how a structurally adequate functional analysis can provide an explanation of a capacity or set of capacities. Given such a functional analysis, one important way in which a set of *incapacities* can be explained is by positing that one of the normally operating constituent capacities can no longer be exercised. Reconsidering our functional analysis for omelet making (see Figure 5) will make this point clear. Given a deficit in any of the functional components underlying a constituent capacity, it is easy to predict exactly what will happen to the output. This is so because each of the constituent capacities makes its own particular contribution to the eventual output. Thus if a constituent capacity cannot be exercised, its particular contribution to the output will be missing.

Sometimes this contribution is direct, as in the case of stirring the omelet (results in the omelet's being fluffy), seasoning the omelet (results in the omelet's being seasoned), adding butter to the pan (results in the omelet's not sticking), etc. Sometimes, however, the contribution is indirect; the exercise of a constituent capacity may not be reflected directly in the output but instead may be a necessary condition for the subsequent normal exercise of another constituent capacity. Thus

Functional deficit		*Output result* (normal unless otherwise specified)		
C1	no shells	bowl clean	5 slightly battered whole eggs with butter and seasoning on shells	pan clean
C2			omelet non-homogeneous in texture	
C3			omelet not done, not fluffy	pan not hot, with liquid residue
C4			omelet sticks to pan	pan with more than normal egg particles on it
C5	(Same as C3)			
C6		bowl filled with egg mixture	no omelet	clean pan
C7			omelet not fluffy	
C8			omelet not seasoned	
C9				burned pan

Figure 5   Possible Functional Deficits of Omelet Making

breaking the eggs into the bowl is a necessary condition for stirring the eggs to produce an omelet which is homogeneous in texture.

What makes a functional system work at bottom is the existence of structures and causal mechanisms which realize that system. Similarly, what makes a functional system break down is that some of these structures and causal mechanisms fail to operate normally. When this happens, there are four possible results. First, one of the functional components of the system may simply fail to operate, resulting in inability to exercise its constituent capacity. This case is exemplified in Figure 5. Second, each functional component may operate normally, but the order in which they operate may be abnormal. Third, the underlying structural or casual change may transform one of the components into what is in effect a different functional component with a different constituent capacity. Or fourth, what amounts to a new functional component may be added to the system. The existence of a functional analysis of how a system or organism has some capacity C, which provides an explanation of the *normal* range of output resulting from exercise of C, is sufficient to provide an explanation of pathological output only in the first two cases. In the third and fourth cases, we must resort to information outside the scope of the functional analysis of normal behavior to account for the deviant output. Either a functional analysis specific to the abnormal organism must be provided, or the explanation of deviant output must occur at a non-functional level, i.e., at the level of causal mechanism. In our omelet-making system, for example, severe lack of attention by the human element of the system might result in $C9$'s being modified to sprinkling detergent on the omelet. The result would be a clearly deviant output, but the nature of the deviance in this case can only be accounted for by knowing about the character of the change, in particular, about the properties of detergent in combination with egg mixture in combination with the human palate. Knowing about the normal functional system does not help us in this case to explain the output. Likewise, if a severe earthquake occurred between steps $C6$ and $C7$, accounting for the nature of the resulting output (e.g., a gooey mess on the floor) would require knowing something about earthquakes and how they affect objects like pans and stoves.

It should be clear that when faced with a pathological or deviant output of a system or organism, we cannot always explain that deviance in terms of a deficit in one of the functional components required for *normal* operation of the system. However, what is important for our purposes is that although positing a deficiency in a normal functional component is not the only possible explanation of pathology, it is often the *best* available explanation. Where it does constitute the best available explanation, we are justified in inferring the existence of the functional deficit on the basis of the pathological evidence. To be more precise: given a functional-deficit hypothesis H that the functional component in O with constituent capacity c is deficient, we are justified in regarding H as *established* on the basis of evidence of pathological behavior P just in case

(1) P is correctly interpreted as the failure to exercise some capacity C.
(2) There exists a functional analysis A of how it is that O normally has C which includes c as a constituent capacity.
(3) A provides the best available explanation of how O has C.
(4) Operation of the program described in A, minus the operation of the functional component with constituent capacity c, results in P as an output.
(5) There is no better available explanation for the existence of P.

Note that (3) calls for the functional analysis to provide not only an explanation of how O has C but also the best available explanation of how O has C. It is unclear precisely what is involved in meeting this stronger requirement. Roughly speaking, what we want is an explanation which is not only adequate "locally," that is, for the capacity under study, but also provides the best possible "fit" with available explanations of other capacities of the organism. Apparently the structural adequacy of a functional analysis does not ensure that the analysis constitutes the best available explanation for how *O* has *C*. A functional-component model incorporating *A* may map onto the structure of the organism (and hence be true of the organism according to our definition) and yet still be un-felicitous. Again the omelet example helps to make the point. Suppose we have a machine capable of cooking a variety of things in a skillet, including omelets. Suppose further that our functional analysis of omelet making treats salting the omelet and peppering the omelet as separate constituent capacities; likewise, the functional-component model incorporating this analysis includes a component for salting and a component for peppering. Now such a functional-component model might be true of our skillet cooking machine (that is, the machine might have a part which salts and a part which peppers) without providing the simplest function description of the machine, given its other capacities. The simplest description might be that the machine has as one of its parts a seasoner, namely, a device which sprinkles whatever it is given as input onto whatever is in the skillet. To reflect this fact, our original functional analysis of omelet making must be changed. Where it posited originally two constituent capacities, namely, the capacity to salt and the capacity to pepper, it now will have only one, namely, the capacity to season.

Conditions like (1) to (5) have an important role to play in scientific practice, although it is often left to the philosopher to make both the conditions and their role explicit. In debating the relative merits and demerits of competing functional-deficit hypotheses, it is such conditions which are ultimately appealed to when a case is made for accepting or rejecting a candidate hypothesis. The appeal can be made in two ways. If there is strong evidence that a candidate hypothesis fails to meet one of the conditions, this failure constitutes grounds for rejecting the hypothesis. If we have neither sufficient evidence to claim that all the conditions have been met nor sufficient evidence to rule out any of the candidate hypotheses on the grounds that it fails to meet some condition, the case is more complicated. In the early stages of research on the neural realization of language, this situation will be typical for functional-deficit hypotheses. This is because in the early stages of research, little or nothing will be known bearing on the question of structural adequacy implicitly required by condition (3). Even in this situation, however, the conditions for regarding a functional-deficit hypothesis as established have a role to play. While we shall not be in a position to claim that any candidate hypothesis meets all the conditions, we may be in a position to choose hypothesis H_1 over hypothesis H_2 on the grounds that, given the total available relevant evidence, the probability that H_1 meets the conditions is higher than the probability that H_2 does. The functional-deficit hypothesis to which we assign the highest probability of meeting conditions (1) to (5) might be regarded as the *best available working hypothesis*.

How we ought to determine such probabilities is an important topic for further research. One possibility is that given two functional-deficit hypotheses H_1 and H_2, each of which meets conditions (1), (2), and (4) and presupposes a functional analysis that constitutes a *possible* explanation of how O and C, we ought to assign the highest probability to the one which (a) constitutes the best available possible explanation of how O has C, and (b) is such that there is no better available possible explanation for the existence of P.

A case study To show how such considerations can be applied, we shall consider a neurological case study reported in Geschwind and Kaplan (1962) and subsequently discussed in Geschwind (1969). Geschwind uses the case to consider two alternative interpretations of what is standardly known as "agnosia." He suggests the classical interpretation of agnosia as a "recognition" deficit is wrong and that instead it should be regarded as an "associative disorder." Both interpretations presuppose (implicit) functional analysis. We shall attempt to make these functional analyses explicit and then raise the question of choosing between them. We shall argue that an updated version of the classical view can be defended against Geschwind's alternative. The reason is that there exists psychological evidence on naming gathered from normal subjects which is difficult to account for on the associative analysis but is compatible with the recognition analysis. Thus Geschwind's interpretation seems to be ruled out because the functional analysis which it presupposes fails to provide the best available possible explanation of the relevant normal capacities.

The classical interpretation of agnosia is that it involves a "recognition" deficit. In effect what is being presupposed is that naming an object can be functionally analyzed into four basic stages: perceiving the object, recognizing it, finding its name, and articulating its name. In contemporary information-processing terms, these four stages might be:

> *Stage I:* Computing a modality-specific representation of the object.
>
> *Stage II:* Computing a modality-neutral "conceptual representation" of the object.
>
> *Stage III:* Searching an internal lexicon for the name of the object on the basis of a conceptual access code.
>
> *Stage IV:* Finding or compiling an articulatory motor program of the name and executing that program.

According to Geschwind, neurologists typically have employed a certain set of criteria for calling a disturbance an agnosia. Interpreting these against the background of our functional reconstruction of the classical view is particularly instructive. Geschwind writes:

> First, it is necessary to show either (1) that elementary sensation is intact or (2) that if an impairment of elementary sensations is present it is not sufficiently severe to explain the disturbance of recognition. [Geschwind (1969), p. 114.]

Satisfying this first condition clearly rules out a deficit in Stage I. He goes on:

> Assuming this to have been demonstrated, how has it been possible to demonstrate that the failure of recognition was not simply a failure of naming? (p. 114)

The problem then is to distinguish cases of Stage II deficit from cases of Stage III deficit, where the former constitute cases of agnosia. Although Geschwind does not mention it specifically, patients presumably are examined for articulatory dysfunction in order to rule out a Stage IV difficulty. According to the classical view, Stage II and Stage III deficits can then be distinguished as follows:

a. A naming deficit is not modality-specific; a recognition failure may be. In terms of our information-processing reconstruction this can be easily understood: the conceptual representation computed in the "recognition" stage is computed from a modality-specific representation. The computational path from, say, a tactile representation to a conceptual representation might be deficient; whereas a similar path from a visual representation might be intact. In contrast, a Stage III deficit would not be modality-specific. If the lexicon cannot be searched on the basis of the conceptual-access code, then no matter how the conceptual representation was arrived at (that is, on the basis of no matter what modality-specific representation), naming cannot occur.

b. Where there is inappropriate naming, the substitutions resulting from a Stage II deficit are different from the substitutions resulting from a Stage III deficit. The former may be "perceptual" in character ('a small package' substituted for 'a book') whereas the latter are usually "linguistic" ('chair' for 'table'). Again this difference can be made sense of in terms of our model. A recognition deficit will involve either failure to compute a conceptual representation or computation of the wrong one. Where the wrong conceptual representation is computed, the stimulus may be misidentified as something which shares many of the perceptual features of the actual stimulus (that is, whose modality-specific representation is similar). In the case of a naming deficit, the lexicon is searched on the basis of the appropriate conceptual-access code, but the lexical-selection mechanism is not entirely accurate. For example, instead of finding 'chair' for the conceptual representation of chair, a lexical item belonging to the same semantic category is chosen. Such semantic substitutions are common in normal speakers [Garrett (1975)].

c. When given a choice of names, one of which is correct, the patient with a Stage III deficit will choose the correct name;

whereas the patient with a Stage II deficit probably will not. The Stage III deficit patient presumably has available the conceptual representation of the object but cannot use it to search the lexicon. But given a phonological or orthographic representation, he *can* search the lexicon. When presented with a list of names, he finds all the appropriate entries in his lexicon, retrieves the relevant conceptual representations, and compares each of these with the conceptual representation of the stimulus object until he finds a match. A list of names will not help the Stage II deficit patient; he will not have available the appropriate representation for match-mismatch operation because he cannot compute a conceptual representation of the stimulus object in the first place.

d. The Stage III deficit patient describes his difficulty as: "I know what it is but I can't find the name," whereas the Stage II deficit patient claims that things look different to him.

e. The Stage II deficit patient cannot show the use of the object when input is limited to the deficient modality; whereas the Stage III deficit patient can. This makes sense in terms of our model because "showing the use" of an object requires conceptual identification.

Geschwind and Kaplan's patient exhibited the following pattern of behavior. When an object was placed in his left hand, he later could draw it with his left hand or select it from a group of objects presented either tactually or visually (although when an object was presented in another modality or tactually to only the right hand, object naming was normal). Under these circumstances (a) he could not produce the correct name of the object; (b) naming errors were arbitrarily related to the correct response ('rubber band' for 'screwdriver'); (c) he could not select the correct name when presented with a choice of names; (d) he gave inappropriate descriptions of what he perceived; and (e) he could "handle" objects normally.

Although four out of the five classical criteria for agnosia are satisfied in this case [(e) is not satisfied], Geschwind argues that the patient is suffering from a "naming defect resulting from disconnexion from the speech area" and ought not to be diagnosed as an agnosic. To understand his argument, we must

look more closely at the model which he proposes as an alternative. It is essentially Wernicke's model. According to Geschwind, when a child learns to name, he learns a set of auditory-
visual and auditory-tactile associations. Once learned, these
associations are stored. When presented with an object to be
named, a person first forms a modality-specific representation
of the object (tactile or visual), searches his store of associations
for the association containing that modality-specific representation as the first member of the associated pair, and then
retrieves the second member of the pair, the auditory associate,
as the basis for articulating the name. To handle laterality
effects, Geschwind must posit that the initial stage of forming a
tactile (or visual) representation of a tactile (or visual) stimulus
occurs bilaterally, but that the tactile-auditory associations are
stored only in the left hemisphere. See Figure 6.

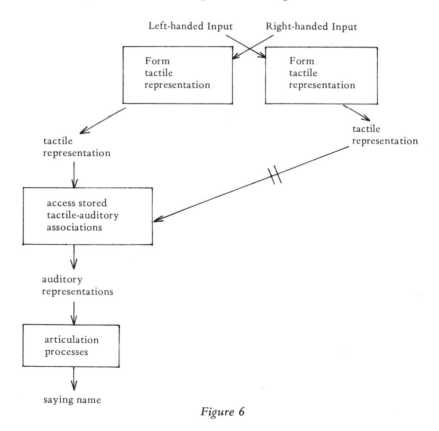

Figure 6

What is functionally deficient in the patient, according to Geschwind, is some process necessary to accessing the stored tactile-auditory associations on the basis of the left-field tactile representation. Given this model, the various classical symptoms of agnosia can all be accounted for.

The modality-specificity of the symptoms are accounted for because tactile-auditory associations are distinct from visual-auditory associations and it is only the accessing mechanism to the former which is deficient. Naming errors are arbitrarily related to the correct response because access to the "naming center" has been cut off. If "the speech area is fully disconnected from the right hemisphere, there is no reason why the speech area should select the correct term. It is obvious that the ability to select the correct word depends on there being some connection between the site of perception and the speech area. The ability to select the correct word from a group when the patient cannot find it spontaneously indicates a lesser degree of disconnection. Phrased in another, diagrammatic way, one could conceive that when one offers a word to a patient he in some way compares the images or memories aroused by this word with the sensations he is receiving from the object. If there is no site for such comparison, the patient will not recognize the correct word when it is offered." Furthermore, "If the patient's speech area is disconnected from a site of primary perception why should his speech area be able to describe what is going on at the site of the primary perception? Clearly, it should not." [Geschwind (1969), p. 118.]

Yet there is good reason to call the deficit a naming deficit because it is precisely the computational path which performs the retrieval of the "name" which is not operational. Furthermore, nothing corresponding to the stage of "recognition," as posited by the classical model, exists.

How does Geschwind's model compare with the classical one? Geschwind argues that the classical model is inadequate on two grounds. First, it assumes

That 'the patient' is an entity. But in someone whose two hemispheres operate as independently as this patient's, the word loses its ordinary meaning. There is no answer to 'Did the patient recognize?' There are, however, clear answers to 'Under what conditions did the right or left hemisphere recognize?' (p. 116)

If we interpret this remark as saying that the classical model cannot account for the right-left asymmetries exhibited by the patient, the point is well taken. Lateralization of function clearly must be incorporated into a classical model. But this can easily be done. A lateralized version of the (updated) classical model is representated in Figure 7. Given this model, what accounts for the patient's behavior is a deficiency in the functional component which computes a conceptual representation of the object on the basis of the left-field tactile representation. Again all the symptoms of the patient can be accounted for.

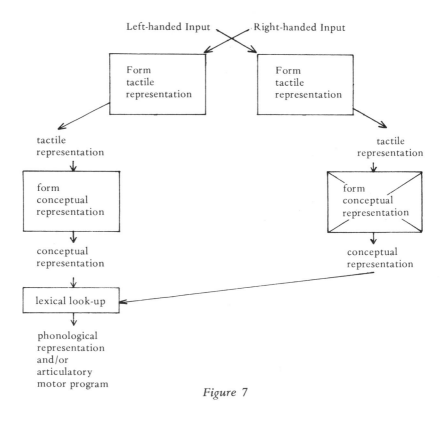

Figure 7

(Without the relevant conceptual representation, the patient has no appropriate basis upon which to search the lexicon and hence cannot access the correct name. When a name is selected nonetheless in order to satisfy the demands of the task, it is selected at random. The correct name cannot be chosen from a set of presented names because, if we posit that a match is done at the conceptual level, there is no basis for making the correct match. If computing a conceptual representation of what one perceives is the basis for finding apt descriptions of perceptual input, then clearly without an appropriate conceptual representation such apt descriptions will not be forthcoming. To account for the fact that the patient could "handle" objects correctly, we need only assume that many motor responses are directly programmed to the level of tactile representations. We suggest that truly "showing the use" of an object where this involves understanding what the object *is* would be deficient in this patient even though some modes of "handling" might still be appropriate.)

Note that the only real difference between the two models at this point (since nothing has been said to distinguish accessing a stored tactile-auditory association from lexical look-up) is the existence of an additional stage in the classical model, namely, one forming a conceptual representation on the basis of the tactile one. This, of course, constitutes the classical stage of recognition. Geschwind registers his strongest objections precisely against this stage. He writes:

> The fundamental difficulty has been in the acceptance of a special class of defects of 'recognition,' lying somewhere between defects of 'perception' and 'naming.' What indeed are the criteria for 'recognition' and is it a single function? I believe in fact that there is no single faculty of 'recognition' but that the term covers the totality of all the associations aroused by any object. Phrased in another way, we 'manifest recognition' by responding appropriately; to the extent that any appropriate response occurs, we have shown 'recognition.' But this view abolishes the notion of a unitary step of 'recognition;' instead, there are multiple parallel processes of appropriate response to a stimulus. To describe the behaviour

correctly we must describe the pattern of loss and preservation of responses to each particular type of stimulus. (p.
115)

Although it is unclear what Geschwind's argument is here, his
view seems to be something like this: unless some account can
be given of the classical notion of recognition as a separate stage
that makes sense conceptually, and unless there is empirical
reason to believe that such a stage exists, we ought to prefer a
simpler associationist model. Furthermore, he seems to suggest
that no such account has been given and that no such reason
exists.

But this is simply false. As we noted above, once we begin to
think in current information-processing terms, it is natural to
explicate perceptual recognition as the assigning of a conceptual
representation to the stimulus object. Recent work in cognitive
psychology gives us considerable empirical reason for believing
that such a stage of representation exists, at least for naming a
visually presented stimulus.

The existence of an abstract conceptual mode of
representation in human cognitive processes, in addition to
other more imagistic or verbal modes of representation, has
been argued for by numerous investigators, including Seymour
(1973), Kahneman (1973), Gibson and Levin (1975), Atkinson
et al. (1974a and b), Lachman (1973, 1974), Bartram (1973,
1974), Nelson (1974), Carpenter and Just (1975), Collins and
Loftus (1975), and Potter and coworkers (1975, 1976). That
such conceptual representations figure in the naming of objects
is supported most persuasively by the work of Potter. It has
been known for some time that naming a drawing of an object
takes longer than reading its name (according to Potter,
260 milliseconds longer). On the sort of model that
Geschwind suggests, such a result is somewhat difficult to
explain. Why should retrieving an auditory associate from the
set of stored verbal visual (i.e., orthographic)/auditory associations take less time than retrieving an auditory associate from
the set of stored nonverbal visual/auditory associations? An
associationist might argue that it is because both members of
the associated pair are verbal in the first case but not in the

second. Potter suggests a better explanation. The extra time in the case of drawings comes from the fact that in order to be named, a drawing is first recognized (that is, a conceptual representation must first be assigned to it). This conceptual representation is then used to search the lexicon in order to access the phonological and articulatory information necessary for uttering the name. In contrast, such phonological and articulatory information can be retrieved more directly in the case of the word on the basis of its visual form. To test this conceptual coding hypothesis, Potter carried out a category-matching experiment. In this experiment, subjects were given the name of a category (e.g., furniture) in advance and then presented with either a picture of something belonging to that category (e.g., chair) or the name of such an object. The task was to say whether the presented item belonged in the category or not. Potter reasoned that if a conceptual mode of representation common to both verbal and nonverbal stimuli existed, then the comparison necessary to perform this task would be done at the conceptual level for both pictures and words; hence the 260-millisecond advantage for words would disappear. Precisely this happened [Potter and Faulconer (1975)]. In contrast, an associationist model must predict that the advantage for words would persist in order to be consistent with the only possible explanation it can offer of the 260-millisecond difference for object naming.

Thus the information-processing account of naming that provides us with the best available account of this set of facts about naming in normal subjects is one which involves the classical stage of recognition. There is no reason to believe that a similar account will not be required for stimuli presented in the tactile mode. The moral is clear: to be considered even as a good working hypothesis, a functional-deficit hypothesis must do more than provide *an* account of the pathological data. The functional analysis presupposed by the hypothesis must be able to account for the normal range of output in the relevant domain. It is on this score that Geschwind's hypothesis appears inadequate.

Localization   Having established that some functional-deficit hypothesis H is the best available working hypothesis, what conditions, if any, justify the inference that the functional component F_c (the component with constituent capacity c) claimed to be deficient in H is normally localized or realized by brain structure S, the site of the lesion? In other words, under what conditions, if any, is an argument of the following form a good one?

> *Localization argument*
> H: There exists a deficit in O in functional component F_c.
> L: There exists a lesion in O in brain structure S.
> FLH: Therefore, under normal conditions, brain structure S would be the structural realization of F_c in O; or brain structure S would have constituent capacity c in O.

We shall first consider whether there is reason to believe that no such conditions exist. The history of aphasiological research is typically portrayed as a long-standing controversy between so-called localizationists and antilocalizationists. It is curious, therefore, to discover upon examining the literature, that most of the arguments and considerations offered in support of the antilocalizationist view in no way impugn the validity of the localization argument. Instead, they seem to fall into two basic categories: arguments against localization of a *particular sort of function* (in contrast to arguments against the legitimacy of localization of function in general), and arguments against *generalizing* from what has been learned about localization of function for one individual to all normal individuals.

Consider, for example, the argument put forward by Henry Head. Head claims that the conception according to which "various functions generated in different areas of the cortex are brought together like fragments of a mosaic to produce some higher form of activity" is "completely untenable and is not justified by the facts either of experiment or of clinical observation." [Head (1963), p. 498.] In fact, however, the facts of clinical observation which he adduces are directed at a slightly different assumption, namely, that "by examining the clinical manifestations, we [can] discover the synthetic elements out of which speech is composed;" where by a "synthetic element" he had in mind speaking, reading, and writing, or "motor," "sensory," "emissive," or "receptive" phenomena. In the terms of our framework, the objectionable assumption comes to this: for each capacity C that can be disturbed in an aphasic patient, there exists a single functional component F which has that capacity directly. Note that given this assumption and the fact that patients exhibit incapacities in speaking, reading, and writing, the method of functional localization can be utilized to infer the existence of functional components (i.e., centers) with functions (i.e., with capacities) such as speaking, reading, and writing. Head rightly objects to the assumption on the grounds that it does not comport with the clinical facts. The assumption predicts that a deficit in F alone in a patient should result in: (a) isolated absence of the capacity C (b) absence of capacity C under all circumstances and (c) no "positive" symptoms. Head discovered that

(a) "A disturbance of one aspect of speech is invariably associated with some other disorder in the use of language or allied functions." (p. 199)
(b) The patient often "succeeds in reading or writing under certain conditions, although he fails completely if the task is presented to him in a different manner." (p. 207)
(c) A lesion may have positive as well as negative manifestations, where, according to Head, positive manifestations may reveal activities which under normal conditions are controlled or suppressed.

Head clearly has a strong argument against localizing such functions as speaking, reading, or writing. But note that none of his clinical evidence in any way counts against localization of function in general. In fact, if we examine what Head proposes to substitute for the traditional "centres," we find that he himself engages in localization. He writes:

The so-called 'centres' in the cortex are not conglomerations of cells and fibres where some particular and more or less exclusive function is initiated, to be abolished by their removal. They are points where the progress of some mode of action can be *reinforced, deviated or inhibited*; in fact they are *foci of integration*. (p. 498)

It turns out that his localization hypotheses simply involve a different set of functions.

An example of the second category of argument is to be found in Geschwind (1969). After describing a patient with a lesion in Wernicke's area but none of the symptoms of Wernicke's aphasia, Geschwind gives four reasons why such a case ought not be taken as an argument against localization. One patient may differ from others in the way some particular task has been learned, in the fact that he manifests duplication of function in the right hemisphere, in his use of alternative pathways to perform the function in question, and in his ability to preserve performance via the mechanism of "external" cuing, utilizing some normally functioning modality. What Geschwind is defending is not the legitimacy of localizing function in an individual but rather the validity of generalizing to all patients functional-localization hypotheses derived from a single patient or small group of patients. His strategy is to show that such generalizations can be maintained in the face of apparent counterexamples such as Kleist's patient because there are legitimate exceptions to such generalizations. We shall return to the problem of generalizing from a small patient sample shortly. For the moment the important point is that the question of the legitimacy of generalization is different from the question of the legitimacy of localization. Many so-called antilocalizationist arguments have in fact been concerned with the former rather than the latter.

Does the fact that the anti-localizationists have failed to address the real localization issue mean that localization arguments are unproblematic? Unfortunately not. Some rather deep problems exist on which we will touch briefly. Like arguments purporting to support functional deficit hypotheses, localization arguments are best construed as inferences to the best explanation. Hence, for a localization argument to count as a good argument, it must be the case that (a) the functional localization hypothesis figures in an explanation of why there is a functional deficiency in F_c, and (b) no better explanation of why there is a deficiency in F_c is available. It is because of (b) that difficulties arise.

The only support available for (b) comes from seeking and

ruling out (on empirical grounds) as many alternative explanations as possible. The seeking can be seriously hindered by lack of theoretical imagination; the ruling out, by serious methodological obstacles. Consider two of the most obvious possible alternative explanations.

Alternative explanation (1): S is the structural realization of some other functional component F_c'. However, normal operation of F_c' is necessary for normal operation of F_c. Hence, the lesion in S produces a deficit in F_c' which, in turn, produces a failure in F_c.

Alternative explanation (2): there is a lesion in some other brain structure S' as well as in S. S' rather than S is the structural realization of F_c. Hence, there is a deficit in F_c.

To rule out the first alternative, it suffices to establish the following:

(i) No functional component whose normal operation is necessary for the normal operation of F_c is deficient.

Evidence relevant to (i) is, in principle, obtainable from a careful examination of the functional analyses used in arriving at the functional deficit hypothesis. In particular, it should be possible to ascertain when there is a significant probability of (i)'s being false. For example, in our functional analysis for omelet making the pathological output consisting of a cold pan containing a raw egg mixture can occur either because there is a deficit in the component which turns on the heat under the pan (C5) or a deficit in the component which places the pan on the stove (C3). In both cases, however, the pathological output is accompanied by a failure of C5 to operate properly, once for intrinsic reasons and once because of the failure of a previous component. Given a functional analysis that reveals failure could be due to a deficit in any of several components, we obviously cannot with full confidence maintain (i).

One way to rule out the second alternative is to satisfy the following condition:

(ii) There are no other brain lesions in O.

Although this condition poses no real difficulties with regard to verification, it is often useless since aphasia patients frequently exhibit more than one lesion. Fortunately, (ii) is stronger than necessary. What is required is that no other *relevant* brain lesions exist. How to specify relevance is, of course, problematic. One way to capture the weaker requirement is this:

(iii) Any other brain lesion in O is such that had it occurred unaccompanied by any other lesions, a deficit in functional component F_c would not have occurred; further, had the lesion in S occurred unaccompanied by any other lesions, a deficit in F_c would still have occurred.

Because of its counter-factual character, (iii) introduces some rather interesting difficulties. First, since we can never examine the functional consequences of the very lesions which exist in O occurring in different circumstances, we must assume that lesions can be categorized by type and that lesions of the same type will have the same kind of functional consequences. This introduces the difficulty of determining the relevant types. Second, because functional deficits are, in general, not recoverable, and more importantly, because of the ethics of research on human subjects, evidence for (iii) will probably come from an individual other than the one directly under study. Such evidence will be relevant to the individual under study only if the neural, functional, and structural organization of the second individual is similar in all relevant respects to that of the first. If not, the evidence will be extremely misleading.

Thus we are faced with the problem of generalization. If human beings are vastly different in either functional or structural organization, our ability to gather the necessary evidence for inferring localization of function in a particular individual will be seriously impaired. Note, however, that even in this dire situation, functional localization hypotheses for particular individuals can in principle be established. The difficulties introduced will be pragmatic ones.

There is no reason to believe that the situation with respect to generalization is dire. It is problematic, though, not so much for logical reasons, as for factual and methodological ones. Human brains simply differ in various ways, just as other human body parts do. Generalization from one individual to another always must take account of individual differences, plasticity of function, neural reorganization and so forth. In addition, whether or not strong correlations of structure and function will be forthcoming depends heavily on whether we have the terms of the correlation right, even where no individual differences exist. Getting the terms right is particularly problematic on the structural side. Gross anatomical features simply may not do. A better index may be the origin of morphological development, but this is in practice impossible to determine in human beings. All this will require careful consideration in any fruitful program of research.

Implications for biology of language If our analysis of the logic of functional localization is correct, it carries an important implication for the conduct of research in the biology of language. The primary research aim of the biology of language at this time is to investigate the neural realization of LRCS. Such investigation currently relies heavily on the method of functional localization. Examining the logic of this method reveals that *in order to develop adequate functional-localization hypotheses in the domain of human linguistic capacity, the joint participation of linguistics, psycholinguistics, and neurology is absolutely essential.*

The argument has two sides. On the one hand, linguistics and psycholinguistics are required for the construction of functional-localization hypotheses which have the status of the best available working hypotheses. The reason is this. For a functional-localization hypothesis to be regarded as the best available working hypothesis, it must in turn be based on a functional analysis of how the organism has the capacity under study, which constitutes the best available possible explanation of that capacity. It is precisely the business of linguistics and psycholinguistics to provide such functional analyses and to test them with respect to the range of data from normal subjects, thereby determining their explanatory role.

On the other hand, neurology is required to ensure that the functional analyses put forward by linguistics and psycholinguistics count as more than possible explanations of how human beings have linguistic capacity. For a functional analysis to count as an (actual) explanation, we have seen that it must be structurally adequate; that is, it must be part of a functional-component model for which a structural realization exists. But this can be determined only by the use of such neurological techniques as the method of functional localization.

A strong dependency among the disciplines exists. It should be clear that if this dependency is ignored in the conduct of research on the neural realization of language, significant progress will be impossible.

2

The Linguistic Interpretation of Aphasic Syndromes

MARY-LOUISE KEAN

Traditionally the most prominent area of study of the biological foundations of language has been research on the neuro-anatomical localization of linguistic functions. The question that was raised for us in this area was: can one provide accounts of the language deficits caused by focal lesions in the brain which are rigorous in terms of universal theories of the knowledge and use of language? We had no doubt that clinicians employ essentially universal characterizations of aphasic syndromes, but it was not clear to us that these could be "translated" into the terms of current linguistic theory in a way which was not trivial and which offered meaningful new insights into the neuroanatomical organization of linguistic function.

Our approach to this topic was first to establish to our satisfaction that there were qualitative differences in the linguistic deficits associated with lesions in various areas of the brain. Having done that, we then focused on one particular aphasic syndrome to see whether or not a perspicuous characterization of that syndrome could be given with respect to the linguistic theory which we had presupposed. The main body of the text to follow deals with the latter enterprise.

The aphasia we considered was Broca's aphasia. We argue here that the recent characterizations of Broca's aphasia as a language deficit involving the compromise of phonetic, phonological, syntactic, and semantic functions is untenable. It is our hypothesis that the manifested linguistic deficits of Broca's aphasia can be accounted for only in terms of the interaction between an impaired phonological capacity and otherwise intact linguistic capacities. Our argument for this hypothesis is two-pronged; we argue on the one hand that it is the only possible grammatical interpretation of the syndrome and on the other that this is the only systematic account consistent with what is known of the structure of the language-processing system.

Our argument is first made in terms of the grammatical system. We begin by discussing certain aspects of the linguistic deficits of Broca's aphasics which are fairly generally taken to be evidence of a phonological deficit. We then turn to those aspects of the observed linguistic deficits of Broca's aphasics which have been argued to be evidence of compromises to other aspects of the normal linguistic capacity. We focus in particular on agrammatism, the tendency of Broca's aphasics to omit grammatical morphemes and function words in their speech. We argue that the pattern of omissions can be given a uniform account as the phonological simplification of a sentence into the minimal string of "phonological words" within the sentence.

Having given this grammatical account of the syndrome, we then show that the capacity to construe items as phonological words is part of the normal capacity for linguistic processing. It is our argument that by assuming all aspects of the language faculty to be intact, save for the phonological, we can predict that there will be systematic variation in the likelihood of omission of function words and grammatical morphemes which parallels the variation in the way these elements are treated within the normal processing system. Not only are the data on language processing consistent with our claim that Broca's aphasia is a purely phonological impairment, they also directly support that argument, in that they show that many of the "deficits" of Broca's aphasics are, in fact, simply reflections of the normal, intact language-processing system.

In the last chapter we discussed the theory of functional localization in some detail, illustrating that discussion with the functional analysis of a neurological deficit outside the proper domain of language. In this chapter we want to turn to the possibility of doing detailed studies of "localization" of linguistic function, as such studies can be pursued in the context of the study of aphasic syndromes. We shall, for the most part, concern ourselves with the domains of LRCS which are characterized by the theory of grammar, domains which we take to be involved in the theory of linguistic performance (see Chapter 1).

Aphasias typically arise from lesions in the dominant (i.e., left) hemisphere. Based on this observation and other data, it is argued that the left hemisphere has a privilege for language not shared with its right counterpart. Once we have localized language in the left hemisphere, the question arises as to whether linguistic function is neuroanatomically represented as an equipotential function for all components of the system across some area of the left hemisphere, or whether various components of linguistic function [e.g., phonology (for production or perception), syntax] are distinctly represented neuroanatomically. In the case of phonetic functions, we know that there is not a single phonetic center in the left hemisphere, but rather one for the control of movements of the vocal apparatus (in the lower portion of the motor strip) and one for the control of speech recognition (in the temporal lobe). Thus we know that there is not complete equipotential representation of linguistic functions. However, what we do not know is whether the "higher" linguistic functions may also be characterized in terms of distinct neuroanatomical domains.

There is good clinical evidence that there is some neuroanatomical division of linguistic domains; above the level of phonetics, focal damage in the left hemisphere does not lead to an across-the-board reduction in linguistic capacity. Lesions in different areas of the left hemisphere lead to qualitatively distinct aphasic syndromes. For example, let us consider the two most commonly known aphasias: Broca's aphasia and Wernicke's aphasia. [In the aphasia literature there is considerable terminological diversity in the designation of these two syndromes. Broca's aphasia is also known as motor aphasia, a contiguity disorder, etc.; Wernicke's aphasia is also referred to as sensory (motor) aphasia, syntactic aphasia, receptive aphasia, posterior aphasia, etc. Goldstein (1948), Head (1963), Jakobson (1964, 1966), Luria (1966, 1970), Weisenberg and McBride (1964), Wernicke (1874).]

Clinicians distinguish these two syndromes behaviorally in terms of such things as a patient's speech *fluency*. Fluency does not refer to the contentfulness or appropriateness of a patient's speech but rather to such factors as the typical length and grammatical well-formedness of the patient's utterances. Wernicke's aphasics typically are fluent; their utterances are fairly long, and their sentences are generally well formed. Broca's aphasics are typically nonfluent; they speak in short, halting phrases, and their sentences are generally not syn-tactically well formed on the surface. In spite of this variance in fluency, it is Broca's aphasics and not Wernicke's aphasics whose verbal output is more generally appropriate and makes sense. Broca's aphasics tend to speak in an interrupted sequence of noun(ish) words which are apropos to the discourse in which they are engaged; Wernicke's aphasics often speak at length in a discourse (having what is known as a press of speech), but their discourses are often like a sequence of non sequiturs, to the extent that they are germane, and jargon words (words which have the form of, for example, English words but which are in fact not English words) are used.

In normal adults, Broca's aphasia arises from a lesion in what is typically called Broca's area, the posterior part of third (inferior) frontal gyrus (Brodmann's areas 44 and 45) immediately in front of the motor area controlling the vocal tract (see Figure 1). Wernicke's aphasia is generally associated with a lesion in Wernicke's area (Brodmann's area 22) in the temporal lobe in the auditory-association cortex adjacent to the auditory cortex (Heschl's gyrus).

While there is some debate in the literature over the exact circumscription of the cortical areas associated with these syndromes, in the clinical reports that we are aware of, the occurrence of these syndromes is associated consistently with brain damage involving these areas. The precise definition of these areas is a problem for neuroanatomy; it is sufficient for our present purposes that there are qualitatively distinct

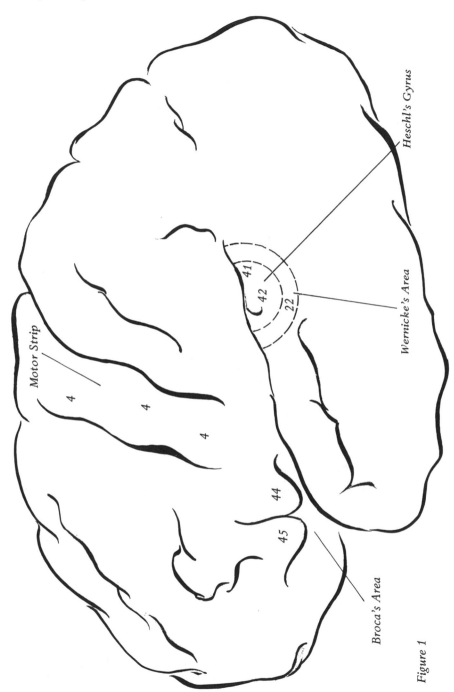

Figure 1

syndromes associated with distinct areas of the brain. While characterizations of the verbal behavior of Broca's and Wernicke's aphasics such as those given above are clinically viable, they are not perspicuous in terms of our understanding of the exact linguistic functions of these areas. Having observed that there are such distinctions to be made in the performance of aphasics, we must ask in what sense are the areas correlated with these deficits committed to linguistic functions. We must inquire, for example, as to whether we can associate each of these syndromes with particular domains of LRCS. This is essentially to ask if particular areas of the left hemisphere have differential commitments to various linguistic functions, e.g., phonological production or syntactic perception.

It is beyond the scope of this report to consider each of the aphasias. We shall focus in detail on one syndrome, Broca's aphasia, as an example of this type of inquiry. We shall argue that this syndrome can be interpreted as a deficit to a specific component of LRCS, the component concerned with the phonological (not phonetic) domain of language. Our argument cannot be interpreted as being a claim that Broca's area is the "home" of phonological language production; from the data on Broca's aphasia we can conclude only that it is necessary that this area be intact for continuous normal language use; there may well be other areas, as yet unspecified, that also play an important role in phonological function.

The material to follow can be broken down into four major sections. In the first section we shall elaborate on the characterization of Broca's aphasia given above. In the second section our argument is put forward. This section may be somewhat difficult for the reader who is not particularly familiar with phonological theory. In order to make our argument, it is necessary to develop some of the fundamental concepts of phonological theory; we have attempted to introduce these concepts with a minimum of formal considerations so that the reader will be able to understand the basic points at issue. We shall, in particular, be concerned with the mapping from the phonological representation of a word in the lexicon to its phonetic representation [see Chomsky and Halle (1968)]. In the third part of the chapter we shall review some recent articles on Broca's aphasia. In the course of this review additional data on the nature of the deficit will be introduced, and these data will be shown to be consistent with the hypothesis that Broca's aphasia is a phonological deficit. In the articles to be discussed in the second section, the interpretation of the syndrome offered is what we might call the traditional interpretation, a view that Broca's aphasia is a deficit that affects virtually all the domains of LRCS—phonetics, phonology, morphology, syntax, semantics, etc. Therefore, in this part we shall also be concerned with pointing out the advantages of our interpretation of the syndrome over the traditional interpretation. The fourth, and final, section briefly covers issues in neuroanatomy which arise in connection with discussions of Broca's aphasia. We shall focus on two issues. One is the debate over whether it is the surface size or the depth of the lesion which is the critical factor in determining the degree of the deficit. The other issue on which we touch is the relation of Broca's area to other areas in the left hemisphere which are associated with linguistic functions.

A Characterization of the Syndrome of Broca's Aphasia

Broca's aphasia is generally characterized in terms of the "typical" difficulties of Broca's aphasics in language production. One of the most striking characteristics of the speech of Broca's aphasics is the relatively high frequency of segmental (literal, phonemic) paraphasias—e.g., saying [tayn] for [taym], 'time.' These segmental substitutions are taken as providing evidence that in Broca's aphasia this is at least a phonological deficit [Jakobson (1968), Lecours and Lhermitte (1969), Blumstein (1970, 1973)]. This hypothesis is further supported by the fact that there is typically no phrasal or sentential stress or intonation in the sentences produced by these patients (i.e., it is dysprosodic). So-called word-boundary bound morphemes (e.g., the plural marker *s* in English as in *boy<u>s</u>*, tense marker, e.g., *ed* in *want<u>ed</u>*, comparative marker *er* in *tall<u>er</u>*) are often omitted, and it has been argued from this omission that Broca's aphasics also have a morphological deficit [Goodglass and Berko

(1960), Gleason et al. (1975)]. In addition, it has commonly been agreed that Broca's aphasics have a syntactic deficit [Goodglass (1973), Goodglass et al. (1972)] because of the typical agrammatism (telegraphism) of the sentences they produce. The term agrammatism is usually employed to refer to both the putative morphological deficit and the omission of "function" words, e.g., *the, will,* in sentences. Finally, it has been suggested that Broca's aphasics also have a lexical deficit because they experience word-finding difficulties [Zurif and Blumstein (1976)].

Each of the deficits listed above shows up not only in speech but also in other modalities of language use. The types of errors observed in the reading aloud and writing of Broca's aphasics parallel those of their spontaneous speech. In comprehension tests there is evidence of lack of attention to word-boundary morphemes and function words [Parisi and Pizzamiglio (1970), Lesser (1974), Goodenough et al. (forthcoming)]. On so-called metalinguistic tasks (for example, tests which require a subject to parse a sentence) Broca's aphasics also show inattention to word-boundary morphemes and function words [von Stockert (1972), Zurif et al. (1972)]. All the linguistic behavior of Broca's aphasics is generally effortful and labored, and typically they are acutely aware of their linguistic deficit.

This picture is further complicated by the results of some recent phonetic studies on articulation and perception. Blumstein, Cooper, Caramazza, and Zurif have found that the speech production of Broca's aphasics is somewhat different from that of normal subjects (as shown by comparative acoustic analyses), and that while Broca's aphasics categorically perceive speech segments, they have difficulty in correctly identifying them. These data have been taken as showing that Broca's aphasics have a phonetic deficit.

The picture that emerges in the literature then is that of a syndrome which is characterized by impairment to all components of the linguistic system in all language modalities (see Table 1 for summary).

It will be argued here, however, that the usual grammatical descriptions of the impairments of Broca's aphasics do not accurately characterize their linguistic deficits. We propose that all the deficits of Broca's aphasia can be characterized systematically in terms of the phonological component of the grammar. Furthermore, it will be argued that this is the only systematic grammatical interpretation of the syndrome which is plausible, either in terms of the particular language of a Broca's aphasic or in terms of universal grammar (the theory of the possible grammars of natural human languages—see the second part of Chapter 1).

Broca's Aphasia: A Phonological Deficit

The phonological component of the grammar assigns to sentences their sound interpretation. On the one hand, it specifies the segmental sound shape of the individual words, for example, distinguishing the initial segment (sound) of 'pun' from the initial segment of 'fun.' On the other, it specifies stress and intonation patterns of the words in a sentence and of sentences as a whole. It is the former function of the phonological component which provides a natural context for explaining both the segmental paraphasias and the agrammatism of Broca's aphasics.

The phonological component of the grammar must provide a phonetically unambiguous interpretation of how sentences sound. There is a level of generalization at which we want to say that the initial sound of 'pan' is the same as the final sound of 'nip.' However, in English, voiceless stops (*p, t, k*) are

Table 1

	(Spontaneous) speech	Writing	Reading out loud	Reading silently	Comprehension of speech
Effortful	+	+	+	+	+
Segmental paraphasia	+	+	+		
Dysprosody	+		+		
Agrammatism	+	+	+		+

pronounced with aspiration when they are in initial position in words such as 'pan' (a comparatively large volume of air is expelled in their release) and without aspiration when they are in final position, as in 'nip.' Consequently, a complete sound representation of a sentence which contains 'pan' will include the specification that the initial segment is aspirated; conversely, the sound representation of a sentence with 'nip' must include the information that the *p* is not aspirated.

Among languages there is variation in the degree to which various phonetic properties of sounds are present in the realization of sentences. These variations are, however, consistent within languages. Thus, in English when a vowel is followed by a nasal sound (e.g., [m], [n], or [ŋ]) it is nasalized (the former two symbols represent the sounds which we usually write with the letters *m* and *n*, and the last one symbolizes the nasal sound in 'think' and 'thing.'). But when a vowel is flanked by nonnasal segments it is not nasalized at all. The degree of nasalization found in English vowels is less than that which is found in some other languages. For example, in Guarani (a South American Indian language), nasalization is a much more pervasive phenomenon. In articulatory terms variation in the degree of nasalization of vowels is a function of the amount of air which is allowed to pass through the nose during the articulation of the vowel. Since the degree to which a vowel will be nasalized varies from language to language, this variation must be specified within the grammatical system of the language by some system of rules which assigns scalar specifications to the properties of sounds.

We have discussed two levels of segmental representations: the level of lexical representations (where, for example, the generalization that the *p*'s in 'pan' and 'nip' are the same is captured) and the level of phonetic representations where the presence or absence of the properties of speech sounds is specified in degrees (and the two *p*'s have different representations)—see Chomsky and Halle (1968) for further discussion of the distinction between lexical and phonetic representations. If there were a true *phonological* deficit, we would expect both these levels of representation to be affected. In cases where the deficit is not so extreme as to leave a person without the ability to produce sentences, the deficit in phonetic representation would manifest itself as articulatory variation from the norm, in the degree to which (some) properties of sounds are present in a given segment. Thus the data reported by Blumstein et al. (1977), which show that the articulation of Broca's aphasics (without articulatory deficits such as dysarthria) is deviant from normal segmental articulation, is consistent with the hypothesis that Broca's aphasics have a phonological deficit. The discrimination and categorical perception of segments is a phonetic capacity; therefore, it would be expected that an individual with a language-related deficit which is not perceptual or phonetic in character would perform normally on discrimination and categorical-perception tasks. However, since the naming of a segment requires assigning a phonological interpretation to the perceived acoustic signal, an individual with a phonological deficit would be expected to perform more poorly than normals on tasks which involve the identification and naming of perceived segments. It is exactly this pattern in speech recognition that Blumstein et al. found; so these data too are consistent with the hypothesis that Broca's aphasics have a phonological deficit. At the level of representation of segments in the lexicon, a phonological deficit would involve the incorrect "identification" of a segment in a word, that we might think of as a misreading of the phonological information about a segment which is stored in lexical entries. Such misreadings would involve, for example, "reading" the voicing specification of the *p* in 'pan' not as voiceless but as voiced, leading the person to say 'ban' instead of 'pan.' Thus the fact that Broca's aphasics typically make segmental paraphasias is also consistent with the hypothesis that they have a phonological deficit.

Not only can we distinguish between the degrees to which some sound has, or does not have, some phonetic property, we can also classify sounds with respect to the degree to which they are members of general classes. The ancient Sanskrit grammarian Panini organized the segmental system of Sanskrit in terms of what is known today as the sonorance hierarchy, a ranking of sounds from the most vowel-like (vowels) to the least vowel-like (stop consonants). The glides *w* and *y* are the most vowel-like nonvowel sounds, because in their articulation the air flow through the oral cavity is relatively unimpeded. Next in the ranking come the liquids, *l* and *r*; while the flow of air through the vocal tract is somewhat impeded in producing these sounds, it is not radically obstructed. Nasal consonants are ranked next; in their production the oral cavity is completely closed but the air flow is diverted through the opened nasal cavity. Fricative consonants (e.g., *f, v, s, z*) are ranked after the nasals; fricatives are produced with a radical, and often noise-producing obstruction, but not with a complete closure in the oral cavity, and the nasal cavity is blocked. Finally come the stop consonants (*p, t, k, b, d, g*) which are produced with a momentary, but complete, closure in the vocal tract. This sonorance hierarchy ranks sounds by what is traditionally called their "manner" of articulation. Acoustically, the ranking correlates with the relative energy of a sound with respect to adjacent segments.

In natural languages phonological processes which are sensitive to "manner" (such as aspiration in English) never affect classes of segments which are not adjacent on the sonorance hierarchy. Thus, for example, no single rule of the phonology of any language applies only to liquids and stops. The sonorance hierarchy is frequently characterized in less detail than above as a ranking of three classes of segments: vowels and glides (no impedence of air flow), liquids and nasals (nonradical impedence of air flow), and fricatives and stops (radical impedence of the air flow).

Many of the morphological omissions of Broca's aphasics are conditioned by the sonorance hierarchy. In general, consonantal morphemes, such as the *-s* of the plural in English, are least likely to be deleted in the speech of Broca's aphasics after the most sonorant segments (vowels), and most likely to be deleted after the least sonorant segments (fricatives and stops). The likelihood of their deletion when preceded by liquids (and possibly nasals) appears to be greater than when preceded by vowels, but less than when preceded by consonants. As far as we have been able to ascertain in reviewing the literature, this area has not been very extensively investigated beyond the basic research of Goodglass and Berko (1960), who found that postvocalic consonantal morphemes were more likely to be retained. Experimental paradigms already well established in aphasia research (e.g., repetition tasks) provide appropriate frameworks for detailed and systematic study of this area. (This issue is discussed further below.)

The examples of aspiration and nasalization given earlier illustrate that the phonological component of the grammar is context-sensitive; that is, some of the properties of the sounds in a sentence are determined by the position of a given sound in a string of sounds. Let us now consider a somewhat more complicated case. The case in point is the contraction of *is* onto a preceding element, as is illustrated in (1).

a. Tom's cooking dinner
b. Bea's on vacation
c. Pat's intelligent
d. Bruce's out to lunch (1)

As is shown in (2), the sound of *'s* differs depending on the preceding sound. The *'s* in both (1a) and (1b) have the sound of *z* when said; however, in (1c) *'s* has the sound of *s*, and in (1d) it is realized as a sequence of sounds [əz].

a. Tom[z] cooking dinner
b. Bea[z] on vacation
c. Pat[s] intelligent
d. Bruce[əz] out to lunch (2)

These alternate realizations of the contracted *is* are regular in English: after strident coronals (segments produced with the tongue approaching the area ranging from the alveolar ridge across the hard palate, and with acoustic turbulence) it is realized as a syllable, [əz]; after a voiceless segment other than a voiceless strident coronal it has a [s] sound; and after every other sound which is neither a strident coronal nor voiceless it is realized as [z].

There must be a level of grammatical representation in which all the sentences in (1) contain the verb *is*, because the sentences in each pair in (3) mean the same thing as the sentences in (1,2); the distinction between (1,2) and (3) is a relatively minor one.

a. Tom is cooking dinner   : Tom [Iz] cooking dinner
   Tom's cooking dinner   : Tom [z] cooking dinner
b. Bea is on vacation   : Bea [Iz] on vacation
   Bea's on vacation   : Bea [z] on vacation
c. Pat is intelligent   : Pat [Iz] intelligent
   Pat's intelligent   : Pat [s] intelligent
d. Bruce is out to lunch   : Bruce [Iz] out to lunch
   Bruce's out to lunch   : Bruce [əz] out to lunch   (3)

The grammar of English must provide an account for these data. The account proposed has two steps: the first step, which describes a process called cliticization, attaches *is* (under certain conditions) to the preceding word; the second step is the specification of the sound realization of the attached *is*. By cliticization a structure such as (4a) is mapped onto a structure such as (4b).

a. $[_{S}\# \; [_{N}\# \; \text{Tom} \; \#_{N}] \; [_{Aux} \; \text{is} \; _{Aux}] \; [_{VP}\# \; \text{cooking dinner} \; \#_{VP}] \#_{S}]$

b. $[_{S}\# \; [_{N}\# \; [_{N}\# \; \text{Tom} \; \#_{N}] \; \text{is} \; \#_{N}] \; [_{Aux} \; ^{*} \; _{Aux}] \; [_{VP}\# \; \text{cooking dinner} \; \#_{VP}] \; \#_{S}]$ (4)

At first it may seem odd to think of *is* becoming part of a noun. However, if we consider other areas of English we find strong support for this analysis. For example, consider the italic words in (5), (6), and (7).

a. two *hams*   :   ham[z]
b. the seven *seas*   :   sea[z]
c. too many *cooks*   :   cook[s]
d. hanging *judges*   :   judge[əz]   (5)

a. *Basil's* church   :   Basil[z]
b. The *bee's* knees   :   bee[z]   (note: knee[z])
c. the *cat's* meow   :   cat[s]
d. *Morris's* beard   :   Morris[əz]   (6)

a. the cad sometimes *robs* poor widows   : rob[z]
b. I don't know what she *sees* in him   : see[z]
c. Parthenia never *rats* on anyone   : rat[s]
d. he *closes* his mind to all innovation : close[əz]   (7)

The nouns in (5) are regular plurals ending in -s; the nouns in (6) are marked by the genitive (possessive), 's; the verbs in (7) all carry the third person singular present tense marker, -s. Just as is the case with contracted *is,* the phonological realization of these markers after strident coronals is as [əz]; after a voiceless segment which is not a voiceless strident coronal, they are realized as [s]; and after a segment which is neither a voiceless one nor a strident coronal, these markers, like contracted *is,* are realized as [z].

It is important to notice that no matter what sound ends a word which immediately precedes another word beginning with [əz], [s], or [z], these sounds are not altered, as is illustrated in (8) to (10). [The sentences in (8) to (10) are organized in a parallel fashion to those in (2), (3), (5) to (7). The (d) sentences have words ending in strident coronals preceding the [s], [z], and [əz]; the (c) sentences have words ending in voiceless nonstrident consonants preceding [s], [z], and [əz]; and the (a) and (b) sentences have words ending in other segments preceding the [s], [z], and [əz]. A * before a string means that it is ungrammatical.]

   Usric   :   [əz] ric
a. the boss said that we should can Usric
   *the boss said we should can [z] ric
b. Arnold walked to Usric's house
   *Arnold walked to [z] ric's house
c. it's not easy to survive with a name like Usric
   *it's not easy to survive with a name like [s] ric
d. there are few people as clever as Usric   (8)

   soft : [s] oft
a. a warm soft puppy
   *a warm [z] oft puppy
b. dance to soft music
   * dance to [z] oft music
c. speak softly
d. it is difficult to screech softly
   *it is difficult to screech [əz] oftly   (9)

zebra : [z] ebra
a. a small zebra
b. three zebras
c. a ridiculously fat zebra
   *a ridiculously fat [s] ebra
d. only mean people tease zebras
   *only mean people tease [əz] bras   (10)

Since we do not find the [s], [z], [əz] alternation across words [examples 8 to 10] but do find this alternation in the suffixes of words [examples 5 to 7], there is strong *prima facie* evidence that when *is* is contracted, it becomes a suffix of the immediately preceding word. Cliticization of *is* therefore can be seen as a process which takes a sequence of a word followed by *is,* and turns that structure into a word structure that is the same as that of a noun with a possessive or plural suffix or of a verb with the third person present suffix. The cliticization of function words is quite pervasive in normal spoken English; where cliticization is possible, it generally occurs. The second sentence of each of the pairs in (3), and not the first, is typical of nonemphatic English.

To provide a systematic description of the form of languages, it is necessary to develop notational conventions for representing the structure of sentences. For example, the symbols used to represent the sound of language, e.g., *p,* are notational conventions, as is the use of [ ] to set off phonetic representations of segments, e.g., [p], and the use of / / to set off phonological representations, e.g., /p/. As the examples just discussed show, we need some notation for distinguishing one word from another, a notation to separate words. The notation conventionally used in linguistics for this purpose is #; # (called a word boundary) is assigned to the right and to the left of every word which is in a major lexical category. The major lexical categories are all the syntactic categories other than those of so-called function words; thus noun (N), adjective (A), verb (V), and adverb (Adv) are major lexical categories, but determiner (Det)—the category of articles 'a' and 'the', preposition (P), etc., are not. The information specifying the category of a word is marked as a subscript on [ ], which appears to the left and right, respectively, of words. Some examples of these notations are given in (11).

$[_N \# \text{boy} \# _N]$
$[_{Det} \text{the} _{Det}]$
$[_V \# \text{run} \# _V]$
$[_A \# \text{soft} \# _A]$
$[_P \text{up} _P]$ (11)

The plural marker, the possessive, and the third person verbal marker all attach to words to make "new" words. The structure of a word plus one of these suffixes is, by the notational system developed here, like that of the words in (12).

$[_N\# [_N \# \text{boy} \# _N] \text{s} \#_N]$ (*boys,* plural, or *boy's,* possessive)
$[_V\# [_V \# \text{run} \# _V] \text{s} \#_V]$ (*runs*) (12)

To account for the phonological similarity of contracted *is* and these markers, under contraction a word plus *is* is assigned an analogous structure.

$[_N\# [_N \# \text{boy} \# _N] \text{is} \#_N]$ (*boy's* as in 'the boy's [boy is] late for school') (13)

It is because of the occurrence of # between the word and its suffix in the items in (12) that the plural, possessive, and verb markers are called here word-boundary morphemes. Since the phonological structure of a word with contracted *is* is the same as that of a word with one of these suffixes, we can say that contracted *is* is a derived word-boundary morpheme. The similarity of the structure of the items in (12) and (13) is purely phonological. The affixes which Broca's aphasics are typically most likely to omit are those which are phonologically word-boundary morphemes.

Not all suffixes and prefixes are word-boundary morphemes. There is another class of affixes which we can see in such latinate words as *permit, remit, submit, reject, subject,* and *object.* Unlike, for example, the plural *-s,* the prefixes *per-, re-, sub-,* and *ob-* do not attach to words. (The prefix *re-* in *remit* is different from the prefix *re-* in *rewind;* while the latter *re-* roughly means "again;" the former does not.) These prefixes attach to stems, morphemes which do not occur on their own as words—e.g., *-mit* and *-ject*—to make words. Our convention for the assignment of word boundaries (#) is that one is assigned to the right and one to the left of major lexical items. Since stems such as *-mit* and *-ject* are not major lexical items (i.e., they are not nouns, verbs, adjectives, or adverbs), the prefixes which attach to them cannot be word-boundary morphemes. That is, by the notational conventions introduced above, a # will not intervene between one of these prefixes and the stem which follows it. Because, for example, *sub-* and *-mit* are independent formatives of a word and each can combine with other formatives, for example, *-ject* and *per-*, respectively, we want a notation which will capture the fact that these words do have internal structure. The symbol + (called a formative boundary) is used in characterizing the internal structure of such words; a + separates the prefix from the stem in, for example, [$_V$ # sub + mit # $_V$]. In the speech of English-speaking Broca's aphasics non-word-boundary morphemes such as these typically are not omitted.

If the hypothesis that Broca's aphasia is a phonological deficit is to be maintained, we must establish that there is an interesting phonological difference between words that have word-boundary affixes and words which have non-word-boundary affixes. That is to say, there must be a phonological motivation for the notational distinction between + and #, and we must find this distinction realized in some fashion in the speech of Broca's aphasics.

In English, the basic difference between word-boundary affixes and non-word-boundary affixes is that the former do not affect the stress pattern of a word, while the latter do. The nominalizing suffix *-ness* is a word-boundary suffix in English, and the adjectival suffix *-ive* is a non-word-boundary suffix. When *-ness* is added to a word there is no change in the place where stress occurs on a word; but when *-ive* is added to a formative, there can be a change in the place where stress occurs, as is illustrated in (14).

a. définite   définiteness
   désolate   désolateness

b. trepidácious   trepidáciousness
 définite   defínitive
 illustrate   illústrative
 cóntemplate   contémplative   (14)

We introduced the notion of word-boundary morpheme simply to identify affixes which attach to what we intuitively feel are words. Retaining the structure we assigned above to words with word-boundary morphemes, we shall further refine the concept by saying that word-boundary morphemes are those affixes which do not affect the stress of a word (in English). This is to say that in the word *definiteness, definite* is phonologically a word, but that in *definitive* the word *definite* is not a word phonologically.

The notion of "word" we are using here is, of course, not the ordinary usage of that term; in English a phonological "word" is the string of segments, marked by boundaries, which function in the assignment of stress to a word. In *definiteness* (and all other *-ness* words) the presence of *-ness* is ignored phonologically for purposes of stress assignment, but in *definitive* the presence of *-ive* plays a crucial role in determining the placement of stress. The affixation of the plural, possessive, or verbal markers to a word never affects the placement of stress on an English word, nor does the cliticization of *is*. In the speech of Broca's aphasics the stress pattern of words is normally retained. Therefore, we can say of English-speaking Broca's aphasics that they have a tendency to omit those affixes which do not play a role in the assignment of stress to words.

There are several different sources for words with word-boundary morphemes. Some words are derived morphologically by rules for the formation of lexical items; for example, plural nouns and words with *-ness* are derived by the word-formation rules of the lexicon [see Aronoff (1977) for an extensive discussion of such rules]. In other cases the presence of a word-boundary morpheme is a function of the syntactic structure of the sentence or phrase. For example, the gerundive morpheme *-ing* (as in 'his sing*ing* is off key') occurs only as a nominalizing suffix attached to verbs in certain syntactic configurations. Such syntactically derived morphemes are called inflectional morphemes, and in English all inflectional morphemes are word-boundary morphemes. The comparative marker (as in 'happi*er*') the genetive marker, the passive -*ed* (as in 'that was cook*ed* by Bocuse'), and the markers of present and past tense ('she work*s* hard,' 'she work*ed* on Saturday') are all inflectional morphemes. A third source of words with this structure is the cliticization rule which attaches one word to another. Word-boundary morphemes form a natural class (that is, a unified class) only in terms of the phonological properties of a language. If we were to claim that the omission of word-boundary morphemes in Broca's aphasia was a function of a deficit in word formation, we would have no clear explanation as to why the formatives in words such as *permit* are not likely to be omitted; whereas formatives such as -*ness* seldom occur: the rules of word formation are concerned with both types of words. It is only in their phonological structure that these two classes are distinguished. Thus in terms of the structure of English there are two arguments which support the hypothesis that the omission of word-boundary suffixes in Broca's aphasia is the result of a phonological deficit: the first is that although there are many different sources for these affixes, what unifies them is their phonological properties; the second is that at some levels in the grammar, e.g., the level of word formation, there are different types of affixes which are affected differently in the verbal output of Broca's aphasics, and those classes can be distinguished in terms of phonological structure.

It has been observed that Broca's aphasics generally retain proper word stress. This is, of course, consistent with our hypothesis that they ignore material which does not affect stress. In a sentence function words do not carry stress or affect the stress pattern of the sentence; for example, there is no intonational difference in the two sentences of (15) (where 1 represents the intonationally most prominent element of the sentence, and 2 and 3 represent decreases in relative prominence).

$$\overset{2}{\text{a. Boys}}\ \overset{3}{\text{climb}}\ \overset{1}{\text{trees}}$$

$$\overset{2}{\text{b. Boys}}\ \overset{3}{\text{run}}\ \overset{1}{\text{home}}$$

```
        2  3      1
```
c. The boy ran to school

```
        2  3      1
```
d. The boys climb up trees   (15)

Thus function words, like word-boundary affixes, are not sensitive to stress. We noted above that the # boundary was associated to the left and right of major lexical items, but not function words. To capture the phonological parallelism in stress sensitivity between function words and word-boundary affixes, a # is assigned not only to the left and right of every major lexical category (N, A, V, and Adv) but also to the left and right of every phrase and sentence which contains a lexical category. By this extension of our notation, the sentences in (15a,c) will be assigned the structures in (16a,b). [In (16) S stands for "sentence," NP for "noun phrase," VP for "verb phrase," and PP for "prepositional phrase."]

The structure of the phrase 'the boy' is the mirror image of the structure of the plural 'boys': in both cases we have a noun, *boy,* flanked by [# and #], to which an element not flanked by [# and #] is attached.

a. $[_S\# \ [_N\# \ [_N\# \ boy \ \#_N] \ s \ \#_N] \ [_{VP}\# \ [_V\# \ climb \ \#_V] \ [_N\#$
$[_N\# \ tree \ \#_N]s \ \#_N] \ \#_{VP}] \ \#_S]$

b. $[_S\# \ [_{NP}\# \ [_{Det} \ the \ _{Det}] \ [_N\# \ boy \ \#_N] \#_{NP}] \ [_{VP}\#[_V\# \ ran$
$\#_V] \ [_{PP}\# \ [_P \ to \ _P] \ [_N\# \ school \ \#_N] \ \#_{PP}]\#_S]$ (16)

a. [# the [# boy #] #]
b. [# [# boy #] s#]   (17)

Using the # notation and category brackets, we can now make a general statement about the phonological process(es) which affect the placement of stress in English: the process(es) by which stress is assigned take into consideration only strings of segments which are flanked by [# and #], and between which no #'s occur. The # symbol is simply a notational device which is used systematically to distinguish classes of structures in phonology.

Recall that we said a phonological word was defined in

English as the domain over which the assignment of stress took place. Given this characterization, function words, like the plural marker *-s* and the nominalizing suffixes *-ness* and *-ing,* are not phonological words. Having shown that function words, contracted *is,* and word-boundary affixes have the same phonological structure; i.e., they are not phonological words, we can now give a systematic account of the inattention to these items by Broca's aphasics (agrammatism).

> Items which are not phonological words tend to be omitted
> in the language of Broca's aphasics.   (18)

The force of (18) is the claim that only those items which are phonologically the most salient are maintained with regularity in the speech of Broca's aphasics.

As we have stated it, (18) suggests that an English-speaking Broca's aphasic may reduce *definiteness* to *definite* but will not reduce *definitive* to *definite* or *object* to *ob* or *ject.* However, this suggestion cannot be accepted; it is empirically falsified by the fact that suffixes such as *-ive* are deleted in spite of the fact there is not an analogous truncation of words like *object.* There is a fundamental difference between *definitive* and *object.* The lexical rules which account for the structure of *definitive* relate it to another word in English, *definite;* the rules which characterize the morphological structure of *object* do not, however, relate either *ob* or *ject* to some word (*ob* or *ject,* respectively) which does occur in English. Therefore, in terms of the structure of the lexicon, as characterized by the rules of word formation, *definitive* and *object* are quite different [Arnoff (1977)]. We therefore must revise (18).

> A Broca's aphasic tends to reduce the structure of a sentence
> to the minimal string of elements which can be lexically
> construed as phonological words in his language.   (19)

Embodied in (19) is the claim that there is no impairment to the grammatical structure of the lexicon in Broca's aphasia. Thus (19) correctly predicts that Broca's aphasics will not speak in jargon. While jargon words have the phonological form of a word in a person's language (e.g., *blick* has the form of an English word), they are not words—items in the speaker's lexicon. If the grammatical structure of the lexicon were impaired in Broca's aphasia, we would have no explanation as to why jargon is not found in the speech of Broca's aphasics. It is also implicit in (19) that there is no syntactic deficit in the so-called agrammatism of Broca's aphasics; the syntactic structure of the sentences of a Broca's aphasic are assumed to be well formed. The apparent lack of well-formedness arises not from a deficit which is intrinsically syntactic but rather from the reduction of the phonological structure of a sentence.

The structure of the mechanisms of language production (above the level of phonetics) is studied through the analysis of the spontaneous speech errors of normal individuals [Fromkin (1971, 1973); Garrett (1975, 1976)]. The logic of this approach to the study of production is quite straightforward: if, as is assumed, the mechanisms of language production are structured, then the pattern of speech errors will not be random—the structure of the language production mechanisms will constrain the set of possible errors; therefore, speech errors will reflect the organizing principles of the system of language production. If Broca's aphasia is truly only a phonological deficit, then all "nonphonological" realizations of the deficit must be accounted for in terms of the interaction of the components of the language system, and in terms of the nonphonological resources of that system.

Central to our hypothesis, (19), is the notion of "construal," which is not a phonological concept. Therefore, to maintain (19) in its strongest possible form, it is necessary to show that "construal" is part of the normal language system. Evidence that it is comes from the consideration of speech errors. The relevant class of errors are those which involve the exchange of two elements in a sentence; some examples of this type of error are given in (20).

a. McGovern favors *push*ing *bust*ers   (busting pushers)
b. I'm not in a *read* for *mood*ing   (mood for reading)
c. she's already *trunk*ed two *packs*   (packed two trunks)

(20)

In normal speech errors one does not find nonphonological words exchanging with phonological words; thus the examples in (21) illustrate impossible speech errors—errors which people do not make.

a. * they *paper*-mitted *sub*s   (submitted papers)
b. * the *ex*-s *boy*-pected to win   (boys expected)   (21)

Both *sub* and *ex* are possible phonological words in English, as is shown in (22).

a. Rickover encouraged the senators to appropriate funds for more nuclear *subs*.
b. My *ex's* new wife is a very attractive woman.   (22)

The data in (22) would appear to refute the claim that the sentences in (21) represent impossible speech errors because they involve the exchange of phonological words with non-phonological words. However, there is a crucial difference between *sub* and *ex* in (21) and *sub* and *ex* in (22). In the former case *sub* and *ex* appear as prefixes in the words *sub-mitted* and *expected;* it is because of the context of these occurrences and morphological conditions on possible words in English that the *sub* of *submitted* and the *ex* of *expected* cannot be construed as possible phonological words in (21), The data in (21) and (22) show that segmental isomorphism with occurring words is not a sufficient criterion for delimiting the class of possible exchanges, and that the internal structure of possible words provides a determining factor.

Consider now the following exchanges:

a. . . . be made a lot of money in*telephon*ing *stall*s (installing telephones)
b. my *froz*ers are *should*en (shoulders are frozen)
c. I had in*stay*ed *tend*ing (intended staying)   (23)

In each of these exchanges a string of segments which is, phonologically, a possible word (though not an actually occurring one) has been exchanged with an actually occurring phonological word. In each case the material which has been "left behind" consists of actual and possible word-boundary morphemes. We can characterize a "possible word-boundary morpheme" in this context as a sequence of segments which has the phonological shape of an occurring word-boundary morpheme and which is in a context such that if it is construed as a word-boundary morpheme the prosodic structure of the whole word is not changed materially. For example, the word *shoulders* has the lexical structure [#[# shoulder #] s #] and is stressed on the first syllable (shóulders); in (23b) *shoulders* has been construed as if it had the structure [# [# [# should #] er #] s #]. The construal of *er* in *shoulders* as a word-boundary suffix is possible because there is an occurring suffix -*er* (as in *dealers*) and -*er* does not effect stress. It follows from our definition of possible word-boundary morphemes that when such a construal is made, the nonword which is being treated as a word (e.g., [# should #]) must have the phonological structure of a possible word; that is, if some element of a word is construed as a word-boundary affix, then the remainder of the word must be phonologically construable as a word itself. The reason for this is that if the segmental material not construed as an affix did not have the shape of a possible phonological word, it could not be stressed as a phonological word, and there would therefore be a change in the prosodic structure of the whole word.

Given this analysis of the errors in (23) in terms of construal as a possible word-boundary morpheme, we can account for the nonoccurrence of errors such as that in (24).

    * they choring sals   (they sing chorals)   (24)

For such an error to occur it would require that *sing* be treated as if it had the structure [# [# s #] ing #] by analogy with, for example, [# [# want #] ing #]) and *chorals* as if it had the structure [# [# [# chor #] al #] s #] (by analogy with, for example, [# [# [# arrive #] al #] s #]). The word *sing* cannot be construed as [# [# s #] ing #] because [# s #] is not a possible phonological word in English and therefore cannot be prosodically analyzed as a word. The construal of *chorals* as [# [# [# chor #] al #] s #] is blocked for different reasons. While *al* has the segmental form of an occurring word-boundary suffix and *chor* has the segmental shape of a possible phonological word, the *al* of *choral* cannot be construed with the suffix -*al* because such a construal would require a material change in the prosodic structure of the word. The stress in *choral* falls on the last syllable (i.e., on *al*) and not on *chor;* if *chorals* were construed as [# [# [# chor #] al #] s #], it would have to have the stress pattern *chórals.*

These data, (20) to (24), show that the construal of a string of segments within a word as a phonological word is part of the normal linguistic capacity of individuals. Under (19) this normal capacity for construal plays a crucial role in how a Broca's aphasic can minimize the phonological structure of sentences. The "strategy" of language production employed by Broca's aphasics is the maximization of the capacity for construal, consistent with the lexical morphological structure of a sentence.

It has been observed that English-speaking Broca's aphasics notice the omission of the genitive marker and the third person present verbal marker with less frequency than they notice the omission of the plural marker [Goodglass and Hunt (1958)]. This differential pattern of recognition of omissions which is paralleled in production (i.e., the plural is less likely to be omitted than the genitive or third person verbal marker) would appear to provide evidence against the hypothesis (19), since by (19) all three morphemes have the same status. However, rather than being evidence against (19), such data are in fact consistent with it; the differential pattern of omissions simply reflects one aspect of *normal* language processing in production. In normal speech errors inflectional affixes (such as the genitive and third person verbal morphemes) pattern differently from derivational affixes (such as the plural). To use the apt terminology of Bradley (1976), derivational affixes are "epoxied" to the words to which they are attached.

This terminology is used not to suggest that there are no speech errors involving derivational affixes but rather to capture the fact that derivational affixes are less likely to be moved or omitted than are inflectional affixes. In English this can be most clearly seen in errors involving adjective/noun words which are historically, but not synchronically, derived from verbs. There is in English a large class of adjectives which resemble the past participles of verbs in that they typically end in *-en* or *-ed.* That these adjectives are distinct from the verbs with the participial affix can be illustrated by adjectives which end in *-en/-ed* but are not related to any actually occurring English verb. The first sentence of each set in (25) contains an adjective; and the second, the same adjective in a participial context. The (c) sentences contain an underived adjective to show, by way of contrast, that the *-en/-ed* adjectives of (a,b) have the same distributional properties of underived adjectives.

a. *Bedridden* people must vote by absentee ballot
   * Glenda has *bedridden* for the last six years
b. *Underhanded* deals happen less frequently than most cynics claim
   * The sleazy businessman has *underhanded* another deal
c. *Small* people should not feel intimidated by tall people
   * Alice has *small* (ed/en) seven pounds on her latest diet (25)

Some adjectives in *-en/-ed* are homophonous with the past participles of verbs. While these adjectives are historically related to verbs, in modern English they are not derived productively from verbs. Such adjectives have acquired special idiosyncratic meanings which are not transparent from the meaning of the verb. It is important to keep in mind here that most past participles can function as adjectives. Consider the pairs of sentences in (26).

a. A *reserved* book cannot be removed from the library
   Prof. Grill has *reserved* those books for students in his class
b. A *reserved* manner is considered a virtue in many cultures
   *Prof. Grill has *reserved* his manner with students   (26)

In the sentences of (26a) the word *reserved* is the past participle of the verb *reserve*; in the sentences of (26b) *reserved* is not a past participle of *reserve*; rather it is an adjective ending in *-en/-ed* which is historically related to the verb but which is synchronically a lexical item that is not productively derived from the verb.

Just as there are "irregular" past participles (i.e., ones which do not end in *-en* or *-ed*—'that dress has *shrunk* two sizes'), so too are there "irregular" adjectives in the *-en/-ed* class. The adjective(/noun) *drunk* is an example of an "irregular" lexical item which is related to a verb but which is not productively derived from that verb in modern English. The lexical item *drunk* has a special meaning having to do with alcoholic beverages which the verb *drink* does not necessarily have. There is nothing odd about the sentence in (27).

> The family reunion was not half over before Uncle Fred had *drunk* too many mint julips, and his grandson Willy had become sick from having *drunk* too many glasses of lemonade.   (27)

In the context of (27) we might well want to call Uncle Fred a drunk, or say he got drunk, but we would certainly never say that Willy was a drunk or that he got drunk at the family reunion.

Phonologically, the adjective/noun *drunk* has the same internal structure as the participial form of the verb *drink*. In modern English new past participles are formed by the suffixation of *-ed* (*-en* now being associated with an essentially fixed class of verbs). That both the adjective/noun *drunk* and the participle *drunk* have the same internal structure—the structure of participles—is illustrated by the speech errors in (28).

a. I don't have to get *drinked* to be silly   (drunk, A)
b. You're the first Virginian I've met who's [who has] never *drinked* bourbon   (drink/drunk, V)   (28)

The claim that derivational affixes (such as that in the adjective/noun *drunk*) are "epoxied" and that inflectional affixes (such as that of the participle *drunk*) are not, is, extensionally, the claim that (29a) is not a possible speech error but that (29b) and (29c) are.

a. * The scoundrel stole the *money-ed's drink* (drunk's money)
b. The scoundrel stole the *money's drunk* (drunk's money)
c. Uncle Fred had *martini-ed* a *drink* (drunk a martini)   (29)

In (29a) a derivational affix has been separated from *drink* (in the noun *drunk*). It is an empirical hypothesis that (29a) is an anomolous speech error because of this separation. In (29b) the noun *drunk* has been exchanged with noun *money*, stranding the inflectional marker *-s* of the genitive; in (29c) the verb *drink* has been exchanged with the noun *martini*, stranding the inflectional affix of the participle. In both cases the stranded material is not within the class of "epoxied" derivational affixes. In fact when lexical items with inflectional affixes are exchanged, the inflectional material must in general be stranded. In this respect function words are like inflectional morphemes in the way they are processed. Thus (30a to c) are not "well-formed" speech errors; the error paradigm for another, analogous, case is given in (30d).

a. * The scoundrel stole the *money drunk's* (drunk's money)
b. * Uncle Fred had *martini* a *drunk* (drunk a martini)
c. * The scoundrel stole *money the drunk's* (the drunk's money)
d. intended:
   I'm not in the mood for reading
   errors:
   I'm not in the *read* for *mood*ing
   * I'm not in *for reading the mood*
   * I'm not in *for read the mood*ing
   * I'm not in the *reading* for *mood* (30)

There is a hierarchy of the degree to which a bound morpheme adheres to the item to which it is attached. The degree of separability is, first, determined by whether the morpheme is inflectional or derivational, only the former class being necessarily stranded. Among the derivational affixes themselves there is a hierarchy of strandability. The more productive a derivational affix in the language, the more likely it is to be strandable. Productive affixes are those affixes which can be freely and transparently used in linguistic innovations. Affixation which has as its phonetic realization a change in the vowel quality of an element of a word [e.g., *foot; feet* (foot#plural)] is totally unproductive in modern English; one would not, for example, make up a new noun in English *doot* and assume that its plural form is *deet*. The most "epoxied" of all derivational affixes are perhaps those not only where there is a change in vowel quality in an item but also where the item has been lexicalized independently of its original "source." The example *drunk* is such a case. At the other extreme is the plural marker *-s;* the *-s* plural is productive in English—the natural plural of *doot* would be *doots*. Even the plural marker *-s,* probably the most productive derivational affix in English, need not be stranded, though it can be. Thus both (31a) and (31b) represent possible speech errors.

a. . . . the unicorns and the butterfly . . . (the butterflies and the unicorn)

b. . . . the unicorn and the butterflies . . . (the butterflies and the unicorn)   (31)

It is our hypothesis that Broca's aphasics have a normal linguistic capacity in all domains save one, the phonological, and that the central realization of this deficit is in the minimization of the phonological structure of a sentence. Under this hypothesis, as we noted above, it is necessary to show that any aspects of the deficit which do not follow from the nature of phonological structure must be accountable for, and predictable from, nonphonological aspects of *normal* linguistic capacity. From the data on speech errors it is predicted that inflectional affixes and function words (elements which are never "epoxied") will be more "deletable" than derivational affixes and that among the derivational affixes, productive affixes (such as the *-s* plural) will be deleted more often than affixes which are integral to the base word form of a lexical item. That is, we would predict that a Broca's aphasic would not simplify the adjective/noun *drunk* as *drink,* and that the plural morpheme *-s* would have a more stable pattern of realization than inflectional morphemes such as the genitive or the third person singular present verbal morpheme (subject, of course, to the phonological structure of the deficit, e.g., the sonorance hierarchy). That this is, in fact, the pattern we find in the speech of Broca's aphasics should not be viewed as merely a happy coincidence for the hypothesis we put forward in (19). We could not maintain our hypothesis that Broca's aphasia is a purely phonological deficit if it were found, for example, that the normal hierarchy of affixal adhesion is not retained in the linguistic performance of Broca's aphasics.

Given that there is a hierarchy in normal production of the degree to which an affix is attached to a word, it must be predicted that this hierarchy will be retained under the conditions of any deficit which is not a direct deficit to that aspect of the language system of which the hierarchy is a part. That is to say, in putting forward any hypothesis about the nature of a linguistic deficit, it is necessary to show not only that the areas of deviance can be accounted for in terms of the hypothesis but also that all other aspects of the normal linguistic capacity which are presumed to be intact do function normally.

We have as yet to offer any account for the dysprosody which is frequently associated with the speech of Broca's aphasics. Whether or not a particular phrase or sentence is produced dysprosodically is a direct function of the rate of speech and fluency of the aphasic in producing that phrase or sentence. When a Broca's aphasic speaks at a (near) normal rate over the duration of a phrase or a sentence, normal intonation is present; but when a Broca's aphasic speaks slowly, when speech production is effortful and marked by pauses and hesitations between words, there is no normal phrasal or sentential intonation. The same contrast between the presence and absence of intonation arises in the utterances of normal speakers, depending on the rate of speech output. A normal speaker who pauses between words in a sentence, like the hesitating Broca's aphasic, speaks dysprosodically when producing declarative sentences. In making a statement, a normal speaker who is pausing between words can only produce the focusing, or emphasizing, effects of normal sentence intonation by employing artifacts of intonation on single lexical items—increasing the pitch and/or loudness of a particular word or words. The statement as a whole appears to have no melody.

The situation with questions is a bit more complex than that of statements. When pausing between words, a normal speaker will often produce a question with a parody of normal intonation. However, when this is done, the rate of speech of particular words within the question is lengthened. That is, to say "why are you going to the store?" pausing between words, but maintaining a semblance of normal intonation, the time which elapses over the production of each word in the sentence is lengthened both over that which is found in normal utterances and over that which is found where there are pauses between words and no intonation.

Dysprosody, like the hierarchy of morphemic omissions, is then nothing more than a reflection of an intact component of the language capacity of the Broca's aphasic. A Broca's aphasic generally speaks slowly and in an effortful fashion as a consequence of his difficulties with coping with the phonological structure of language *and* his strategies for over-coming those difficulties. As a consequence of this, he is in essentially the same situation as the normal speaker who pauses between words in a sentence he is producing. (We discuss the prosodic pattern of sentences further below.)

The last several sections have focused primarily on the structure of English. Our goal here, however, is to provide not simply an account for the verbal behavior of English-speaking Broca's aphasics but rather an account of the syndrome which is general and independent of particular languages. By taking (19) to be such a general account, we make falsifiable predictions about the verbal behavior of all Broca's aphasics, and not just those who speak English. In this section we shall briefly consider some data from languages other than English to show that (19) does in fact make the appropriate predictions.

In many languages there is a rich inflectional system on both verbs and nouns, the verbs being marked for number (singular/plural), person, tense, etc., and the nouns carrying markings of number, gender, and case (nominative, genitive, accusative, etc.). Russian is such a language. In Russian by a productive process a stem may be inflected as either a noun or a verb, as is shown in (32).

rod-	verb:	rod + i + t'	'to give birth'
		rod + i + l + a	'she gave birth'
	noun:	rod	'generation' (nom., sing., masc.)
		rod + a	'generation's' (gen., sing.)
xod-	verb:	xod + i + t'	"to walk'
		xod + i + t	'he walks'
	noun:	xod	'walk' (nom., sing., masc.)
		xod + a	'walk's' (gen., sing.)

frant-	verb:	frant + i + t'	'to act like a dandy'
		frant + i + t	'he acts like a dandy'
	noun:	frant	'dandy' (nom., sing., masc.)
		frant + a	'dandy's' (gen., sing.)

(32)

As these examples show, the stem is segmentally isomorphic with the nominative, singular, masculine form of nouns; therefore, *rod, xod,* and *frant* are phonological words in Russian. By (19) it is predicted that Russian-speaking Broca's aphasics will generally delete all overt conjugational and declensional endings, and their sentences will have the appearance of being a string of nouns in the nominative singular masculine. In fact, this seems to be what is found; to quote Luria (1970): "in attempting to repeat sentences, such a patient [a Broca's aphasic] is only able to reproduce a few words, usually substantive [i.e., nouns]. His spontaneous speech is transformed into serial naming [nominatives] . . . verbs are altogether absent (so-called telegraphic style)" (p. 189). Thus Luria's characterization of the agrammatism of Russian-speaking Broca's aphasics is consonant with our predictions.

In Russian, unlike English, the inflectional affix of the third person singular present tense form of the verb does play a role in the assignment of stress to a word. In our consideration of the agrammatism of English-speaking Broca's aphasics, the effect of bound morphemes on stress assignment was one of the central areas discussed. There is, however, no inconsistency in our analysis. In English all inflectional morphemes are stress-neutral word-boundary morphemes; this is a property of English and not a necessary property of all languages. In Russian, as is the general case in highly inflected languages, the inflectional morphemes are not stress-neutral. There is in languages a correlation between the richness of the inflectional system and whether or not inflectional morphemes are word-boundary morphemes.

The claim made in (19) is totally independent of stress; what we claimed was that a Broca's aphasic tends to minimize the phonological structure of a sentence in a fashion which is consistent with the structure of his language. A lexical entry is a complex structure (see Chapter 4); it contains not a single word but also characterizes productive relations between words. There is an essential difference between the relation of, for example, the noun *drunk* and the verb *drink* in English, and that of the noun *frant* ('dandy') and the verbs derived from the stem *frant-* in Russian. It is only in the latter case that both items are productively part of the same lexical entry; presumably there is no lexical entry of the noun *frant* which is independent of that of *frant-*. This is not the case with the noun *drunk* and the verb *drink*. To minimize the phonological structure of a word means here the selection of the phonologically simplest form within the lexical entry which includes the word in question. Since there are productive and systematic meaning relations between major class items within a lexical entry, it is by strategies exploiting these relations that the meaning of an utterance is essentially retained even in the degraded production of Broca's aphasics. Thus one might think of agrammatism as the minimization of phonological redundancy.

We find a similar situation with Japanese, which is unrelated to Russian and English.

Japanese

ryoori	verb:	ryoori + suru	'cook(s)' (pres. tense)
	noun:	ryoori	'cooking' (nom.)
		ryoori + na	'cooking's' (gen.)
ai	verb:	ai + suru	'love(s)' (pres. tense)
	noun:	ai	'love' (nom.)
byooki	verb:	byooki + ta	'is sick'
	adject:	byooki + na	'sick'
	noun:	byooki	'sickness' (nom.)
hukoo	verb:	hukoo + ta	'is unfortunate'
	adject:	hukoo + na	'unfortunate'
	noun:	hukoo	'unfortunateness' (nom.)

(33)

If (19) is the correct account of agrammatism, it should be the case that the speech of Japanese-speaking Broca's aphasics, like that of those who speak Russian, is "transformed into serial naming;" that is, it is predicted that the nominative forms of nouns will predominate in their language use. Supporting this prediction, Jakobson (1973) reports that a Japanese Broca's aphasic "exhibits a considerable deficiency in suffixes" (p. 36).

Based on our general hypothesis that Broca's aphasia is a phonological deficit, and (19) as a specific characterization of agrammatism, we can make falsifiable predictions as to the types of errors which Broca's aphasics who are speakers of languages other than English, Russian, or Japanese will make. In all cases we would expect there to be the same sorts of segmental deficits, e.g., segmental paraphasias. At the level of agrammatism we would expect a general tendency to omit function words. It is in the case of agrammatism which arises from the omission of a bound morpheme that our predictions will vary.

In the case of a language like Korean, which is in all relevant respects like Russian and Japanese, we would predict that Broca's aphasics would tend to produce nominatives instead of inflected verb forms, genitive nouns, or derived adjectives.

Korean

yori	verb:	yori + ha + ta	'cook(s)' (pres. tense)
	noun:	yori	'cooking' (nom.)
		yori + ii	'cooking's' (gen.)
sarang	verb:	sarang + ha + ta	'love(s)' (pres. tense)
	noun:	sarang	'love' (nom.)
		sarang + ii	'love's (gen.)
py η	verb:	py$\supset\eta$ + i + ta	'is sick'
	adject:	py$\supset\eta$ + tin	'sick'
	noun:	py$\supset\eta$	'sickness' (nom.)
		py$\supset\eta$ + ii	'sickness's' (gen.)

(34)

German nouns, like those of the other languages we have discussed in this section, are marked for case declensionally. The declensional paradigms of German nouns and the definite article are illustrated by the classic textbook examples in (35).

a.

sing.	pl.	der Mann 'the man' (masc.)
der Mann	die Männer	(nom.)
des Mannes	der Männer	(gen.)
dem Manne	den Männern	(dat.)
den Mann	die Männer	(acc.)

b. sing.	pl.	die Frau 'the woman' (fem.)
die Frau	die Frauen	(nom.)
der Frau	der Frauen	(gen.)
der Frau	den Frauen	(dat.)
die Frau	die Frauen	(acc.)
c. sing.	pl.	das Haus 'the house' (neut.)
das Haus	die Häuser	(nom.)
des Hauses	der Häuser	(gen.)
dem Haus	den Häusern	(dat.)
das Haus	die Häuser	(acc.) (35)

We would predict that German nouns would be realized by
Broca's aphasics in their nominative/accusative singular form,
the phonologically simplest word in the paradigms. As a
consequence of this, coupled with the predicted failure
regularly to realize function words (for example, the definite
article), distinctions between the gender of nouns would be
expected to be effectively lost in the speech of German-
speaking Broca's aphasics.

German verbs are inflected for both number and person.

sing.	pl.	gehen 'to go'
gehe	gehen	
gehst	geht	
geht	gehen	(36)

From simply inspecting the conjugational paradigm in (36), it is
impossible to make any prediction as to what form of the verb
is most likely to be realized in the speech of Broca's aphasics.

The -en which occurs in the infinitive forms of verbs is not an
inflectional marker of the infinitive; rather it is part of the
lexical derivation of a word (analogous to the -s of the English
plural in being a productive derivational affix). The -en is
essentially a word-forming suffix on verbal stems, and it is
present on the surface in some forms and not others [see
Aronoff (1977) for a discussion of the deletion of derivational
material]. Because -en is a derivational affix and not an
inflectional one, it is predicted that the predominant form of
verbs in the speech of German-speaking Broca's aphasics will be
the -en form. We predict, for example, that a German-speaking

Broca's aphasic will typically not say *Er singt* ('he sings/he is singing'), saying instead *(Er) singen*.

In German, as in English, there is a prepositional particle, *zu* ('to'), associated with the infinitive. Unlike *to* in English, *zu* occurs only in some syntactic constructions.

a. Er sagte, daß wir Peter halfen, die Geschichte
   he said that we   helped the   story
       zu erzählen
       to tell
b. * Er sagte, daß wir Peter halfen, die Geschichte erzählen
c. Er sagte, daß wir Peter die Geschichte erzählen halfen
d. * Er sagte, daß wir Peter die Geschichte zu erzählen halfen

                                  (37)

Since *zu* is a function word, we would expect it to be typically omitted in the speech of Broca's aphasics; that is, ceteris paribus, an agrammatic German speaker would probably use (37b) rather than (37a) but would not use (37c) instead of (37d).

The nonconjugational *-en* forms do not only occur as infinitives; they also occur as neuter nouns. The contrast between nominals and infinitives is illustrated in (38).

a. Das Singen ist mir immer eine Freude
   the singing is to me always a   joy
b. Es ist mir immer eine Freude, zu singen
c. * Zu singen ist mir immer eine Freude
d. * Es ist mir immer eine Freude, das Singen
e. * Es ist mir immer eine Freude, singen   (38)

When the infinitive occurs in initial position in such sentences, *zu* does not appear on the surface. Consequently, (39) is ambiguous between a nominal and an infinitival reading.

   Singen   ist mir immer eine Freude
   to sing
   singing   (39)

Being a function word, *das* would be expected to be omitted in the speech of German-speaking Broca's aphasics. Therefore,

(39) is the predicted realization of (38a) for Broca's aphasics, ceteris paribus.

The linguistic deficits of Broca's aphasics were outlined above. Let us review those deficits in the light of the hypothesis that Broca's aphasia involves an impairment to a physical system which subserves at least part of the phonological domain of the language-responsible cognitive structure (the LRCS of Chapter 1).

Phonology, as it is viewed by linguists, is not simply the study of the systematic relations which are found in the surface phonetic representation of language, though that is surely an important aspect of phonology. The grammar must provide an account of the sound-meaning relationships of sentences in human language. Consequently, the phonological component must be integrated into the whole theory of the structure of language, which includes the syntax and the morphology. It is because of this integration of the components of the grammar that we can begin to understand why an array of seemingly disparate deficits in fact have an interpretation in terms of only one component of the grammatical system.

The phonetic deficit of Broca's aphasics is, we have claimed, a direct function of the fact that the phonological component of the grammar must provide a phonetically unambiguous representation of sentences. We have ascribed the frequent occurrence of segmental paraphasias (substitutions) to a more abstract level of sound representation, the phonological representation of words at the level of the lexicon; on this point we agree with other proposed interpretations of Broca's aphasia [e.g., Blumstein (1970)]. It is in terms of this level of representation that we propose the word-finding difficulties of Broca's aphasics are to be explained; to use Luria's (1970) description, "the inner sound schemata of words" (p. 186) has been impaired. We have claimed that agrammatism can be accounted for on the basis of the sound structure which exists between words and between a word and its affixes. The central concept developed in this regard was the notion of a phonological word; the domain of all phonological processes is characterized in terms of phonological words. The other apparently deviant aspects of the speech of Broca's aphasics, e.g., dysprosody, are claimed to be not inherently deviant but rather to arise as a consequence of the interaction of normal intact components of the linguistic system with the impaired phonological component.

In Chapter 1 we put forward the hypothesis that LRCS was essentially uniform across all normal members of the species. It would, of course, be absurd to suggest that there is equivalence between the actual linguistic knowledge of, say, a speaker of French and a speaker of English—what a French speaker knows is French, not English; what an English speaker knows is English, not French. What they have in common, under our theory of language, is an equivalence in their capacities to acquire and use knowledge of a natural human language. Therefore, the knowledge of language which each acquires will be in terms of equivalent sorts of structures. That all Broca's aphasics have qualitatively parallel deficits lends support to our general hypothesis of the uniformity of LRCS as a biological endowment.

The phonological component of the grammar characterizes one of the domains of LRCS. The interpretation of Broca's aphasia we have put forward here relies exclusively on universal aspects of word-level phonological structure—segments, boundaries, and phonological words. Not only are these all aspects of word-level phonological structure—segments, boundaries, and phonological words. Not only are these all aspects of phonology, they are the set of properties which define the domain of phonology. Consequently, we are making the implicit claim that there is, in some sense, a one-to-one of language. This is not to claim that Broca's area is necessarily the only area of the brain involved in phonology; rather it is to say that Broca's area is necessary to normal phonological capacity across the domain of the phonology, leaving open the question of if, and to what extent, other areas might be directly implicated in normal phonological capacity. The fact that Broca's aphasia can be identified with a lesion involving a particular area of the brain is consistent not only with the hypothesis that LRCS is biologically uniform—part of the genetic program of normal individuals—but also with the hypothesis that LRCS is neuroanatomically uniform. Thus the theory of language we have adopted has served an important heuristic purpose in furthering our understanding of the functional neuroanatomy of language.

Some Recent Perspectives on Broca's Aphasia

Goodglass, Gleason, Bernholz, and Hyde (1972) argue that a subset of the syntactic system is impaired in Broca's aphasia. This conclusion is based on the performance of a 22-year-old Broca's aphasic on the Story-Completion Test. The subject "had sustained a gunshot wound in the left frontoparietal region of the brain while serving in Vietnam" (p. 194). The test was administered to the subject five times during four months. Because the subject was allowed to change his responses, and because all responses were counted, there were more than five responses to each of the twenty-eight items on the test. (The test is repeated here as Table 2, and a summary of the subject's response patterns is given in Table 3.)

Table 2 Story-Completion Test with Target Sentences and Sample Response

Target sentences	Typical aphasic response
1. Imperative intransitive—VP	
a. My friend comes in. I want him sit down. So I say to him: What? (Sit down!)	Sit down.
b. My cousin is at the door. I want him to come in. So I open the door and say: What? (Come in!)	Come in
2. Imperative transitive—VP + NP	
a. My little son eats lunch. He has not touched his milk. I want him to drink it. So I say: What? (Drink your milk!)	Boy, drink the milk.
b. The grass needs to be cut. I give my son the lawn mower, and I tell him, What? (Cut the grass!)	Boy, mow the grass.
3. Declarative intransitive—NP + VP	
a. A baby has a toy. I take the toy away. What happens? (The baby cries.)	Baby crying.
b. The baby smiles. I want the baby to laugh. I tickle the baby. What happens? (The baby laughs.)	And baby, baby, laugh.

4. Declarative transitive—NP + VP + NP
   a. Dogs always chase cats. A dog is in the street. A cat comes along. What happens? (The dog chases the cat.) — Cat and dog, get running and dog.
   b. Mr. Jones wants to hear the news. The radio is off. What happens? (He turns the radio on.) — Father, father turn on radio.

5. Direct + indirect object—NP+VP+NP+NP
   a. She owes her friend a dollar. She goes to see her friend. She takes out a dollar. What next? (She gives her friend the dollar.) — And give 'em to dollar to person.
   b. My dog is hungry. I get a bone to give the dog. What next? (I give the dog the bone.) — Dog and uh bone, he gimme.

6. Yes-No question—AUX + NP + VP + NP
   a. John is in his room. He thinks he hears his mother call. So he goes downstairs to see if she called him, and he asks . . .What? (Did you call me?) — Mother, you call?
   b. Mother sent Johnny upstairs to wash and brush his teeth. When he came down, she wondered if he brushed his teeth. She asks: What? (Did you brush your teeth?) — Johnny, you brush teeth?

7. WH question—WH + BE + NP AUX + NP + VP + NP
   a. Jane can't find her shoes. Her mother has just cleaned the room. She knows her mother put them somewhere. So she asks: What? (Where did you put my shoes?) — Mother, where are my shoes?
   b. The father broke the toy. He couldn't fix it. But his son fixed it and the father wondered how. So he asked: What? (How did you fix it?) — Boy, how you fix it?

8. Future—NP + AUX + VP (+NP)
   a. John works every Saturday. He worked last Saturday, too. And next Saturday . . . What? (He will work.) — John work next week again.
   b. Father smokes his pipe every evening after supper. Supper is just over now. What will happen now? (He will smoke his pipe.) — Father smoke pipe again.

9. Embedded sentence—(NP + VP) + S S→NP + TO + VP + ADV + NP
   a. The children were being noisy. Mother was annoyed. She wanted . . . What? (She wanted them to be quiet.) — Mother, uh, the kids, uh, be quiet.

Table 2 (continued)

b. The soldier's gun was dirty. The sergeant was annoyed. So he called the soldier and told him . . . him he wanted . . . What? (He wanted him to clean the gun.)   . . . To do again, he wanted do it again.

10. Passive—NP + AUX + PP

a. A man was walking on the railroad tracks. A train came along. The man didn't hear it. What happened to him? The man . . . What? (The man was killed by the train.)   A man, the man got killed.

b. A little girl went too near the angry dog. What happened to her? She . . . What? (She was bitten by the dog.)   She got bit on a dog.

11. Comparative—NP + BE + ADJ + ER

a. Little Johnny couldn't reach the cookies. He wasn't tall enough. He called his sister and she reached the cookies for him. How come? (She was taller.)   The girl tall and uh boy little.

b. Mrs. Jones tried to open the jar. She wasn't strong enough. So she called her husband and he did it the first try. How come? (He was stronger.)   Because Father, uh, strong.

12. Cardinal number + Noun — NP

a. There are some cups on the table. There are twelve of them. What is on the table? (Twelve cups.)   Twelve cup on the table.

b. There are books on the shelf. There are thirteen of them. What is on the shelf? (Thirteen books.)   They thirteen on the shelf.

13. Adjective + Adjective + Noun — NP

a. He told a story. It was funny. He told a . . . What? (A funny story.)   A funny story.

b. I picked up a dish. It was dirty. What did I pick up? (A dirty dish.)   A dirty, dirty, dishes.

14. Adjective + Adjective + Noun — NP

a. I sold her a small car. The car was red. In other words, I sold her . . . What? (A small red car.)   Little car and little car and white.

b. They bought a large house. The house was white. In other words, they bought . . . What? (A large white house.)   A white house, a large house.

Source: Goodglass et al. (1972) pp. 197-199, 201.

Table 3 Scores Obtained on Story-Completion Test Items

Syntactic type	Total at-tempts	a b	Percent conven-tional	a b	Percent gramma-tical	a b	Percent criter. feature	a b
Imper. Trans	10	5 / 5	90	100 / 80	100		100	
Imper. Intrans.	11	6 / 5	73	67 / 80	82	67 / 100	100	
Indic. Intrans.	17	11 / 6	0		12	18 / 0	71	73 / 67
Indic. Trans.	20	14 / 6	0		0		65	57 / 83
Dir.+Indir. Obj.	15	6 / 9	0		0		47	67 / 44
Yes-No Inter.	14	6 / 8			14	33 / 0	86	83 / 88
WH-Inter.	15	7 / 8	33	57 / 13	40	71 / 13	87	86 / 88
Future	17	11 / 6	0		0		47	36 / 67
Emb. Clause	23	12 / 11	0		22	25 / 19	61	58 / 63
Passive	19	10 / 9	21	10 / 33	47	50 / 44	47	40 / 56
Compar.	15	7 / 8	7	0 / 13	33	29 / 38	73	71 / 75
Number + N	18	9 / 9	0		6	0 / 11	56	56 / 56
Adj. + N	15	5 / 10	27	80 / 0	73	100 / 60	73	100 / 60
Adj.+Adj.+N	16	9 / 3	13	11 / 14	19	0 / 43	44	56 / 29

Grammatical responses to many of the test contexts required that the subject produce a word-boundary morpheme—the plural, the third person singular present, the passive, or the comparative. Typically the subject failed to produce any of these suffixes in his responses. In a study of the realization of some word-boundary morphemes, Goodglass and Berko (1960) found that aphasics were most likely to produce these morphemes when they were suffixed to a word ending in a vowel. As a pretest for the Story-Completion Test, the Berko-Goodglass Inflectional Morphology Test (a repetition task) was administered to the subject. As with the subjects reported by Goodglass and Berko, the subject in this study showed a marked tendency to omit word-boundary morphemes when they were attached to a word ending in a consonant. On only one of his six trials on the Berko-Goodglass test where a postconsonantal plural marker was required did the subject give a correct response. On three of his six attempts at responses requiring a postvocalic plural marker the subject did realize the plural morpheme. The distinction between consonants and vowels is phonological and not syntactic or morphological. The subject's responses on the Story-Completion Test were consistent with the overall phonologically specified condition that Broca's aphasics are more likely to produce postvocalic word-boundary morphemes than postconsonantal ones.

Two of the story contexts require responses in which a cardinal number is followed by a plural noun—"twelve cups" and "thirteen books." In only one of his eighteen responses did the subject produce a grammatical string; in ten of his eighteen responses he produced the cardinal number followed by a noun not marked for plural; the other sources of ungrammaticality are not enumerated. In both these contexts the nouns to which the -s is to be affixed end in consonants. Thus the failure of the subject to produce the plural marker is predicted by the phonological criteria put forth by Goodglass and Berko.

The hypothesis that the subject's errors with word-boundary morphemes were phonological and not morphological or syntactic is lent further support by consideration of the subject's responses to contexts where the third person present verbal marker was required for grammaticality. In all his attempts at sentences which required a postconsonantal third person verbal marker (e.g., "the baby laughs," "he turns on the radio," "she gives her friend a dollar"), the subject failed to produce the verbal suffix morpheme. On only two of fourteen attempts at the sentence "the dog chases the cat" did the subject use "chases." The verb 'chase' ends in a consonant, [s], the vowel [ə] which shows up in 'chases' appears only in the third person present. Often in responding to the context meant to elicit this response the subject used the verb 'run' instead of 'chase'; a consequence of this substitution is that the verbal marker must be realized in postconsonantal position. There were two truly postvocalic environments for the verbal marker: "the baby cries" and "where are my shoes?" In the former case the subject did not produce the -s verbal marker, instead frequently using 'crying.' In the latter case, the subject produced fully grammatical responses in all six of his attempts.

One factor which appears to interact to some degree with the phonological conditioning of the realization of morphemes is redundancy. De Villiers (1974) found that the more redundant a morpheme was in a sentence, the less likely it was to be produced. In the case of the plural marker, in a string where there is a cardinal number there is redundancy of number between the number itself and the noun marking; the word 'one' directly preceding a noun means that the noun is singular, and any number greater than one preceding a noun means that the noun must be plural. In the case of the third person present verbal marker, whenever a sentence has an overt third person singular subject and the sentence is in the present, the -s marker is predictable (note that it is only in the present that there is any person-number distinction made on verbs, and then only for the third person singular).

Two contexts on the test are intended to elicit passive sentences in response ["the man was killed (by the train)" and "she was bitten (by the dog)"]. The subject did somewhat better on responses using the passive than he did on active indicatives (47 percent of the passives grammatical, 7 percent of the actives grammatical). The putative explanation for the disparity between the active and passive responses is that the active is more problematical because it "requires verb inflection" (p 211). This cannot possibly be the correct explanation, since the passive requires verb inflection, tense, and person marking on the copula *be,* or on *get,* and for example, the -ed on 'killed' or the -en on 'bitten.' The subject typically did not realize the passive morpheme on 'bite.' Verbs such as 'bite' are called strong verbs; the characteristic of strong verbs is that the quality of the vowel of the verb changes in some tenses and in different moods, e.g., [bayt] 'bite'/[bIt] 'bit'/[bIten] 'bitten,' [swIm] 'swim'/[swæm] 'swam'/[swʌm] 'swum.' While for the so-called standard dialect of English the verb 'bite' is 'bitten' in the passive, there are dialects where it is realized as 'bit' in the passive. Goodglass et al. do not consider that the use of a strong verb is a confounding variable in their test, nor do they comment on the dialect of the subject. The latter point may be of some moment, since the subject did produce 'bit' instead of 'bitten.' Redundancy might also be an explanation for why the suffix was omitted; for many strong verbs there is no passive suffix -en, e.g., 'drink'/'drank'/'drunk'; 'hang'/'hung'/'hung.' On almost all his attempts at the other passive sentence the subject did use 'killed.' That the subject did so well with the form ' killed," especially in comparison with his performance with other postconsonantal consonantal morphemes, is quite suggestive. The only plausible explanation for this lies in the fact that [1] is a sonorant continuant, as are vowels, and stands relatively close to the vowels on the sonorance hierarchy. The subject's performance here suggests that the Goodglass and Berko generalization should be relativized to the sonorance hierarchy. This is an area which should be studied in future research.

The only other case in the tests which required a word-boundary morpheme was in the response to contexts which required comparative responses: "she was taller" and "he was stronger." Rather than using the comparative marker, the subject used adjectival contrasts: "the girl tall and uh boy little" and "because father (uh) strong." While the comparative data are of interest in that they suggest the patient avoided using at least some inflectional morphemes, they shed no direct light on the issue of the realization of word-boundary morphemes.

There are no apparent structural generalizations to be inferred from the subject's performance which would indicate a syntactic deficit of any systematicity. For example, while the subject failed to give any grammatical responses where an active indicative sentence with a direct object was required, on all ten of his attempts at imperatives with direct objects he gave grammatical responses. Similarly, while the subject did not produce grammatical sentences regularly where the response required was in the indicative and had an intransitive verb (i.e., a verb without a direct object), in nine of his eleven attempts at imperatives with intransitives he gave grammatical responses. The active indicative sentences all required the third person present verbal morpheme; the imperative requires no verb inflection. In many of his imperative responses, the subject initiated the response with a stressed vocative, e.g., "bóy, drink the milk," "bóy, mow the grass." Imperatives, unlike indicatives, begin with a prosodically prominent element. There is considerable research evidence which indicates that speech is facilitated for Broca's aphasics when a sentence begins with a stressed element. In spontaneous speech Broca's aphasics frequently begin a sentence with a stressed 'and.' This 'and' is not used as a conjunction but rather as a (production-facilitating) stressed sentential operator. This function is analogous to the aphasic's use of the vocative in commands.

The subject also used vocatives to initiate yes/no questions, e.g., "mother, you call?" and "Johnnie, you brush teeth?" The expected responses for these sentences were "did you call (me)?" and "did you brush your teeth?" respectively. Goodglass, Fodor, and Schulhoff (1967) showed that *do* is frequently omitted. In a repetition task, they found that Broca's aphasics did significantly worse on yes/no questions which began with an unstressed *do* form than they did on yes/no questions beginning with stressed negatives (e.g., "aren't you hungry?"). In the light of the earlier studies of deletion of unstressed material, the subject's performance on the yes/no questions in the Story-Completion Test is a pattern which would be expected. Stress is, of course, a phonological and not a syntactic variable.

There were also so-called wh- questions on the test. One response required was "where are my shoes?" As we noted above, the subject gave five correct responses (in seven attempts, all grammatical); as with the imperatives, he frequently initiated his response with a vocative, "móther, where are my shoes?" The other wh- response that the test was designed to elicit was "how did you fix it?" The subject gave only one grammatical response in eight attempts at this sentence. He typically said, for example, "how you fix it?" omitting the unstressed *do*. The pattern of omission of un-stressed elements was further revealed by the omission of the pronominal subject of the embedded sentence of "he wanted him to do it again" and "he wanted him to clean the gun."

While these data suggest that stress plays an important role in determining which words can and will be deleted in the speech of Broca's aphasics, at this point our understanding of the role of stress is a simple taxonomy of where elements are likely to be deleted. On a repetition task, Goodglass et al. (1967) found that the initial element of a sentence beginning with an iamb (the poetic term for a sequence of an unstressed element followed by a stress-bearing element, e.g., "the bóy") was omitted 70 percent of the time. This is contrasted with only 14 percent omission of function words when they occur in a trochee (a sequence of stressed element followed by unstressed element which is in turn followed by a stressed element, e.g., "clóse the doór," "só can yóu," "clóse, if ópen," "cán't he dańce?"). It was also observed that in strings which were anapests (two unstressed or weakly stressed elements followed by a stressed element, e.g., "in the hoúse," "we all wént") both initial elements were deleted 52 percent of the time; there were only 9 percent deletions of the initial word alone. In the six items on the repetition task where all the elements of the sentence could carry the main stress of the sentence and where each carried word stress (e.g., "cóws éat gráss") there were no errors. These results parallel the observations of deletions in the spontaneous speech of Broca's aphasics made by Goodglass, Quadfasel, and Timberlake (1964).

The question which remains open is whether there is a real metrical pattern to the omission of elements in a sentence. Goodglass, Quadfasel, and Timberlake suggested that the Broca's patients initiate sentences with the first salient, i.e., stressed, element of the intended utterance. While this does account for much of the data, it leaves unexplained the pattern of such sentence internal deletions as those found on the Story-Completion Test—"he wanted φ do it again" for "he wanted *him* to do it again." In the study of poetic meter, generalizations about metrical form are missed if one restricts the characterization of such forms to a correlation of 'weak' with 'unstressed' and 'strong' with 'stressed' [cf., for example, Halle and Keyser (1975)]. It is argued that there are poetically regular patterns of meter in which 'weaks' are sometimes stressed and 'strongs' sometimes unstressed. While it is not obvious that any metrical study of the speech of Broca's aphasics would yield interesting generalizations about the pattern of omission, to ignore the possibility that such generalizations might emerge seems unwarranted.

Two of the context sets on the Story-Completion Test involved adjectival modification of nouns. In one context set the subject was supposed to supply an Article-Adjective-Noun sequence. Eleven out of fifteen responses (75 percent) for these contexts were grammatical (e.g., "a funny story"). The other set of contexts required Article-Adjective-Adjective-Noun responses. On this set only three of sixteen responses (19 percent) were judged to be grammatical. Instead of saying, for example, "a large white house" the subject would say "a white house, a large house." The disparity between these types of responses cannot be accounted for in terms of English syntax, limitations on the number of adjectives which can be "stacked" not being a property of grammar. It might be the case that there is stress interference in the response pattern; in the first case the phrases have a ˝ pattern, while in the second the strong element is the fourth item in the phrase, ˝. [The authors note somewhat enigmatically that the subject "showed [in spontaneous speech] none of the problems he had with adjective order on the Test" (p. 207).]

In their discussion of the subject's performance on the Story-Completion Test, the authors do not ignore that there is a phonological explanation for at least some of the errors in sentence production. Furthermore they note: "He continues to correct himself only until he has maximized his approach to grammaticality and very rarely rejects a correct production in favor of a less correct one" (p. 209). In spite of this finding and the fact that the test is essentially a test of sentence production, the authors conclude: "We cannot, however, accept the view that syntactic competence is intact" (p. 209). The absence of inflection is characterized as a syntactic deficit. The subject's difficulty with sentences containing complements is taken as showing "the partial integrity of the simpler construction [the imperative]," though there is no linguistic sense in which the imperative is a "simpler construction" (p. 204). There is virtually nothing in the test results obtained which supports the conclusion that the subject had a syntactic deficit. The pattern of omission of function words and word-boundary morphemes can be systematically addressed only in terms of phonological structure. The deleted items almost invariably have the phonological structure of word-boundary morphemes; the prosodic contour of a sentence plays an important role in determining which items will be omitted—items with primary word stress are not omitted, but stressless items are omitted in some metrical structures; finally, the segmental shape of a word and a following word-boundary morpheme affect the pattern of omissions—word-boundary morphemes which consist simply of a consonant (e.g., the plural-s) are most likely to be omitted when they occur postconsonantally. There is an interaction between the segmental and prosodic factors; since word-boundary morphemes such as the plural can never carry primary stress (or even emphatic or contrastive stress), they are, for prosodic reasons, the elements of a sentence which are most likely to be subject to omission, irrespective of their segmental environment.

A far more radical view of the deficit of Broca's aphasia is taken by Schnitzer (1974). Schnitzer bases his discussion on two "empirical assumptions" (p. 303):

(1) Brain damage may cause disruption, impairment, impoverishment, or simplification of the normal linguistic system; it does not cause enhancement, enrichment, or complication of that system.
(2) The previous postulate [(1) above] notwithstanding, an aphasic may sometimes develop a system or subsystem which is more complicated than the normal system had been, in order to compensate for what has been lost or damaged.

Schnitzer, expounds on (2) saying, "Thus an aphasic who has lost access to the rules of plural formation, but not the category 'plural,' could develop a rule of plural formation which is more complicated than the normal one" (p. 303).

He assumes that the only interpretation which can be assigned to linguistic deficits is in terms of impairment of particular rules of grammar rather than in terms of the notions of particular components of universal grammar. The particular rules of the grammar of, for example, French or Chinese are of course quite different from those of the grammar of English. Therefore, under Schnitzer's approach it would seem that it is purely accidental that the linguistic characteristics of various aphasic syndromes are, within a syndrome, the same across languages. That is to say, the fact that the characteristics of Broca's aphasia outlined at the beginning of this chapter are essentially the characteristics of the speech of all Broca's aphasics, including those who are speakers of English, is not predicted by Schnitzer's model. His theory cannot, therefore, capture significant generalizations about the nature of particular syndromes.

The subject of Schnitzer's study was a 21-year-old whose symptoms led to a diagnosis of "cerebral thrombosis with right hemiplegia and motor [Broca's] aphasia" by the Tyrone (Pennsylvania) Hospital (p. 300). Three aspects of the subject's spontaneous speech are considered: omissions of the "copula," omission of subject pronouns, and omission of articles.

Schnitzer observed that the full present tense forms of the "copula" were always omitted, where by copula he meant any version of be—as an auxiliary element or as a verb in a copular construction. When a present tense form of *be* was realized in the subject's speech, it had been cliticized (as in, "they're too hot"). Past tense forms of *be* were only occasionally omitted in spontaneous speech (as in "I driving a truck"). Schnitzer considers three possible analyses for this array of data: (a) an optional contraction rule precedes an obligatory rule for the deletion of uncliticized present tense forms of *be*, (b) optional *be* deletion precedes obligatory cliticization, or (c) there is a rule which obligatorily inserts past tense forms of *be* and optionally inserts present tense forms, and this rule precedes a rule of contraction which is obligatory for present tense forms but optional for past tense forms. Schnitzer argues that (c) is the best analysis since there is not a rule of copula deletion in standard English; that is, both (a) and (b) are analyses which entail proposing that there had been an elaboration of the subject's "preaphasic" grammar, and by assumption (1) there can be no such elaboration. Solution (c), by hypothesis, represents an impairment or impoverishment of the normal system.

However, within the context of the theory of grammar there is no evidence in standard English which provides a basis for arguing that there is a *be* insertion rule. Linguistically such a rule would be unmotivated complication in the grammar of English. The various syntactic forms *be* do not constitute a natural class. Therefore, to admit such a rule would require increasing the expressive power of transformations and/or expansion of the substantive theory of syntactic categories. It has been argued in linguistics that all the forms of *be* are present in initial (deep) structures of standard English. In normal spontaneous speech, a present tense form of *be* is always cliticized unless it is being focused (subject to certain constraints); in some dialects of English past tense forms of *be* are also contracted.

Schnitzer suggests that unlike normal speakers of English, the subject contracted past tense *be* as in "I's [I was] up by New York," and "that's last time I's [I was] driving a truck." Since there are dialects in which this form occurs, this may simply be a reflection of the subject's normal dialect rather than any linguistic pathology. No mention is made of any of the work on the deletion of unstressed elements or of the work on the segmental conditioning of omissions which are cited above. In the examples of the subject's speech which Schnitzer provides, the pattern of omission is consistent with the phonological account; for example, in "I's . . ." and "they're . . ." the contracted element is unstressed but follows a vowel. At one point, before arguing for (c), Schnitzer suggests that perhaps "only redundant information is omitted" (p. 304). As is noted above, de Villiers (1974) argues that redundancy plays a large role in deletion/omission in the speech of Broca's aphasics. The speech of Broca's aphasics is labored throughout; therefore, the redundancy/omission relation may be in part a performance strategy designed to reduce the length and phonological complexity of sentences.

The subject generally omitted pronominal subjects of sentences "(a) when the subject would have been *I*, or (b) when the reference of the subject was derivable from the previous discourse" (p. 304). Here again the data can be characterized with respect to stress. The pattern of omissions corresponds well to the pattern of omissions found in Goodglass et al. (1967). For example, in "[they] oil them too much" there is deletion of a sentence initial prosodically weak element which is immediately followed by a strong element, the first element of a sentence initial iamb frequently being subject to deletion in the speech of Broca's aphasics. Furthermore, this sentence was the second in a brief discourse by the subject, and the antecedent of the subject of the sentence was explicit in the first sentence. In this case, as in the one above, it does not seem unreasonable to suggest that the subject was using a strategy in which the facilitation afforded by initial stressed material was mediated by communicative needs.

Schnitzer, however, does not take such an approach. Rather he says that these data provide evidence for there being a transderivational rule of subject pronoun insertion in English. This is yet another instance of his assuming (a) that a systematic error pattern must reflect some systematic part of the speaker's particular syntax and, by inference, (b) no systematic processing systems or heuristic strategies are available to both normals and aphasics. The evidence strongly contradicts both these assumptions.

In the case of determiner omission, Schnitzer again makes no reference to stress. He simply notes that *a* and *the* were omitted when the definiteness of the following noun was determinable from other elements in the sentence or from the discourse. From this he concludes that there must be "transderivational semantic rules" in the grammar of English for article insertion (p. 308). While no one would deny that there are systems for understanding and producing coherent discourses, whatever the nature of those systems may be, they are not part of sentence grammar but rather are part of a person's pragmatic competence.

Schnitzer had his subject perform a sentence-classification task in which he was asked to determine the grammaticality of "several hundred English sentences and non-sentences" (p. 300). Unfortunately, Schnitzer does not provide the reader with any more detailed information about the test material. According to Schnitzer, the subject made both types of possible errors. His judgments of the grammatical sentences generally corresponded to those of a normal speaker, with the exception of "certain long, embedded or conjoined grammatical sentences," which he judged to be ungrammatical (p. 300). Of more interest is the set of nonsentences which he judged to be grammatical. That set consisted of three distinct types of sentences: sentences with a deleted *be*, sentences with deleted subjects, and sentences with deleted determiners. That is, his errors in grammaticality judgments paralleled his errors in sentence production. Since the errors in sentence production are systematic with respect to phonological structure, then so too must be the "same" errors in his grammaticality judgments. These briefly summarized results suggest that a productive line of research might involve the systematic study of the performance of Broca's aphasics on sentence-classification tasks.

Schnitzer is not the only researcher who has found that on "metalinguistic" tasks (i.e., tasks which require a subject to make grammaticality judgments, parse sentences, etc.) the performance of Broca's aphasics parallels their spontaneous speech performance. On metalinguistic tasks which require sentence parsing, the subjects generally focus on the nouns and verbs of a sentence and not on the function words; that is, their attention is on those items in a sentence which can, minimally, carry primary word stress. They do not attend to those items which do not carry stress and which, in phonological structure, are word-boundary morphemes. The ungrammatical sentences which Schnitzer's subject classified as grammatical (with the exception of the very long sentences) were those sentences where function words were omitted. Thus a uniform phonological account can be provided not only for the speech production of Broca's aphasics but also for their capacity on "metalinguistic" tasks.

Zurif, Caramazza, and Meyerson (1972) compared the

performance of Broca's patients with that of normals on a sentence-parsing task. Three Broca's aphasics, each with a right hemiplegia (like Schnitzer's subject), and four normal controls were tested. In a pretest it was determined that all the subjects could read aloud. The reading of the Broca's aphasics was effortful and larded with awkward articulation and literal paraphasias; however, "when their attention was focused on each word of a sentence, they invariably read the sentence correctly, including grammatical formatives."

The test involved showing a written sentence to the subject. On a separate card three words from the sentence were displayed triangularly with no violation of the left-to-right word order of the sentence. All possible three-word combinations for each sentences were presented one at a time to the subjects. After each, the subject was asked to point to the two words on the card which went together best. This method of testing was decided on so as to circumvent the speech-production deficit of the Broca's subjects. The results were organized in the form of a relatedness matrix.

In the sentence "the baby cries" the normal subjects grouped *the* and *baby* together while the Broca's grouped *baby* and *cry* together. Because of the testing technique this was taken as evidence that inattention to articles was not simply a sentence-production phenomenon. This conclusion was supported by the word clustering of Broca's aphasics on other sentences. These data are consistent with Schnitzer's subject's performances on the grammaticality judgment test and the production errors observed generally in Broca's aphasics.

The sentence for which the Broca's aphasics parsing was closest to normals was "where are my shoes?" Here again the results are consistent with both Schnitzer's data and observed production.

Zurif et al. (1972) conclude from their study that "since the agrammatic aphasic's tacit knowledge of English syntax appears to be as restricted as his use of syntax, we may presume that agrammatism reflects a disruption of the underlying language mechanism" (p. 416). However, their results do not entail that Broca's aphasics have a syntactic deficit which leaves them with only "some residual memory of grammatical form" (p. 415).

These data, like those discussed in the previous sections, can be accounted for in terms of phonological structure; the Broca's subjects attended only to the major class items, which never occur phonologically as word-boundary suffixes and which always bear stress. They did not attend to function words, which are not stressed and which can occur as word-boundary morphemes in phonological structure. Thus the pattern of parsing was based on distinctions in the phonological structure of a sentence and not on the basis of the syntactic structure of a sentence.

Another study which attempted to tap the metalinguistic abilities of aphasics is reported in von Stockert (1972). In this test subjects were presented with sentences such as "the girl from Boston is pretty" where the sentence had been divided into constituent chunks and put on cards; one card, therefore, had *the girl*, another card had *from Boston* and a third card had *is pretty*. In a second condition the sentences were presented

Broca's Aphasics

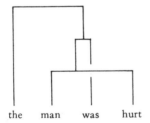
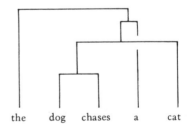

Normals

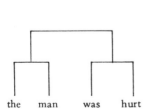
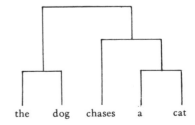

Figure 2

again on cards. This time, however, the sentence was not broken up along constitutent boundaries; for example, one card might have *the* on it, another *girl from*, and the third *Boston is pretty*. In each condition the cards were presented to the subjects in a vertical array in the proper sequential order maintained from top to bottom. It was the task of the subject to put the sentence chunks into normal left-to-right sentence order.

There were two subjects in this experiment: one was a 72-year-old Wernicke's aphasic and the other was a 53-year-old Broca's aphasic. Before the test was given, there were two screening tests, one which looked for the subjects' ability to read and comprehend written material, and the other which tested the subjects' ability to read aloud the sentences that would be used in the experiment. On the general reading and comprehension screening test there were six commands and six yes/no questions. The Wernicke's subject read in jargon and performed correctly only once on the comprehension section.

Broca's Aphasics

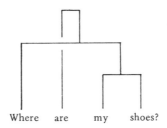

Normals

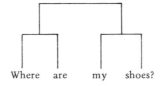

Figure 3

The Broca's subject read telegraphically; e.g., he omitted function words and grammatical suffixes. However, he correctly answered eleven of the twelve questions designed to test his comprehension of the sentences. The second screening test, which used the sentences from the main part of the test, consisted of 12 simple declarative sentences, 12 declaratives "with embedding" (a sentence with a prepositional phrase counted as having embedding), twelve questions (at least some of which were wh- questions), and six imperatives. The reading of the Wernicke's aphasic was once totally jargon; e.g., he read "Arthur talbot and ingel a talbot" for "my father is smoking his pipe."

The interpretation of the subjects' performances in arranging cards with words on them into sentences is somewhat confusing. Both subjects did better when the sentence chunks were nonconstituents. Overall the Wernicke's subject was better at ordering sentences presented in constituent chunks than was the Broca's patient. However, if one looks at the performance of the two subjects on an item-by-item basis, one discovers that only on one category, simple declarative sentences, was the Wernicke's patient actually superior to the Broca's patient; on the other categories the Broca's patient produced more correct responses than the Wernicke's patient. Nevertheless, von Stockert concludes that the Wernicke's patient gets clues from syntactic structure in the absence of any real understanding of the lexical meaning, while the Broca's patient had considerable syntactic disturbance, and he is not helped by lexical meaning. That the Wernicke's subject broke down on "embedded" sentences is purportedly a consequence of their being longer than the simple declarative sentences. Von Stockert offers the following conundrum as his conclusion: (a) the Wernicke's patient has relatively intact syntax, (b) the Broca's patient has a syntactic impairment, (c) both patients performed better with nonconstituents than with constituents; therefore, the "neurolinguistic" reality of constitutents is shown, and (d) the results are consistent with experimental results on normal sentence processing obtained using the "click" paradigm [see Garrett (forthcoming) for a review of the "click" literature]. We do not feel that these conclusions are supported by the data that von Stockert reports.

Broca's aphasics appear to have relatively intact comprehension in conversational situations; however, several studies have demonstrated that they in fact have a comprehension deficit. Many of these tests can show the presence of a comprehension deficit which might well go unnoticed in normal discourse situations, but they are not constructed to address the particular source of the deficit. Two of the most commonly used in the study of Broca's aphasics tests are: the Token Test, and the Parisi and Pizzamiglio test (1970). Each of the 13 Broca's aphasics discussed by de Renzi and Vignolo had comprehension problems on the Token Test. Parisi and Pizzamiglio considered three sets of subjects, all speakers of Italian, in their original study: 30 normal subjects, 30 non-aphasic brain-damaged subjects (15 with right hemisphere damage and 15 with left hemisphere damage), and 60 aphasics (28 Broca's, 5 amnesic, 10 Wernicke's, and 17 mixed or global aphasics). The mean score for the normal subjects was 75.2 out of 80, and for the nonaphasic, brain-damaged subjects 73.9. Of the aphasics, the amnesics had the best performance, their mean score being 71.8. As would be expected, of the other aphasics, the Broca's aphasics had the best performance. However, their mean score of 60 was considerably below that of the normals (four of the patients had scores above 70). The Wernicke's aphasics had the lowest mean score, 49.5, and the mixed/global group had a mean score of 50.8.

The categories were ordered for each aphasic group on the basis of the number of mistakes made within each category. For all the groups the hierarchy of difficulty was essentially the same. [Other authors have noted that the hierarachy of difficulty of syntactic constructions does not vary greatly from one aphasic population to another—see Goodglass (1973), for example.] The exceptions were that Broca's aphasics were better than Wernicke's aphasics with sentences containing relative clauses, but Wernicke's aphasics were better than Broca's aphasics with inflectional morphology, e.g., number (singular/plural). The test results are consistent with the claim

that the comprehension deficits of Broca's aphasics parallel
their production difficulties.

Lesser (1974) administered an English version of the Parisi
and Pizzamiglio test. The performance of English-speaking
aphasics generally was parallel to that of the Italian aphasics.
There was, of course, one expected difference; the English-
speaking aphasics had none of the problems with gender that
Italian-speaking aphasics had. Unfortunately Lesser does not
provide a thorough breakdown of the performance of different
aphasic groups on her replication of this test.

Zurif and Caramazza (1974) report on a study in which they
tested the comprehension of center-embedded sentences using a
picture-identification task. Four types of sentences were used:

(a) The boy is eating the red apple.
(b) The apple that the boy is eating is red.
(c) The boy that the girl is chasing is tall.
(d) The boy that the dog is patting is fat.

In the preliminary testing there were six subjects: two
Broca's aphasics, two mixed anterior aphasics, and two
Wernicke's aphasics. All the subjects showed much better
comprehension on the nonembedded sentences, like (a). The
next best performance was on the sentences in which the
function of the nouns is irreversible such as (b); the aphasics
gave correct responses 71 percent of the time. However, on the
reversible sentences (c), the Broca's aphasics and the mixed
anterior group gave only 64 percent correct responses. As the
authors note, a subject cannot rely on either a word-order
strategy or real-world knowledge for proper interpretation of
such sentences. The worst performance was on the "semantically improbable" sentences such as (d). On these sentences
the Broca's and mixed anteriors performed at chance level (50
percent correct responses).

Sentences with relative clauses are in general harder for all
subjects (including normals) to process than are sentences which
are structurally identical except that they lack relative clauses.
Normal subjects cannot deal well with subject relative clauses
where the complementizer 'that' (and verbal auxiliary *be*) have
been omitted as in "the horse raced passed the barn fell" [i.e.,

the horse [that (was) raced passed the barn] fell]. An overt complementizer greatly facilitates the processing of such sentences. If a subject does not attend to the complementizer, that is equivalent to the complementizer's not being present in the structure at all. From the fact that normals have great difficulty with parallel sentences where there is no complementizer, it follows that a subject who does not attend to function words (and complementizers are function words) will have difficulty with such sentences. Thus the subjects' performance on this test is consistent with our theory that Broca's aphasia is a phonological deficit. That there was variation among the percent correct for the (b) to (c) test items can be accounted for in terms of nongrammatical factors. The sense of sentence (d) flies in the face of a subject's real-world expectations. While boys are not generally red, and apples do not eat other things [as in (b)], it is not the case that dogs generally pat boys [as in (d)]. The responses to (d) may therefore reflect a plausibility effect arising as a consequence of failure to attend to grammatical structure.

The subtlest and most interesting of the comprehension tests is reported in Goodenough, Zurif, and Weintraub, (1977). Their test looks specifically at the comprehension of definite and indefinite articles. In a variation on the Token Test, subjects were presented with an array of three figures: a white circle, a black circle, and a black square. They were then given instructions such as "press *the* white one." Some of the instructions were appropriate, as in the above case, but some were inappropriate, such as "press *the* black one," an instruction for which there was no unique referent in the array. The response latencies of the Broca's subjects did not vary significantly between responses to well-formed instructions such as "press *a* black one" and responses to anomalous instructions such as "press *the* circle." When given the instruction "press *the* black one," they would press the black circle. That is, the Broca's aphasics, unlike other aphasics, treated expressions such as "press *the* black one" the same way they treated expressions such as "press *a* black one." This study gives striking evidence that the comprehension deficit of Broca's aphasics is indeed very similar to their production deficits. Articles do not carry stress except under contrast in English: in phonological structure they are typically word-boundary morphemes attached to the following noun or adjective like a prefix.

In comprehension, in production, and on "metalinguistic" tasks there is an overriding regularity to the pattern of linguistic performance of Broca's aphasics. To reiterate the pattern, major lexical items which carry word stress typically are fully attended to, but function words and bound inflectional morphemes, which occur phonologically as clitics on major lexical items and which do not carry stress, are ignored. It is our argument that the only systematic characterization of the agrammatism, dysprosody, etc., of Broca's aphasia is solely in terms of phonological structure. We have focused on three basic areas of phonology: segmental form, prosodic form, and the phonological boundaries which exist between items. These are the essential phonological variables of the grammatical and processing structure of all languages. Thus we have provided an interpretation of the syndrome in terms of the predicates of universal grammar, and not in terms of the properties of particular languages. As we have noted, the characteristics of Broca's aphasia (e.g., agrammatism) are typical of all Broca's aphasics, not just of those who speak English. Thus the theory we have put forward generalizes uniformly across all modalities of language use, and also across all languages. While the description of the syndrome has always been generalizable across languages, explanations of the linguistic nature of the deficits (particularly agrammatism) in the past have typically focused on the grammatical structure of the language of individual patients and not on the structure of language. The proposal that Broca's aphasia is a phonological deficit is therefore an empirical hypothesis explaining why the description of the syndrome is uniform across languages and across modes of language use.

Some Neuroanatomical Considerations For Future Research

While Broca's aphasia is generally associated with a lesion involving the posterior portion of the third frontal convolution, not every lesion in that area will cause a Broca's aphasia with the characteristics discussed on page 75. Dejerine (1914) observed that a lesion in Broca's area could cause either "pure" motor aphasia (aphemia) or Broca's aphasia. Aphemia is characterized by an initial mutism which is followed by the reemergence of speech that is dyspraxic and effortful. There are two apparent sources of aphemia: damage to Broca's area, and subcortical damage to the pathway from Broca's area to the motor area controlling movements of the vocal tract.

The aphemia resulting from subcortical damage is a disconnection syndrome. Even in the acute phase of mutism, the aphemic purportedly can read, write, and comprehend spoken language normally, unlike the true Broca's aphasic. When speech does return, the phonetic character of the output of the aphemic does not improve significantly, even with imitation. There is no evidence of any linguistic disturbance in aphemia (beyond articulatory phonetic distortion) such as the agrammatism found in Broca's aphasia. That there should exist such a syndrome as aphemia is predicted by the disconnection model developed in Geschwind (1965). (See Chapter 2 for a discussion of this model.) The plausibility of that model has been demonstrated repeatedly; there is Geschwind's work on pure alexia without agraphia, Leipman's research on conduction aphasia, and more recently the work on anosognosia for hemiplegia by Green and Hamilton (1975), all of which support the disconnection model. Even in the absence of any clear data which confirm the existence of the syndrome of aphemia, to deny that such a syndrome could exist is effectively to deny the theory of disconnection, a denial which leaves unexplained research results such as those cited above.

A critical question is then whether the aphemia resulting from damage in Broca's area is the same syndrome as aphemia; that is, can a lesion in Broca's area cause a disconnection syndrome? In a recent series of spectographic studies of the speech of patients with lesions in Broca's area, Blumstein et al. (1977) showed that the speech of these subjects was truly dyspraxic by considering such variables as voice onset time. (Other aphasic populations were shown to have phonetic production like that of normal subjects.) Thus the existence of an articulatory dyspraxis for language does not serve as a way of distinguishing aphemia (as a disconnection syndrome) and Broca's aphasia.

The period of mutism in aphemia is briefer than the period of mutism in Broca's aphasia. While there is a rapid improvement in the quality of speech production in aphemia arising from damage to Broca's area, there apparently is not in aphemia resulting from subcortical damage. Hécaen and Consoli (1973) studied the variation in the severity of language impairments of nineteen patients with lesions in Broca's area with respect to depth of lesion, including the degree of subcortical intrusion. They found these two variables to be strongly correlated; the deeper the lesion the more likely there is to be at least partial impairment, if not complete disconnection, of the pathway from Broca's area to the motor area controlling speech production. Such a correlation is to be expected in the light of the hypothesized disconnection-syndrome aphemia.

An extensive study of the degree of language deficits relative to the extent of cortical damage in Broca's area and adjacent areas has been made by Mohr (1975). That study is based on thirty cases personally observed by the author (and documented by autopsy, CT scan, or arteriogram), autopsy records at the Massachusetts General Hospital for the last twenty years, and a review of the cases reported in the literature since Broca (1861). The author concludes that the transient aphemia arising from a lesion in Broca's area is to be identified with a relatively small and discrete lesion in Broca's area, and that Broca's aphasia is to be identified with a relatively large lesion in that area, with the size of cortical lesion being the critical factor.

It appears then plausible to propose, in terms of lesion site and syndrome, that the aphemia associated with a lesion in Broca's area is a special (mild) case of Broca's aphasia, and that it is an error to collapse this type of aphemia with the aphemia arising from subcortical damage as a single syndrome distinct from Broca's aphasia. Under this hypothesis we would be led to conclude that there is essentially functional "equipotentiality" for phonological language production across Broca's area. While any lesion in that area is a shock to the language system, and in particular to the phonological system, radical impairment appears only when there is destruction of a critical mass of that area. That is to say, even though there is equipotentiality across the area, it is still the case that a certain amount of the area must remain intact for it to be adequately, if not perfectly, functional in speech production.

This theory predicts that, in the initial stages, patients with the aphemia resulting from damage to Broca's area should exhibit, in some degree, characteristics of Broca's aphasia; writing, reading, and comprehension should not be fully normal. With the return of speech, such patients would be expected to speak somewhat agrammatically in the beginning. In therapy, these patients should, like Broca's aphasics, be aided by repetition and imitation. This is, on such grounds, an empirically falsifiable hypothesis.

We argued above that Broca's aphasia was a phonological deficit because (a) the observable impairments all were systematically characterizable with respect to concepts of phonology and (b) they were systematically characterizable with respect to only those concepts. Here we have adopted a localizationist view of the syndrome and associated it with lesions in what is classically termed Broca's area. Furthermore, we have suggested that there is an equipotential phonological commitment across Broca's area. The notion of a cortical area being committed to some function is an ambiguous one. On the one hand, it could be that a function "resides" at a site; on the other, it could mean that the site is simply essential to the function (although not necessarily the locus of that function itself). The former interpretation is a special case of the latter. Unless the latter claim is qualified by a characterization of how the area is essential, it is the weaker of the two claims. So the question must be, in what sense is Broca's area committed to phonological function?

It is beyond the scope of our current enterprise to address this question in any detail and with any precision. However, as it is a central issue in the study of functional neuroanatomy of language, it deserves some elaboration. Our approach has, from its inception, been based on the traditional research model of functional biological studies: if an organism with a biological

"deficit" exhibits deviant behavior, the biological characterization of the normal state of the impaired domain is a description
of a system which subserves the disrupted function(s). As any
function may arise through the interaction of a complex
network of structures and be disrupted by damage to a single
element within that network, one can only claim that the
biologically characterized domain is necessary to carrying out
the function and not that there is a simple one-to-one correlation between the damaged area and the function. For example,
consider the function F, whose biological realization involves
the pathway a to f in Figure 4. Under normal conditions,
demand for F may activate the entire pathway, and each
component of the system a to f may be necessary for the
normal realization of F. Assuming this to be the case, the
realization of F will be deviant if for some reason d is non-
functional. As is illustrated in Figure 4, in such a case it would
be wrong to suggest that d alone underlies F. Since we cannot
know in advance the structure of the biological system underlying language, for any linguistic deficit correlated with a
neurological impairment the only hypothesis that we can make
is that the biological system involved plays an essential role in
the realization of normal linguistic capacity.

Let us take Figure 4 as a hypothetical model of the neuroanatomical systems a to f involved in the normal realization of
linguistic function F. Furthermore, let us assume that d is
Broca's area. We know from the linguistic analysis of the
language use of Broca's aphasics that the functional linguistic
involvement of Broca's area is phonological in nature. We
cannot from this exclude the possibility that a, b, c, e, or f is
also implicated in normal phonological function. The research
question in the functional neuroanatomy of language is then
twofold: to identify the areas of the brain which are directly

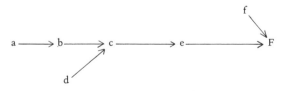

Figure 4

involved in or committed to normal linguistic function and, having done that, to determine the functional commitment of those areas. Having done that, we can then assign to *a* to *f* neuroanatomical and functional characterizations. The research reported here (page 73ff) can be taken as one step in such a research program. That step is not, however, sufficient for any serious attempt to answer the question of how Broca's area is committed to the phonological aspect of linguistic capacity within the context of a (more) complete account of the functional neuroanatomy of language.

We can make a small beginning toward addressing this issue by reviewing what has been hypothesized about the relation of Broca's area to other areas of the brain in the light of our claim that damage to Broca's area causes a phonological impairment. Wernicke observed that the motor regions of the brain are anterior to the Rolandic fissure, and that the rest of the brain (the parietal, occipital, and temporal lobes) has sensory functions. Consequently, he identified the memory, or conceptual image, of articulated (motor) language with Broca's area, and the sensory, auditory image of speech with what is now called Wernicke's area in the temporal lobe. We believe Wernicke's characterization of the function of Broca's area to be essentially correct. The location of Broca's area in the motor-association cortex, immediately anterior to the motor area of the vocal tract, provides prima facie support for the hypothesis that the area is committed to language production. That the nature of that commitment is phonological comes from analysis of the linguistic behavior of subjects with lesions in Broca's area.

If Broca's area functions in speech production, the question arises as to why all other modalities of language use are disturbed as well. Figure 5 [taken from Whitaker (1971) and consistent with that of Baker and Baker (1971)] gives a schematic representation of the areas of the left hemisphere which are identified with various linguistic functions and the connections which exist between those areas. The data on which such representations are based come from the study of various language deficits caused by lesions.

Exner's center is associated with written language. In

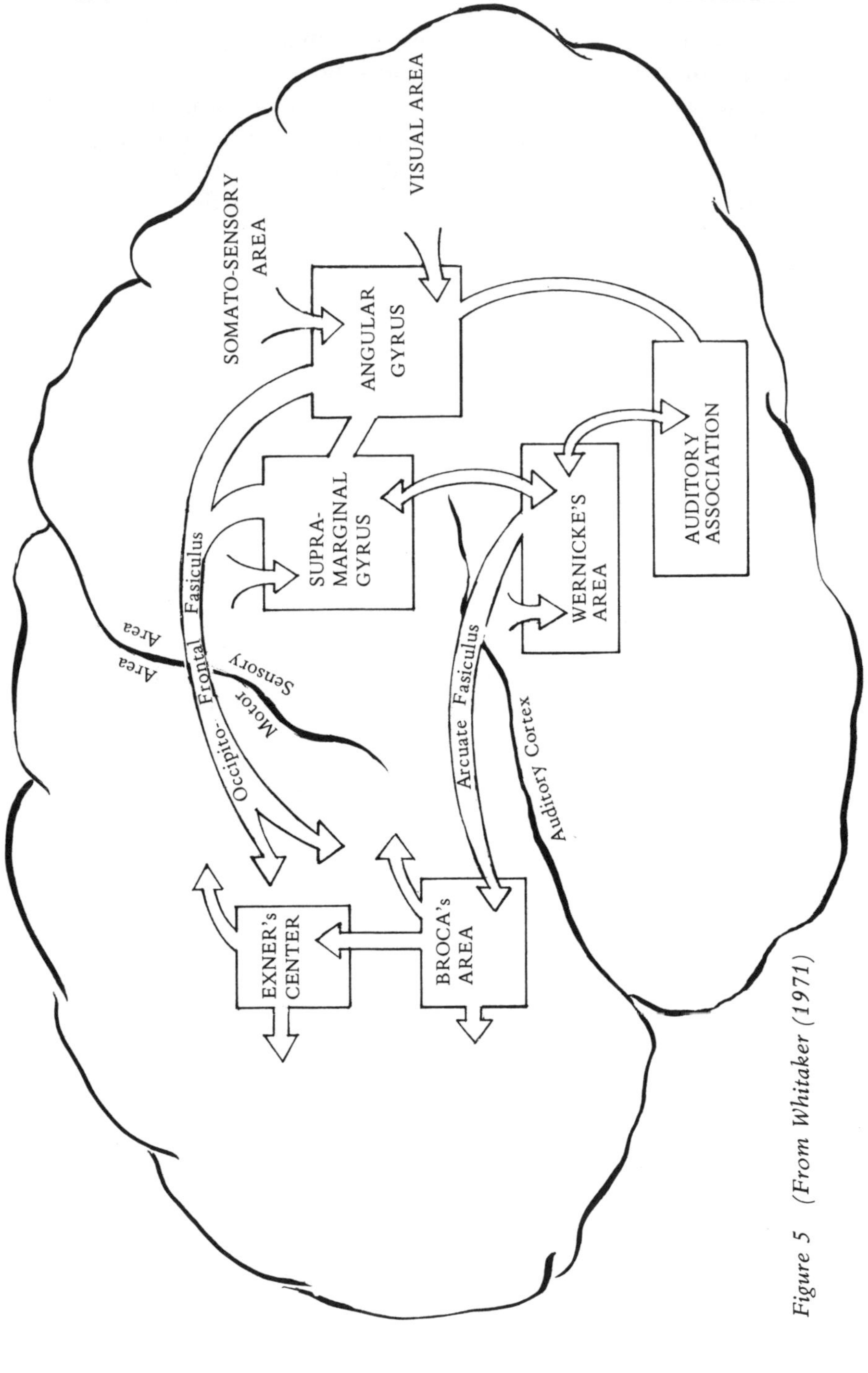

Figure 5 *(From Whitaker (1971)*

languages with alphabets (such as English) there is a correspondence relation between the sounds of the language and the orthographic symbols; in languages with syllabary orthographic systems (such as Hindi) there is also a correspondence between the orthography and the segmental system; however, in languages with ideographies (such as Chinese) there is no systematic relation between the orthography and the segmental system of the language. As illustrated in Figure 5, there is a connection between Broca's area and Exner's center; but it does not follow from this that damage to Broca's area will cause impairment of a patient's written output, since there is also a connection to Exner's center through the speech area via the occipitofrontal fasiculus. It is hypothesized that in a linguistic situation the whole of the linguistic system is activated. (It is this hypothesis which underlies research in experimental psycholinguistics.) Under this generalization it does follow that Broca's area will in some sense be activated in spontaneous writing and dictation of words. However, it should only be the case that there is interference with writing in just those languages where the orthography represents single segments or segmental syllable structure. In a language where there is no such relation, no matter how severe the damage to Broca's area, a phonological production deficit should have essentially no impact on the written output. This is in fact what has been found by Luria (1970) and Sasanuma and Fujimura (1971, 1972).

That there is a relatively secure maintenance of orthographies which are ideographic can be fully accounted for only if one argues that Exner's center has a functional capacity for the "storage" of orthographic representations, at least ideographic ones. If, however, it is claimed that for some languages orthographic representations are associated with Exner's center, then the strongest hypothesis (the most easily falsifiable) is to say that for all literates Exner's center functions crucially in the representation of written language. If, as is suggested in Figure 5, the connection between Broca's area and Exner's center is essentially "one-way" from the former to the latter, then under the hypothesis put forward here it should be the case that damage to Exner's center will have relatively little, if any, impact on speech production; that is, it follows that there should be a syndrome of (relatively) pure agraphia. (We leave aside here any further consideration of the nature of the functional commitment of Exner's center to orthographic representations.)

While we predict impairment on writing tasks where Broca's aphasics must spell, i.e., assign orthographic representations to strings, we also predict that on copying tasks their performance should be somewhat better. To show this we must first distinguish two sorts of copying tasks: those which involve copying strings which are composed of words and possible words, and those which are composed of random sequences of segments. Via the occipitofrontal fasciculus there is a connection from the visual cortex to Exner's center which does not involve Broca's area. Because of this there should be a general "improvement" in writing when it involves only copying written material. However, when what is involved in copying is language, the linguistic system will be activated. Therefore, performance on copying actual language material (be it real words or possible words) should be worse than copying random strings of letters. What is unclear to us is whether, when presented with alphabetic representations of nonlanguage, a subject will, at least initially, treat the copying task as a linguistic task. Since it is at least conventional to associate writing with language, at first a subject would most likely show more errors than he would after the nonlinguistic nature of the task has become evident.

Implicit in what we have said here is that writing is not really translating of a phonological representation into an orthographic one. This implication comes from the claim that, for all literates, orthographic representations are associated with Exner's center, and phonological ones are associated with Broca's area. Therefore, the proposed explanation for the writing deficits of Broca's aphasics is that there is interference of the deficient speech-production system with the orthographic system. It should be noted that little is known about the effects of literacy on the functional representation of language. One area of experimental research which might shed new light on this area would be determination of whether

Broca's aphasics show different patterns of recognition for "ear" rhyme (especially where the rhyme is phonological and not phonetic) and "eye" rhyme (the rhyming of words by virtue of their orthographic similarity).

The claim that the whole of the linguistic system is activated when a person is placed in a linguistic context is hardly novel and should not be subject to debate. Many, if not most, paradigms used in psycholinguistics are based on exactly this assumption: in the context of a linguistic stimulus, a subject is asked to attend to some nonlinguistic phenomenon (such as a click) or to carry out some nonlinguistic task. The assumption of across-the-board activation of the linguistic system in linguistic contexts is an empirical hypothesis which would be falsified if it were the case that brain damage to one area of the brain associated with a particular linguistic function did not impede performance on other linguistic functions. The data which show that Broca's aphasics have impairments which are parallel (if possibly less severe) to their speech-production impairments in comprehension and on metalinguistic tasks are consistent with this hypothesis and therefore can be taken as evidence in support of it. A functional characterization of language-associated areas posterior to the Rolandic fissure is clearly beyond the scope of the present paper, since such characterizations would require analyses parallel to that given above for Broca's aphasia. Whatever the posterior areas with linguistic commitments are, and the nature of their commitments, is actually irrelevant here because we are claiming that in any language situation, Broca's area will be activated for its linguistic function. That in itself is sufficient to cause systematic interference with all modalities of language use.

Turning more directly to the question of what is meant by claiming that Broca's area is functionally committed to phonological speech production, from the above discussion it should be evident that such a claim of functional commitment does not entail the claim that functional commitment of any area to language is necessarily modality-specific with respect to behavior. To say that Broca's area has an orientation toward speech production is to say that its function is in production, but it is not to say that this function is totally independent of

other functions. There is, by hypothesis, an interaction of all
the components of the linguistic system. This hypothesis is
supported by the data on Broca's aphasia. We cannot at this
point go beyond this to the more fundamental question of
whether we want to propose that Broca's area is in fact the site
of phonological representation for speech production, or
whether it is simply an essential subcomponent involved in such
productions.

3

Accessing the Mental Lexicon

KENNETH I. FORSTER

A highly structured information-retrieval system permits speakers to recognize words in their language effortlessly and easily. The results of psycholinguistic research using lexical decision and lexical access paradigms reveal that this system does not employ direct access to the full mental representations of words but is based instead on a structured search of the mental lexicon via various access files. The codes of the phonological, orthographic, and semantic and syntactic access files are constructed in terms of properties of the modality which they represent. Pointers associated with these codes direct the search process to entries in a master lexicon. Entries in this master lexicon are themselves sensitive to such aspects of words as their frequencies of occurrence and their morphological composition.

Some of the deficiencies in lexical access experienced by aphasic patients—semantic confusions, object-naming deficits, and restricted classes of word-finding difficulties—can be characterized as defects in various components of the model for normal lexical processing, augmented by a component allowing independent coding of visually presented objects and by a separate file representing conceptual knowledge.

The discussion of normal and abnormal lexical access presented here points out the importance of considering interactions between the structure of lexical representations and the neuropsychological processes involving those representations when constructing theories of both performance and the underlying capacity on which performance is based.

It is impressive that mature speakers recognize the words of their language so rapidly and so effortlessly. Even *more* impressive is their ability to recognize immediately that even though an item such as *thamon* might be a word (in English), it is not.

This ability involves a highly structured information-retrieval system which apparently has at its disposal extremely rapid search procedures. Characterizing how this system operates obviously is important in formulating a theory of sentence comprehension and production. Perceiving the meaning of a sentence requires that information about each of the words in the sentence be recovered, and on the production side, we obviously cannot speak until we have found words to express our intent. In the larger context of the study of mental processes, such a system is also important, since perception, memory, learning, and thought itself all depend critically on efficient information retrieval.

A psycholinguistic theory of information retrieval from the "mental lexicon" must play a central role in the biology of language, since it is directly relevant both to linguistics and to neurologically committed theories of cognition. Word-recognition experiments should provide data both for theories of *how* information is retrieved from the mental lexicon and for those of *what* is retrieved. The latter information is relevant not only to theories of lexical access but also to linguistic theory, which among other things provides an analysis of some of the kinds of information that must be stored in the lexicon. For example, in the recent linguistic literature, much turns on whether complex nominal expressions such as *destruction* are stored separately or are derived from simpler underlying forms, such as *destroy*, and have entries of their own [see Chomsky (1970) for further discussion of this point].

Finally, a meaningful theory of the psychological processes by which we access lexical memory can scarcely fail to be of critical importance to neurology. First, such a theory must make fundamental claims about how the brain works, at least in

functional terms. Second, the characterization of lexical access
in normal speakers may help provide insights into those neurologically based language disorders in which aphasics manifest,
directly or indirectly, problems in accessing lexical information.

Psycholinguistic Theories of Lexical Access

Direct-access models   The essential feature of associationism
was the claim that familiar stimuli somehow contacted their
appropriate memory traces directly. Thus, when a word is
presented, we automatically produce the meaning of that word,
or the ideas connected to it, or the mediating responses
associated with it (whatever the terminology, the concept is the
same). In this view, words and the mental events that they give
rise to are wired together directly.

The implications of associationism are best understood by
means of an analogy with an ordinary dictionary. It is possible
to predict from the spelling of a word exactly where it will be
listed in such a dictionary. The computational machinery for
making this prediction might use something like the decision
tree shown in Figure 1. The tree is used by descending from the
topmost node via the path labeled with the first letter of the
sequence to be investigated. At the second node, one descends
via the path appropriate to the second letter in the sequence,
and so on until the final "letter" (a blank or #) indicates the
end of the sequence. At this terminal node, from which no
further branches lead, there is an "address," which might be
simply a number telling us which page, column, and lines in the
dictionary we should consult to find the entry for the sequence
in question. If the letter sequence is a word, then that information, plus the meaning, will be found at the address given. If it is
not a word, then there will be nothing entered at the location
specified. Thus, if we were given the test item *atishnet*, we
would trace the path for A, T, I, S, H, N, E, T, and # in
sequence, take the address specified at the terminal node, and
then discover that there was no information in the lexicon at
that address. We would conclude from this that *atishnet* is not a
word.

It is an interesting property of such a dictionary that there would be no real need to have words of similar spelling stored together (although this could be arranged if necessary). Any arbitrary assignment of numbers to terminal nodes would suffice, as long as each address was unique. However, the millions of empty slots required for sequences which are not words of English would make such a dictionary enormously expensive. But at least the exact address of the appropriate information could be computed from the description under which that information is filed (i.e., the spelling), and the dictionary would be *content-addressable*. Recovering information from such a dictionary in memory would thus be by *direct access*. The decision tree described in Figure 1, which is a complex form of direct wiring, could constitute the mechanism of *association*.

It may seem pointless to have terminal nodes which correspond to impossible nonwords or to possible, but not actual, words. These nodes increase the necessary wiring substantially.

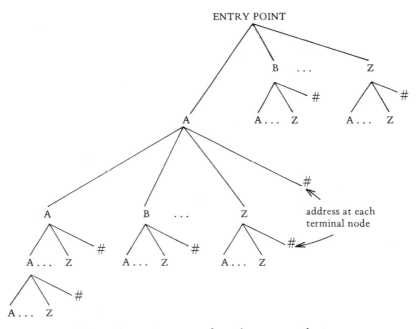

ENTRY POINT

address at each
terminal node

Figure 1   Decision tree for a direct-access lexicon

This difficulty can be easily counteracted by pruning the tree to leave only those branches that lead to actual words. A fragment of such a tree is shown in Figure 2.

The principle by which this tree is constructed can be seen by examining the node at the end of the path A-B-A. Since there is no word beginning *abaa-*, there is no need to have at this node a branch for the letter *a*, nor similarly for *b*. Since there *is* a word beginning *abac-*, there must be a branch for the letter *c*. But for most people, there is only *one* such word (*abacus*); so there is no need to have branches for each of the remaining letters of

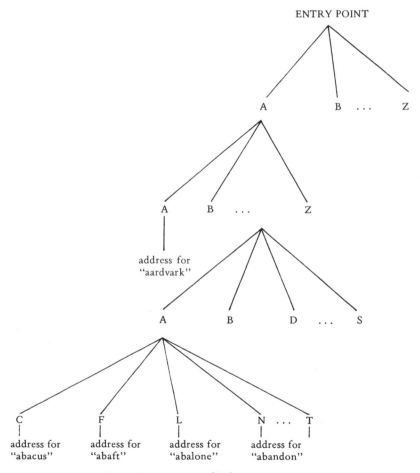

Figure 2   A "pruned" direct-access tree.

that word. All that remains after locating *abac-* is to check that the remaining letters are in fact *-us* (to allow for the fact that *abacan* must be recognizable as a nonword).

Consider what would happen in locating a nonword such as *atishnet*. Descent would be via the path A-T-I (necessary for words such as *atilt* and *atingle*), but there would be no further branch for *s*, since there is no word beginning *atis-*. Hence nonwords will be recognized as such with great efficiency using such a tree. In fact they should be recognized as nonwords more rapidly (on average) than real words will be recognized as words.

By means of *lexical decision* experiments, we can estimate the relative times required to decide whether a letter sequence is a word or not. In such experiments, a letter sequence is presented visually for as long as the subject requires to classify the item as a word or nonword, performing as rapidly as possible. Since there is no way to perform this task without accessing the internal lexicon (with one exception; see below), we can estimate the relative times required for lexical access by measuring the subject's reaction time.

In such experiments, familiar words typically are classified as words in around 500 milliseconds, while nonwords require about 650 milliseconds. That is, nonwords take substantially *more* time to classify than words. This is an extremely robust finding, and it has been reported by a number of investigators [e.g., Rubenstein, Garfield, and Millikan (1970), Stanners and Forbach (1973), Forster and Chambers (1973), Forster and Bednall (1976)]. The only exception to the general rule (first noted by H. Rubenstein) is that *impossible* nonwords, such as *thptxt*, are classified in about the same time as words. Presumably, such items might be rejected by some process in which the lexicon is not consulted at all, such as one relying on rules for permissible letter sequences.

It is not easy to explain the discrepancy between the decision-tree theory and the experimental results. There is no natural way to explain why nonwords require longer to classify, even using the pruned decision tree. Instead extra processes, which always will involve processes occurring *after* the non-existence of a branch has been detected, must be assumed to apply. One such assumption is that the subject is not aware of the status of processing within the decision tree until an address is discovered; that is, he is never aware that no address could be found for a given item. To decide that an item is a nonword, he must set a deadline, after which a "No" decision will be made if no address has been encountered. For error-free performance, this deadline would need to be set so that the addresses of all actual words would be found before the time limit was up.

Although they are ad hoc in this case, the notions of limited awareness of the status of processing and of deadlines have been invoked in a number of reaction-time models and are not implausible. Such a model would explain why nonwords, on the average, take longer to access than words.

Fortunately, it is not difficult to eliminate this and similar lines of argument from consideration, since it can be shown that nonwords do not *always* take longer to process than words. For example, Forster and Bednall (1976) asked subjects to classify items according to whether they have more than one meaning. Orthographically legal nonwords, such as *flink*, were classified faster than either unambiguous words, such as *year*, or ambiguous words, such as *chest*. The correct response to the first two cases is "No" and to the last case "Yes." Similarly, it takes less time to recognize that *to flink* is not a possible phrase in English than it takes to make the same decision about *to year*.

Under the previous assumptions about limitations on conscious awareness, nonwords still should produce longer reaction times than words in such tasks, since the retrieval system cannot indicate that there is no information about these items until the deadline has been passed. The "unpruned" model in Figure 1 would run afoul of exactly the same data, because it implies that words and nonwords should take the *same* time to classify. Hence it seems that this class of modifications to the direct-access model should be discarded.

There is another critical fact that such models cannot explain naturally. Characteristically, words with relatively high frequencies of occurrence are classified faster than those with low frequencies, even when the latter are perfectly familiar to the subjects of the experiment (e.g., *mildew, perspire, radiate*).

Although it is of course possible to arrange the search tree so that *letter* frequency is a relevant parameter (e.g., by changing the order in which the paths are listed), there is no way to arrange the decision trees so that the frequency of occurrence of the whole word *itself* controls access time. In fact, letter frequency itself typically has no detectable impact on decision time [e.g., Chambers and Forster (1975)]. About the only variable that such models clearly implicate is the number of letters in the word, and even this variable is inappropriate, since length appears to play almost no role in word recognition in at least two experimental situations [Frederickson and Kroll (1974), Forster and Chambers (1973), Chambers and Forster (1975)].

Our conclusion then is that if we *do* have direct access to entries in the internal lexicon, it is not via letter-based decision trees of the sort described above. What alternative remains? To our knowledge, there is only one class of direct-access models of lexical access that differs in kind from the decision-tree approach. That is a threshold model. [For a fuller discussion of such models, see Selfridge and Neisser (1960), Morton (1970).]

The essence of such a theory is that a separate detector for each word is selectively sensitive to properties of environmental stimuli. Each detector has its own tuning curve and responds to a variety of inputs. Thus the detector for the word *dog* would be activated to some degree by any letter sequence having an initial *d*, a medial *o*, or a final *g*. It would also be activated, although less so, by sequences having *similar* letters. It might also be activated by any sequence having exactly three letters and, to a lesser degree, by two- and four-letter strings.

Obviously, the presentation of a particular word will activate many detectors to varying degrees, just as would the presentation of a nonword. The problem is to decide which of the many detectors affected is responsive to the word for the entry in question. One method would be to scan and compare all detectors. This alternative has to be discarded since the potentially exhaustive scan it requires is the *antithesis* of direct access. Another method would be to set thresholds on each detector so that a detector would fire automatically when the level of activation reached its threshold. If no detector reached its threshold level, the item would be declared to be a nonword.

There are two problems with this account. The first is that it is technically difficult to ensure that the *correct* detector will always reach threshold first. Because the theory usually assumes that the thresholds of high-frequency words are lower than the thresholds of low-frequency words (to allow for frequency effects), problems obviously will arise when the stimulus is a low-frequency word that is similar to a high-frequency word. In such cases (which are by no means rare), there would be a marked tendency for the detector for the high-frequency word to fire before that for the word actually presented. Of course, this kind of error may sometimes occur in reading, but the point is, such errors happen *rarely* rather than often.

The far more serious problem with threshold models is that we are not entitled to assume nonwords will not activate any word detectors to threshold level. There is now abundant evidence that nonwords which are similar to words take longer to classify than other nonwords [Amey (1973), Novik (1974), Taft and Forster (1975), Chambers (1975), Coltheart et al. (1976), Taft and Forster (1976)]. To take some examples from Chambers (1975), it is known that a nonword formed by permuting adjacent letters of a word causes substantial interference, even though in many cases the permutations produce impossible words, e.g., *vaiation, obttle surpries.* Interference with the correct decision also is caused by changing just one of the letters of a word, e.g., *prinon, destair, abount.*

It is inconceivable that we could explain that nonwords which resemble words are different from other nonwords without postulating that such nonwords activate to threshold level the detector for at least one word. Presumably we could explain the fact that such nonwords are not misread as words by giving up the notion that our percept of a word or a nonword corresponds to, or is controlled by, the first detector that reaches threshold. Instead we might simply regard the set of detectors which reach threshold as plausible *hypotheses* about the correct interpretation of a stimulus item. The hypotheses would have to be checked for veracity as they became available (i.e., as the detectors reached threshold). This subsequent check would fail in the case of nonwords which are similar to words, and the item would be assigned correctly to the category of nonword.

Although this modification of the theory is a quite reasonable one, it gives up the assumption of direct access. If the term direct access means anything, it means that the correct lexical entry is specified automatically, without specifying any other entries as candidates. The modification proposes a search process among a set of candidate entries.

Thus we conclude that lexical access will inevitably involve *some* search process. That is, there must be preliminary processors which specify a subset of the lexicon within which the correct entry for a target item will be found with a high probability. This subset of entries must be searched to locate the entry for the item sought.

This is equivalent to giving up the claim that lexical memory is directly addressable in that the final, precise locating of the correct entry requires a serial examination of a range of entries, each entry being examined for a match between, say, its orthographic properties and those of the target item.

Such a process is very like the procedure we would use to consult a dictionary when asked whether *atishnet* is a word. Initially, we would use only one property of the item, that the first letter is *a*, to guide the access process. This property would fix the probable search area as, say, the first twenty pages of the dictionary. Using the guide words listed at the top of every page, we would then search for the page that must contain *atishnet*. Up to this point, we have merely narrowed the area which will be searched (although a search procedure involving the guide words was used). Now the real search begins; we examine the entries on the page until we find the position where *atishnet* would have to be if it were a word. If any entry were found, a "yes" decision would be made. But since the position is not occupied, a "no" decision is made.

To make this model a satisfactory account of the results so far presented, we need modify only one aspect of the process outlined. The words on each page must not be ordered alphabetically; if they were, then words and nonwords would take the same (or very nearly the same) time to classify in a lexical decision experiment. Instead we assume that the entries on any given page are organized by frequency of occurrence, high-frequency words being at the top of the page, low-frequency words at the bottom. Then we can explain both the effects of frequency (the detailed search starts from the top of the page) and the longer time required for nonword decisions (all entries on a page will have to be searched before a "no" decision can be made).

A search model of lexical access We will now attempt to provide a more detailed model of lexical access, incorporating the assumptions just made. That is, we assume that accessing the mental lexicon differs from looking up a word in a printed dictionary only in its final stages.

The first point to notice is that the lexicon must be accessed under three rather different conditions: reading, listening, and talking. (Writing is perhaps a fourth condition, but we shall defer that issue for the moment.) For reading, it seems sensible to have lexical items organized into pages of *orthographically* similar words. But for listening, it would seem more sensible to organize entries by *phonological* similarity. Finally, when we construct sentences, we need to find words with the desired semantic and syntactic properties and seldom care how the words will look or sound. Therefore, it would seem desirable for the purposes of talking to organize entries by semantic and syntactic properties.

Of course, we cannot organize the same set of entries in three different ways without, in some sense, listing each entry three times. But we can assume that there is only one copy of the lexicon, which we shall call the *master lexicon*, and three peripheral access files referring to the master lexicon, one with words organized by *orthographic* properties, one by *phonological* properties, and one by *semantic and syntactic* properties. An entry for a word in the master lexicon contains all the information that we have about that word. The entries for the same word in the peripheral access files contain descriptions of the appropriate stimulus features of word (the *access code*) and pointers to the corresponding entry in the master lexicon. This situation is depicted in Figure 3.

The first step in accessing the master lexicon is accomplished by finding an entry for the word in question in the appropriate peripheral access file. This process involves preparing a coded description of the target item (the stimulus word) and then searching through the access file, comparing the coded description of the target item with the *access code* in each actual entry. A sufficiently accurate match between these (the criterion of sufficiency being variable) terminates the search. The pointer specified in the entry at which termination occurs is used to access an entry in the master lexicon. Finally, a detailed comparison must be made between the properties of the stimulus item and the properties of the word specified in the master lexicon. We shall refer to this comparison as a *postaccess check*.

As a concrete illustration, let us trace through the steps involved in accessing the entry in the master lexicon corresponding to the visually presented word *henchman*. Initial perceptual operations convert the neural representation of the visual stimulus into a format compatible with the access codes (e.g., there is no point in taking the size of the stimulus into

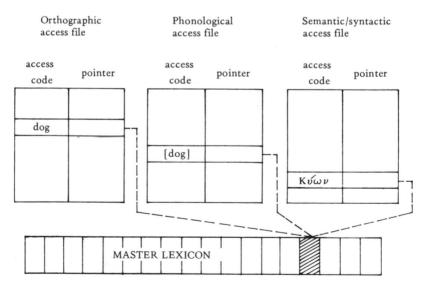

Figure 3   Organization of peripheral access files and master lexicon

account if the word is not listed under a size access code). If we assume that a letter code is required, we need not assume that *all* letters are involved. It would be computationally expensive to make comparisons involving all eight letters of *henchman* when the first four letters, or perhaps the first syllable, might suffice [Taft and Forster (1976)]. We now proceed to search the orthographic access file, comparing *h-e-n-c-h* and the access code at each entry. When the similarity between these exceeds some previously defined criterion, the pointer in that entry directs the system to an entry in the master lexicon. At that point, the full orthographic specification of *henchman* must be extracted and compared with the properties of the input stimulus. (The format of this comparison need not be the same as the one used for access; indeed, if the system has really effective error checks, it might use a quite different format for this comparison.)

As we have already seen, the criterion for a match must be well below the maximum, since nonwords which are similar to words take longer to reject. This presumably is due to the fact that the search incorrectly stops at an entry, and time is lost accessing the master lexicon, performing the postaccess check, and recommencing the search in the original access file.

As we assumed earlier, entries in the access files are grouped together by similarity, and we shall refer to each such grouping as a *bin*. The first stage of lexical access involves calculating to which bin the derived pointer likely belongs. Entries belonging to the same bin obviously will have similar descriptions. The internal structure of an access file is depicted in Figure 4.

The entries within each bin are listed according to frequency of occurrence. Actually, this frequency may vary from file to file. For example, the frequency of the printed form of a given word may differ widely from the frequency of its spoken form, and the relevant frequency of entries in the file used for talking is likely to be that in the speech of the person possessing the lexicon, rather than that in the language at large.

Before going on to consider further properties, we should ask what evidence supports this model of lexical access. At the moment, little is available. One might point out that some people can access words from their orthographic representation without being able to spell the words correctly. Assuming this *is* a fact, orthographic properties must be represented twice—once in the access file (correctly) and once in the master lexicon (incorrectly). This double representation would explain why children can check their oral spelling of a word by writing it down: if the written version leads back to the same entry used to produce the oral version, then it is very likely to be correct. Such phenomena would be very difficult to explain if there were only one representation of orthographic information.

Perhaps the strongest evidence for the model is that arranging the system any other way is counterproductive. For example, it was once assumed that the orthographic file could be discarded by adopting the so-called phonological recoding hypothesis [e.g., Rubenstein, Lewis, and Rubenstein (1971)]. This hypothesis suggested that orthographic representations were converted to phonological representations by rule, taking

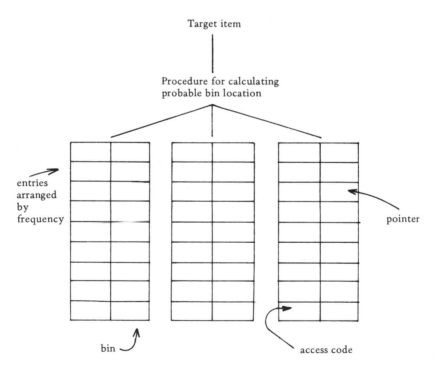

Figure 4   Approximate content addressing.

advantage of the fact that everyone who learns to read already has a phonological access file (i.e., can understand the spoken word). There are many objections to this theory [for a review, see Bradshaw (1975)], but one experimental observation is crucial. If the recoding hypothesis were correct, then it should take no longer to decide, all things being equal, that *trane* is pronounced the same way as an English word than it takes to decide that *train* is an English word. In fact, the former task takes nearly twice as long as the latter [Taft (1973), Bower (1970)]. Thus one cannot collapse the orthographic and phonological access files.

One might wish to collapse either of these files with the semantic and syntactic files. For example, one could imagine a decision tree in which the initial categorization was by semantic category, with a subclassification by orthography or phonology, as in Figure 5. The problem in this case is to make sure that frequency can be represented. If we preserve the bin arrangement originally suggested, with frequency controlling order of search within a bin, then we have constructed a subclassification tree rather than the cross-classification scheme suggested.

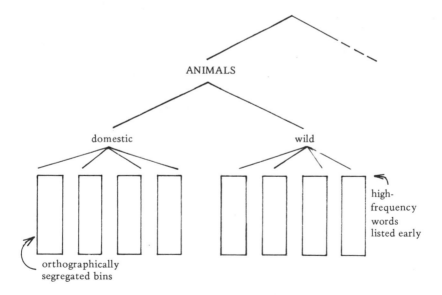

Figure 5   A semantic/orthographic/frequency search tree.

Such a system makes exactly the wrong predictions about frequency. When the semantic category in which a word belongs is known (e.g., in a sentence context), a high-frequency word will be found before a low-frequency word, and normal frequency effects will be observed. But when the semantic category is *not* known (e.g., in a lexical decision experiment in which the words are presented in isolation), the semantic category tree would have to be searched at random, with low- and high-frequency words having equal probability of being searched first, the result being that there should be no frequency effect at all. But the *strongest* effects of frequency are found just when the semantic category is *not* known; so we must abandon either the usual interpretation of frequency effects or the notion that entries are organized into semantic categories with an orthographic subclassification.

We now return to a discussion of further properties of the search model. It should be clear from the discussion of decision times for nonwords that the current model postulates an *exhaustive* search for nonwords and a terminating search for words. The main source of evidence stems from experiments in which the task calls for information that is not contained within any single entry. For example, if we ask whether a word such as *year* is ambiguous, the information in the entry for *year* will not answer the question, unless words are marked as unambiguous. The search must continue beyond the initial entry to find whether a second entry exists for *year*. Similarly, if we ask whether *year* can be used as a verb, an exhaustive search will be required to establish that it cannot. The consequence of such a decision procedure would be that no frequency effects should occur: no matter how quickly the first entry was located, an exhaustive search is still required. This result in fact has been obtained [Forster and Bednall (1976)].

However, these experiments do not indicate whether the search continues only to the end of whatever bin the entry should have been in, or whether more than one bin is searched. What evidence we have suggests that the search extends beyond the initial bin. For example, consider the following nonwords: *xecause, bxcause, bexause, becxuse, becauxe,* and *becausx*. In each case, the nonword is very similar to *because,* and, in each case, this similarity is perceived quickly enough to interfere with the "no" response [Amey (1973), Chambers (1974)]. This implies that the set of entries searched includes that for *because*. It seems unlikely that the same bins would have been searched in every case (a word beginning *xe-* would surely be in a different bin from a word beginning *bx-*), we must assume either that *because* is listed in many different bins, that the bins are *very* large, or that the search continues beyond the first bin if no entry is found.

The last property that needs to be outlined is cross reference between entries. Meyer and Schvaneveldt (1971) have shown that lexical decision time for a word is decreased if it is preceded by another associatively related word. That is, the decision time for the word *doctor* will be faster if it is preceded by the word *nurse*. Within the terms of the search model, this implies that there must be some kind of cross reference between *nurse* and *doctor*. Bednall (1976) has recently shown that the method of access for the second member of such a pair must be quite different from the method of access for the first. She obtained the normal frequency effects for the first member (e.g., *nurse*) but no frequency effect at all for the second (e.g., *doctor*). Bednall also showed, incidentally, that the results do not depend on *associative* connections *per se*. Words chosen from the same semantic field show the facilitative effects, even when they have zero associative connectivity, as defined by word-association norms. (When given *fun* as a stimulus word, nobody responds with *mirth* as an associate.)

The implications of these results are that the first word of a semantically related pair is accessed normally in the orthographic file (hence it shows a frequency effect). But the entry for the second word is found in a completely different way. One possibility is that *doctor* can be accessed directly from the entry for *nurse* by means of a cross reference, the idea being that words in a semantic field somehow are linked. Evidently, it is quicker to find the entry for *doctor* by searching this set of cross references from the entry for *nurse* than by locating the entry for *doctor* via the orthographic access file.

Where is the most appropriate place for such a system of cross references? Presumably it is not in the peripheral access files; if it were, we would have to repeat these cross references at least three times (assuming that the same types of effects apply to all access files). Since the cross references must constitute a very rich system, such duplication would be expensive and pointless if this network could be established over just the entries in the master lexicon.

Such a network obviously extends the power of the access system considerably. Effectively we have defined a different kind of search, one that is semantically organized. This search differs from the syntactic and semantic access file in that the latter serves the need of sentence *production* and hence would be expected to subclassify according to part of speech. However, since we know virtually nothing about the third access file, we should not overlook the possibility that the system of cross referencing in the master lexicon serves the purpose of finding the words needed to express the propositions. Of course, even if it did, we would still need a system that allowed us to *enter* this network at an appropriate place (unless we began the search at random starting points). The third access file may serve this purpose.

This completes our preliminary description of the search model. In the end, the model turns out to be more like that used to find a book in a library than that used to find a word in a dictionary. In both a library and a mental lexicon, the essential problem is to arrange information so that it can be accessed efficiently in a number of *different* ways. For a library, the solution is either to store the information in each location predicted by the various access functions (which means buying several copies of each book) or to have only one set of books and several different catalogs (e.g., one organized by author, one by title, and another by subject area). The books of a library are analogous to the lexical entries in the master lexicon, the catalogs are analogous to peripheral access files, and the reference numbers in the catalog entries are equivalent to pointers.

When Access Fails: Word-Retrieval Problems in Aphasics and Normals

To date our concern has been to explain findings derived from the relatively artificial situations of experiments. The aim of this section is to select a small sample of more "natural" problems of word retrieval and discuss them in the light of the model we have been developing. The question we seek to answer is whether we can learn anything about lexical access by studying aphasic symptoms.

Semantic confusions The most striking aphasic symptom, from our point of view, is that of paralexia. When given a word-naming task (pronouncing printed words), patients often substitute a word from the same semantic field as the target word; for example, they read *college* as *school,* or *drama* as *play* [see Marshall and Newcombe (1966)].

That the error comes from the same semantic field as the target clearly implies that in *some* respects the lexical access mechanisms are performing satisfactorily. One interpretation is that the orthographic access file functions correctly to direct the search to the relevant entry in the master lexicon but that for some reason, semantic cross references are invoked, and the search terminates at the wrong entry. That is, the search continues past the correct entry to one of the cross-referenced entries. The pronunciation of this related, but erroneous, word is determined from its entry; control is transferred to some speech system, and the incorrect word is articulated. Much the same effect could be obtained if the pointer in the access file referred merely to a list of semantically related entries, rather than to a particular entry.

This theory assumes that the error results from a defect in accessing the master lexicon; the search somehow "spills over" from the correct entry to an incorrect entry. Such a hypothesis has two clear-cut implications:

(i) It should be possible to link the semantic facilitation effects described by Meyer and Schvaneveldt (1971) to paralexic error patterns. Both phenomena are mediated by the system of semantic cross references. If a word X is often read as Y by paralexic patients, then lexical decision times by normal subjects for Y should be faster when preceded by X. Since

Rinnert and Whitaker (1973) have shown that semantic-confusion errors are highly predictable from word-association norms, and the magnitude of the Meyer and Schvaneveldt effect is itself predictable from the same norms, the two phenomena are, in fact, very likely related.

(ii) From the assumption that both dictation and speech production require activating lexical entries in the master lexicon, it follows that the paralexic patient frequently should exhibit the same kinds of errors in dictation tests and spontaneous speech. It is difficult to determine from the clinical literature whether this hypothesis is correct. Often the presence of "verbal paraphasia" (semantic confusion errors in ongoing speech) is noted without any indication whether this type of error is made in other tasks.

For the moment, we should remark that the formulation suggested in (ii) above,

if paralexic, then paraphasic

should not be interpreted as a biconditional. That is, we *could* imagine a system that produced semantic confusions in speech but not in word naming because the defect might be in the production access file rather than in the master lexicon. Of course, such a move is absolutely necessary to account for normal language functioning. Normal speakers often make semantic errors in *speech* [see Garrett (1976)] but seem almost never to do so in either listening or reading.

If the facts indicate that it is quite possible to find patients who make semantic errors *either* in a word-naming situation (conversion from orthographic to phonological representation) *or* in a dictation test (the reverse conversion), but not in *both*, then any theory based on malfunction in the master lexicon would have to be abandoned. We would be forced to locate the malfunction elsewhere, the most obvious possibility being one of the access files. This is not a straightforward modification, since a malfunction in, say, the orthographic access file would be expected to produce errors of *visual*, not semantic, similarity. Similarly, errors in the phonological access file would produce errors based on phonological similarity, not on visual or semantic similarity.

To avoid these problems, we must assume that entry to the access file is accomplished successfully. This leaves only one mechanism for the confusion, namely, the *pointer* from the access file to the master lexicon. That is, we would have to argue that an error in the pointer misdirects the search to a semantically related word. This in turn implies that some aspect of the pointer itself has a structure related to meaning.

If the pointer were a number corresponding to an ordinal position in the master lexicon, and if numerically similar pointers referred to semantically similar words, then it would be possible to explain semantic confusions as misinterpretations of the pointer, e.g., reading 3429 as 3439. Of course, such misreadings might not always produce semantic confusions. If 3429 were misread as 8429, the resulting error would be unlikely to be semantically related, since words separated by 5000 entries probably will not bear an obvious semantic relationship.

The most important implication of this pointer theory is that in the master lexicon, entries for semantically related items are functionally "close." Without such organization, misreading the pointer could not produce the required property.

The conclusion of this argument, then, is that if semantic confusions in a given patient can be shown to be restricted to just one type of task, we are strongly committed to the assumption that the master lexicon, or access to it, is physically organized according to semantic principles. Conversely, if semantic confusions can be observed in a variety of tasks for the same patient, we can revert to the weaker assumption that it is not the entries *themselves* that are organized, but cross references between entries. In the latter case semantic confusions are, in some sense, a timing problem in which the search process does not terminate at the right point.

These issues have considerable importance for the study of semantics itself. If one could be completely confident that the storage of information in the brain is organized according to principles of semantic similarity, it is obvious that any semantic theory should be able to explain this principle. On the other hand, if semantic confusions are mediated by a loosely structured system of perhaps idiosyncratic cross reference between lexical entries (such as might account for the word associations that normals produce), then there is less reason to hope that interesting semantic principles will be revealed by studying such errors.

Object-naming deficits   The next type of symptom that we shall consider is the inability to name objects actually presented. The color of an object is frequently very difficult to name, although the patient can complete sentences adequately with color names; e.g., "the color of grass is ———." Similarly, an actual razor cannot be named, although the patient can respond correctly when asked, "what do you use to shave yourself?"

One might be tempted to postulate yet another access file in which the perceptual attributes of objects are listed, with pointers to the entry in the master lexicon corresponding to the name of each object. The formal semantic properties of the word are contained within the entry, as well as a pointer to a section of a general memory structure representing the person's knowledge of the world. The situation in Figure 6 depicts how this conceptual knowledge might be accessed from two different files.

The essential point of this model is that access to knowledge about objects is always through an entry in the master lexicon. Such a model would explain object-naming difficulty as a defective operation in the object file. Even with a defect in the object file, it is still possible that the name of the object will be understood or found from a description of its properties (using the production file).

However, it is clear that this model will not work. Potter (in preparation) has shown that information about an object in the conceptual knowledge system can be accessed faster than the name of the object, a result which certainly does not fit the specifications of Figure 6. Potter had subjects compare objects (pictures of them) or the names of those objects (printed words) according to the relative *cost* of the object. She found that the pictures of objects were compared faster than their names. By itself, this fact could imply merely that the path labeled B in Figure 6 is "shorter" than path A. But it would be difficult to explain Potter and Faulconer's further finding (1975) that pronouncing the name of the object was initiated faster when the name was presented than when the object was presented. Since words are pronounced faster than nonwords, and high-frequency words are pronounced faster than low-frequency words [Forster and Chambers (1973)], lexical access must be involved in these pronunciation times.

It seems that the best way to explain these results is to assume that there is a direct path from the object file to the conceptual knowledge system, as shown in Figure 7. We now assume that the first step in object recognition is to find the representation of that object in the conceptual system (using the object file) and then use the production file to find a word

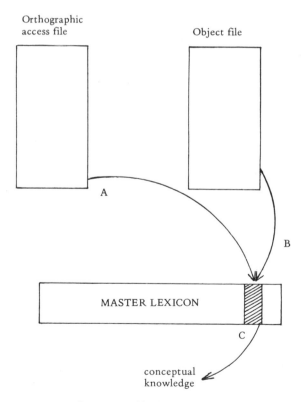

Figure 6   Access to general memory file from either the name of an object or the object itself.

which has the desired property, namely, one referring to the object in question.

In Potter's experiments, classifying an object according to cost requires path *C*, while classifying a *word* according to the cost of the object to which it refers involves paths *A* and *E*. Thus it is possible (although not necessary) that classifying an object could take less time than classifying a word. The distinction of processes is retained if both the object file and the production file are removed to produce the simplified model shown in Figure 8 (the phonological access file is not critical here). The critical implication is that access to conceptual knowledge about objects from their names is made via the master lexicon.

However, Oldfield and Wingfield (1965) have shown that object naming is influenced by frequency; so we need to assume that the conceptual system is searched according to the frequency of occurrence of objects. We shall also need to postulate some procedure by which the master lexicon can be searched when all that is known about the desired entry is some aspect of its meaning. The point of having peripheral access files is to permit several *different* principles of organization of the same

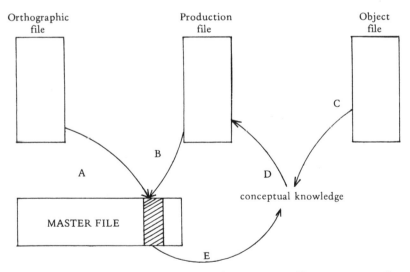

Figure 7   Access path from object file to master file via conceptual knowledge and the production file

set of entries; if we decide to drop one of the access files, we must embed its principle of organization in some other component.

Now let us consider the case of an anomic patient, using the fuller representation of the model shown in Figure 7. The most striking symptom of such patients is their inability to name an object which is presented to them. We could argue that the deficit giving rise to this difficulty lies in path *C, D,* or *B.*

Apparently path *C* can be ruled out, since there is no evidence that anomic patients are unable to recognize the *properties* of the object, e.g., its use. (They may have difficulties in demonstrating its use in the case of apraxia, but this appears to be a separate issue.)

It appears that path *D* can be eliminated also, since it is often reported [e.g., Brown (1972)] that the anomic patient can be cued successfully by a sentence context such as "you shave with a———." This finding *also* implies that path *B* operates successfully, since both *D* and *B* must be involved in accessing the appropriate entry, given a context.

Now we have created something of a paradox: no paths remain which could be defective. Each *component* process appears to be intact. Why then should the patient be unable to prompt *himself* by observing that the object he cannot name is something that he shaves with?

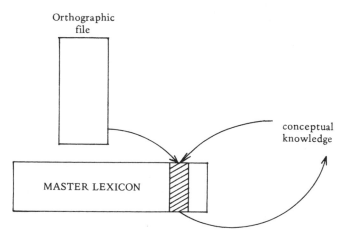

Figure 8 Simplified model for object naming.

Two possible lines of explanation should be pursued. When a patient has word-retrieval problems but can be cued effectively from a functional description of the object, the true nature of the deficit may be simply a blocking of *output*; i.e., the patient is unable to *say* the word. The second possibility is that sentence contexts use words which are themselves directly linked to the desired word by the network of semantic cross references (e.g., shave → razor).

The possibility of using this alternative access route initially appears to be a reasonable proposal, but there are indications that it is probably wrong. Anomic patients often use circumlocutions in which it is not at all unlikely that they might substitute the phrase "the thing I use for shaving" for the word *razor*. If this is possible, why does the correct word not then become available? Above all, why should a prompt provided by the experimenter be more effective than a self-generated one?

Why Does Access Fail At All?

So far, we have concentrated on the nature of the retrieval operations that malfunction. Within the search model, there appear to be only two reasons why any of the access files should malfunction in the first instance. First, it could be that somehow the structure of one of the access files has deteriorated, so that some words become temporarily "disconnected" from the rest of the file. Beyond this somewhat ad hoc remark, there is very little to say (at present) except to observe that we would need to provide an account of the fact that the malfunction is restricted to just one access file and does not apply generally.

The second possibility is that aphasic patients set too high (or too low) a criterion for a match between the best available description of the target word and the entries for the search process to terminate at the right entry. The same comment applies. Why does this not happen across the board? Why is it that the patient has trouble just in finding the *names* of objects?

Perhaps the answer is that word finding of the sort being discussed here is more prone to interference than are other file operations because it involves the production file (or perhaps because it involves several stages). There can be no doubt that this is true for *normal* speakers. Word finding is the one area of language performance that regularly causes problems in spontaneous speech. It is commonplace for normal speakers to be unable to think of the name of an object, concept, or person, but it is most unusual for them to be unable to think of what a familiar word refers to, or what the salient properties of a familiar object are.

Why should this be so? Why should the name of an object be such a fragile item of information? Perhaps it is because the name of an object is a *linguistic* property; whereas other properties of the object are nonlinguistic, whatever their linguistic reflexes. Thus we might expect that the one property of an object that is *not* listed in the conceptual knowledge system is its name, the reason being that linguistic properties are stored in a different system.

Actually, we have already assumed this in making Figure 7. We have assumed in searching for the name of an object that this name cannot be located in the conceptual knowledge system but must be represented nowhere else but in the master lexicon. This implies, of course, that language is served by a distinct neural system from other cognitive activities.

Word-Finding Difficulties in Restricted Categories

One aspect of anomia is of considerable interest, and that is when the *class* of objects which cannot be named is highly restricted. Brown (1972) reports that proper names and abstract nouns are especially prone to error and that colors can be particularly difficult to name (although they can be matched satisfactorily).

The existence of such difficulties makes sense if we consider tasks in which the subject or patient must locate a particular word with designated syntactic and semantic properties. We might presume that access would involve searching a particular area of the lexicon which contains words with similar semantic properties. In other words, we would be arguing that the *production* file was causing the problem. This is not at all unlikely, since the production system is almost bound to have a semantically organized search routine available. Hence there exists the possibility that certain semantic categories may become relatively hard to access. It would not be inconceivable, to take an extreme example, that an anomic patient might have trouble just in finding words that are related to sports (e.g., *baseball, touchdown*) but experience much less difficulty with other types of words.

The plausibility of this line of argument would diminish if it could be shown that the same restricted-category problems are found with other tasks such as word naming. Since it seems most unlikely that word naming involves the production file, there would be no convenient mechanism to explain the effect. That is, if a patient were found who had pronounced difficulty only in reading proper names, the model would be incapable of providing a satisfactory account, since the appropriate access files are assumed not to be organized semantically.

Therefore, one might predict from the existing model that restricted category word naming (reading) difficulties should not exist. While there appear to be no dramatic cases of this sort described in the literature, there are a number of references to *syntactic* variables that appear to affect word naming. Marshall and Newcombe (1966) report more word-naming errors for verbs and adjectives than for nouns, while Weigl and Bierwisch (1970) report more errors for pronouns and function words. These results suggest that we ought to structure a model of the reading process so that syntactic form can influence the outcome. Presumably, one way to do so would be to subclassify the orthographic access file by form class (an otherwise pointless move) and then to assign the separate subfiles so created different properties, so that one can deteriorate, leaving the others intact.

This would imply that in both reading and listening, there are, in effect, separate access files for nouns, verbs, pronouns, function words, etc. The problem with this interpretation is that there seems to be little advantage in so organizing the files. There is no way that one can tell in advance in which file a given test item is likely to be found. That is, there is no way to tell merely by looking at the spelling that the item *the* is likely to be a function word. Hence one would always have to consult the files in some sequence.

Evidence reported by Forster and Bednall (1976) suggests that this line of argument is correct. They required subjects to decide whether phrases such as *the house* or *to card* were acceptable phrases of English (i.e., whether *house* can be used as a noun or *card* as a verb). The critical cases concerned decision times for items such as *to flink* and *to year*. Once might expect that if there were a separate file for verbs, this file could be checked to see whether *flink* or *year* appeared, and if they did not, then a "no" decision could be made immediately for either letter sequence. Evidently this does not happen. The subjects took longer to respond "no" to the item *to year* and thus seemingly were aware that *year* could be used as a noun. Hence they must have located the entry for this word in the noun file. Not only this, if the noun form had *two* separate meanings both of which were nouns (e.g., *pupil*), then subjects took longer still (i.e., *to pupil* takes longer to reject than *to year*). This could only mean that both noun uses were considered before a decision was made.

The most obvious explanation of these results is that the search process is not directed to a particular area containing entries of only a certain syntactic type. However, this is not the only possible inference. It might be that the search *can* be governed by syntactic cues but that the subject of the experiment nevertheless consults all relevant and irrelevant files before rendering a "no" decision.

The question of syntactic cross classification of the lexicon is obviously a most important one, and considerably more evidence is required before even tentative conclusions can be reached. At the moment, the evidence from aphasic symptoms seems to establish a very strong case for some kind of syntactic organization.

What we have said so far presupposes that syntactic organization is established over the orthographic and phonological peripheral access files used for reading and listening. That the *production* file is organized syntactically is another possibility. This suggestion makes more sense, since it is reasonable to suppose that the targets of search in a sentence-production task would be defined syntactially. This interpretation is strengthened when we consider that the clearest evidence for syntactic cross classification of entries in normal speakers comes from the analysis of speeck errors; i.e., errors made during the *production* of sentences [Garrett (1976)].

But this proposal commits us to the view that in aphasics (and possibly in normals), word naming involves the production file. That is, to read a word out loud we use the orthographic access file to find the entry in the master lexicon, then extract some information from that entry, and finally use this information to specify the target for a search in the production file, which, of course, is simply using *another* access file to get back to the same entry we found by the orthographic search.

This procedure would enable us to explain how word-naming difficulties could be confined to a syntactically restricted class of items. It would also help us to explain why many patients show the same kinds of symptoms in word naming and spontaneous speech. However, it does seem a *most* bizarre and irrational computational strategy. It would be equivalent to finding a book in the library by looking up the title in the title catalog, using the location code for the title to find the book, getting the author's name from the book itself, and then looking up the location of the book by using the author catalog.

Of course, the procedure, as it is described, *would* be irrational. But if we imagine slightly different circumstances, perhaps it is not so irrational. If somehow the entry in the master lexicon became fragmented, so that the segment dealing with orthography was temporarily dissociated from the segments dealing with syntactic or semantic properties, then just such a double-access procedure might be necessary. Take the case of reading. The correct entry in the master lexicon might be located normally by using the orthographic access file. But if the entry has become fragmented, and the information we need is contained in an inaccessible or missing segment of the entry, we might well extract whatever information we could and use that to define a new target. We would then use a different access file to search for that new target, hoping that this second access route would enable us to reconstruct the full entry.

Two phenomena which occur in normals suggest that such fragmentation may occur. The first is the so-called tip-of-the-tongue (TOT) state [Brown and McNeill (1966)]. When asked to find a word having a designated meaning, normal subjects often report that they are sure that they *know* the word but cannot determine which it is. However, they *can* report some of the phonological properties that the correct word will have when it is discovered, such as the number of syllables, stress pattern, and even actual segments. When the target is *sextant,* a person in a TOT state might be able to report that *sextet* is very similar to the intended word. This implies that the correct entry in the master lexicon has been located but that the pronunciation of the word (and presumably its orthography) is still inaccessible. This situation sounds very much like that which would result from a temporary fragmentation of the entry in the master lexicon.

The second phenomenon suggesting fragmentation is the pattern of speech errors referred to as malapropisms [Fay and Cutler (1976)]. A typical malapropism would be the substitution of *magician* for *musician* in ongoing speech. The error produced is similar phonologically to the intended word, but it is not produced by simple misarticulation since the erroneous segment always is a *word*. Once again, we must assume that the correct entry in the master lexicon has been located, but the details of its pronunciation are not available. Presumably, in both the TOT state and in producing a malapropism, enough information can be gleaned from the entry to permit the person to initiate another search. This second search apparently has a reasonable probability of hitting an incorrect, but similar-sounding, word.

These phenomena suggest then that it might not be fanciful to suggest that entries in the master lexicon can become fragmented. However, it should be noted that the actual details of the circumstances which produce a TOT state or malapropisms are not at all similar to the aphasic case. The *normal* subjects are given a production task and cannot reconstruct the entire entry, using the production file. The aphasics are given a word-naming task and are unable to reconstruct the full entry, using the orthographic access file.

Furthermore, the normals use the phonological file (presumably) as a backup access system, whereas the aphasics must be using the production file.

Before leaving this issue, it should be pointed out that it is not at all implausible to assume that the production system is employed in *some* reading tasks, namely, those that involve *sentences*. For example, we have already argued that the effects of sentence context on word naming might involve the production system. In addition it is a commonplace observation that reading errors in children preserve grammaticality and sense, at least to some degree. Such mistakes make sense only if we assume the child is using a sentence-production system to generate plausible candidates for the presumed reading of the sentence.

Some Linguistic Implications of The Model

So far, we have concentrated exclusively on outlining possible implications of aphasic word-retrieval problems for a model of lexical access. The trend of the argument may seem to have been that the explanation of these problems is more likely to reveal something about the *mechanisms* of information retrieval than about the structure of the information being retrieved.

Should this be taken to indicate that the study of lexical access has little relevance for linguistics proper? Not necessarily; already a number of studies suggest that it will one day be possible to test linguistic hypotheses about the nature of the information stored in the mental lexicon quite directly. In order to do so, we shall need to be reasonably certain that we understand the characteristics of the information-retrieval system as well.

By way of illustration, we shall consider some lexical access experiments designed to reveal some aspects of the organization of lexical entries and the kind of information they contain. In all these cases, the moral of the illustration is the same: before we can draw inferences about the properties of lexical entries, we need to settle some details of the access process itself.

The first type of experiment concerns the issue of how

related forms are stored; for example, are there separate entries for *cat* and *cats*? From a linguistic point of view, one might expect that plural forms would be derived by rule from the singular and would not be listed separately. Those cases which constitute exceptions to the main rule, e.g., *man-men*, could be marked as such. That is, the entry for *man* would include the information that this word has an irregular plural form, but *men* is not listed separately. From an information-processing point of view, it might be advantageous to list *both* forms, especially if the inflected version is more frequently used than the uninflected form (e.g., *guests* has a higher frequency of usage than *guest*). This assumes, of course, that the storage capacity available to the lexicon is so vast that there is little point in trying to minimize the number of entries.

One might think that this issue could be settled again by testing for the frequency effects we have observed again and again in lexical-access experiments. Suppose, for example, that there is only one entry for *cat* and *cats*. If the frequency effect is influenced by the number of times entries are used, the effective frequency of occurrence of a form would be influenced by the frequency of forms related to it. For example, the "real" frequency of *cat* would be the sum of the frequencies for *cat* and *cats*. This would predict that if we held constant surface frequency (the frequency of occurrence of the particular word) but varied *summed* frequencies, we should observe a frequency effect.

In an unpublished thesis, O'Connor (1975) has shown this to be the case, but only if the item tested is the inflected form. That is, an item such as *towns* is accessed faster than *hills*, even though the two words have the same surface frequency of occurrence; presumably this is because the uninflected form *town* occurs far more often than *hill*. However, the same conclusion did not apply to latencies for uninflected items. For example, *acre* was not accessed faster than *dusk,* despite the fact that *acres* occurred far more often than *dusks*. One might be tempted to argue that surface frequency influences access in this case. However, when summed frequency is constant, and surface frequency varies, reliable frequency effects are not obtained.

The suggestion that, somehow, the frequency of an un-inflected form influences the effective frequency of its related inflected forms, but not vice versa, is also tempting. That is, *towns* benefits from the frequent occurrence of *town,* but *acre* derives no benefit from *acres*. While this principle might cover the facts, it really does not tell us very much about the number of entries for related forms.

Similar results were obtained by Bradley (1976), who focussed on derived, rather than inflected forms. She asked whether access time for deverbal nominals such as *decision* are influenced by the frequency of occurrence of related forms such as *decide* and *decisive*. In her first experiment, she found that words which have similar surface frequencies but belong to semantic clusters of very different frequencies (i.e., summed frequency varies) were nevertheless accessed in the same time. That is, *hesitation* is accessed no faster than *humiliation*, even though *hesitate* and its related forms occur more often than *humiliate* and its related forms. This result implies that each word has its own entry. However, Bradley's second experiment appears to rule out this alternative, since she found that words of differing surface frequency were accessed in the same time, provided they belonged to semantic clusters of similar frequency (e.g., *entertainment* and *advertisements,* with the former having the higher surface frequency).

Obviously, we need to know a great deal more before we can interpret such results. In particular, we need to be sure that we are interpreting the frequency effects themselves correctly. We also need to know more about methods of access. We have already seen evidence in the work of Meyer and Schvaneveldt (1976) that a network of semantic cross references exists. Since both inflected and derived words are usually semantically related to their base forms, one might expect the network to be operative in this situation. For example, there may be a direct link from the entry for *dog* to the entry for *dogs,* so that when one is searching for *dogs,* the access time will be governed by the frequency of *dog,* provided this item is listed first. This would obviously complicate the separate-entry model con-siderably.

A second example of linguistically relevant research concerns the storage and retrieval of prefixed words. Taft and Forster (1975) have shown that attempting morphological analysis of the test item is a necessary first step in lexical access. Briefly, the evidence is as follows:

(i) Nonwords which are the stems of prefixed words (e.g., *juvenate*) take longer to reject as words than nonwords which are not stems of prefixed words (e.g., *pertoire*). This cannot be explained without assuming that the prefix of the lexical entry for *rejuvenate* is somehow ignored or overlooked during search; whereas the corresponding letters of *repertoire* (which do not form a prefix) are not so treated. Thus the probability of falsely identifying an item as a word is more likely when the test entry is *juvenate* than when it is *pertoire*.

(ii) Nonwords which contained a real stem but also contained an inappropriate prefix (e.g., *dejuvenate*) took longer to classify than appropriate control nonwords (e.g., *depertoire*). Once again, we need to explain why the initial letters are overlooked in one case but not in another.

(iii) Real words which are spelled the same as the stems of other prefixed words (e.g., *vent*) take longer to classify than control words, presumably because there is some confusion between the entries. That is, in searching for the entry for *vent*, sometimes a false match is made with the entry for *prevent*. Most interestingly, this effect occurs only if the prefixed word occurs more often than the test word (as *prevent* does). When the frequency of occurrence is reversed (e.g., *card* occurs more often than *discard*), no such confusion appears.

These experiments strongly imply that morphological structure is psychologically real, in the sense that morphology is constantly involved in actual language use, rather than merely a component of speakers' language knowledge. The results also serve to demonstrate convincingly that at least some aspects of linguistic structure can be studied relatively easily in an experimental setting.

Many other issues could be raised at this point, such as the method by which a person decides on the correct pronunciation of a word or the storage of homographs and homophones. All these may bear directly on theories characterizing the contents of the lexicon, but at present explanations of such phenomena are too poorly developed to be convincing. The few experiments we have discussed must serve to illustrate the point.

Conclusion

We have discussed an area of experimental cognitive psychology in order to illustrate some of the research topics that a biologically oriented group might profitably pursue. Although linguistic theory is not directly concerned with lexical access and need say nothing directly about the retrieval of information about words from memory, linguistic theory and theories of lexical access ultimately address common questions, the most obvious being the structure and contents of lexical entries and the structure of the lexicon itself.

Research in lexical access illustrates clearly the differences between structure and function: at every point, we have been compelled to make assumptions both about how information is structured and about how access mechanisms operate. Obviously these are interrelated issues: the structure of information determines, to some extent, the possible access functions to it, and vice versa.

Although a thorough review of the failures of lexical access which aphasics experience is impossible here, we hope we have demonstrated that many aspects of the behavior of aphasic patients can be viewed as resulting from deficits in components of the structural or functional theories of lexical access in normal subjects. Conversely, we hope that in discussing findings from the clinical situation, we have demonstrated at least potential benefit to theories of normal lexical access from the modifications to those theories which parsimonious explanations of abnormal language capacity require.

[A preliminary version of this chapter appeared in Wales and Walker (1976).]

4

A Case Study: Face Recognition

SUSAN CAREY

We can recognize an immense number of faces, and our capacity to do so is impressively insensitive to expression, the passage of time, and the presence or absence of such identifying features as scars, outsize features, or apparel. The study of face recognition is in its infancy; however, the framework developed in this report for studying the biology of language can be generalized readily to reach some general conclusions about the phenomenon, its neural substrate, and its course of development.

Studies of the ability of normal subjects and brain-injured patients to recognize faces reveal that face recognition is supported by neural mechanisms located in the right posterior hemisphere. Furthermore, recognizing faces, unlike recognizing houses, stick figures, or other complex visual stimuli, is particularly sensitive to spatial inversion, but insensitive to such identifying visual features as apparel or distinguishing paraphernalia such as eyeglasses. Rather than being identified by particular features, it appears that faces are encoded with reference to some canonical arrangement of features. This reference to a canonical face allows us to recognize a particular face despite the addition or deletion of garments or jewelry, changes of expression, or gross alteration by time. The ability to recognize faces is not fully developed before age 10, indicating that experience is required to form a canonical face in reference to which individual faces are encoded. To some extent, younger children recognize faces by referring to relatively isolated features, much as adults recognize other complex visual stimuli.

The nature and relation of the canonical representation and the idiosyncratic features by which young children identify faces are only poorly understood and must be considerably refined. Furthermore, the relation of faces to other classes of stimuli must be examined in greater detail. The psychological processes by which faces are encoded with respect to a canonical representation remain to be determined, and the neural mechanisms involved in these processes are yet to be isolated. The relation of these neural mechanisms and their maturation to the development of face recognition is a matter for further study, particularly in comparison to the development of other capacities supported by mechanisms located in the right hemisphere.

Such topics for future research are but a few of those which arise from applying interdisciplinary methods for studying cognitive capacities, and they illustrate the fruitfulness of extending methods for studying the biology of language to the study of other cognitive domains.

In previous chapters of this report, we have presented a general framework for interdisciplinary research on the biology of language. This chapter illustrates how this framework can be used to generate research questions and answers to them in the study of a nonlinguistic cognitive capacity, face recognition. We wish to emphasize in discussing face recognition that the interdisciplinary framework we have developed here is appropriate for studying any cognitive capacity, and that the study of other capacities such as face recognition provides informative contrasts to the study of language.

In the introduction we stated that at least three enterprises are involved in studying the biological basis of a cognitive capacity. First, a theory of the knowledge represented is required to characterize the domain of the capacity. Second, real-time models of how that knowledge is applied in various situations are required in order to characterize the psychological processes involved in its acquisition and use. And third, neurological models are required to relate the biological mechanisms of the organism to the behavior which reveals the cognitive capacity. In the study of language, the first enterprise is further along than the others; in the study of face recognition, all three enterprises are in their infancy.

The relation between the brain and psychological descriptions of a cognitive capacity can take many forms. One can ask which general parts of the nervous system process the information relevant to that capacity. Speaking generally, the occipital cortex is implicated in visual processing, just as the spinal cord and peripheral sensory-motor pathways mediate certain reflexes. In a finer-grained analysis, one can relate the cognitive capacity to particular neural structures within grossly identified anatomical areas. Hubel and Wiesel (1962) have demonstrated a hierarchy of lateral geniculate cells and simple and complex cortical cells which corresponds to a hierarchical analysis of visual patterns composed of low-level visual features. In an even more detailed analysis, networks of neural connections and their mutual excitatory and inhibitory influences can be used to model the details of psychological processes. Spencer et al. (1966) models of the habituation and classical conditioning of spinal reflexes provide an example for simple learning phenomena. In the present state of work on face recognition, the relation of brain and behavior can proceed only to gross localization of function.

The development of a cognitive capacity adds an important new dimension to the study of its biological bases, namely, the role played by genetically determined maturational factors in that development. Particularly relevant to untangling nature and nurture is the study of various forms of plasticity the system exhibits. For example, is experience relevant to the formation of certain neural connections only during some critical period? If the anatomical underpinning of some capacity is damaged, can some other part of the brain compensate? If so, are there critical periods after which this compensation will not take place?

The field of developmental neurobiology is flourishing, and models of neuronal plasticity and the limits thereof are available for many neuroanatomical systems in animals. The specificity of detail in these models varies widely. The most unspecified models are those which correlate the age of functional maturation and the final development of neuroanatomical areas. Such correlations are found by covarying age and the locations of lesions in experimental animals. Goldman's studies of the development of orbital and dorsolateral frontal cortex in monkeys are a particularly elegant example of this method of inquiry [Goldman (1972, 1974)]. In adult monkeys, lesions in dorsolateral cortex produce a marked and specific deficit on delayed alternation tasks. Lesions in orbital cortex result in a syndrome of general problems with simple learning tasks, with delayed alternation not being particularly vulnerable. Goldman found that early lesions (at 6 months) in orbital cortex immediately produced the symptoms of adult damage but that such early lesions (at 6 months) in dorsolateral cortex had no effect on the early development of delayed alternation. However, the same monkeys, tested at age 2 years, began to show a curious pattern of results. Those with orbital lesions began to *improve* on orbital tasks, whereas those with dorsolateral lesions began to do worse (compared to controls) on delayed alternation. Goldman suggests that the dorsolateral cortex does not become "functionally mature" until age 2. Until age 2 the monkey with a dorsolateral lesion appears to have no deficit on delayed alternation because it is only after that age that dorsolateral frontal cortex begins to play a role in normal monkeys' performance on that task. Orbital cortex, in contrast, is "functionally mature" at least by 6 months. An interesting asymmetry in plasticity is associated with early and late functional maturity. Apparently, early-maturing orbital cortex cannot assume dorsolateral cortex's role in delayed alternation, as an early lesion in dorsolateral cortex inevitably leads to a deficit (although the deficit does not appear until age 2). In contrast, dorsolateral frontal cortex can, at the age it becomes functionally mature, begin to mediate some of the functions normally requiring an intact orbital cortex.

The concept of plasticity is used in a slightly different sense in models which relate the tuning of feature detectors to experience and the age at which that experience is incurred. In at least some cases, critical periods for the effect of input have been demonstrated through changes in the characteristics or proportions of single-cell receptor fields resulting from unusual or missing input during that time [e.g., Hubel and Wiesel (1970)].

At least two classes of neural mechanisms underlying plasticity have been proposed. In one, abnormal experience or lesions result in the formation of abnormal connections among normally unconnected parts of the brain [e.g., Schneider (1973)]. In the other, structures which are normally inhibited by competing input are released from inhibition if the sources of that competing input are removed [e.g., Wall (1975)]. In the latter case, no new connections are formed.

As more is known about the development of a cognitive capacity and of the neural basis of that capacity, it becomes possible to try to apply whichever models are relevant from the field of developmental neurobiology as possible models of the biological basis of that development. This, in turn, leads to finer-grained hypotheses about development and about the neural basis of the capacity. For example, Held and his associates are exploring the development of the oblique effect (visual acuity is worse for oblique lines than for horizontal and vertical lines) in terms of the "tuning of feature detectors" model [e.g., Leehey, Moscovitz, Brill, and Held (1975)]. Because the study of face recognition and its neural basis is in its infancy, models of its neurological development are at the level of maturation of whole cortical areas, and questions about their plasticity, as presented in Goldman's model, arise.

In the section that follows, we will review what is known about the phenomenon of face recognition, its developmental course, and its neural substrates. Our main goal is to show that it is possible to outline an integrated theory of the biological basis of face recognition. The components of the theory attain what plausibility they have entirely through the inter-disciplinary approach advocated here. Suggestions from one enterprise are supported in another. Although the theory lacks detail in all three crucial enterprises—description of competence, discovery of processing models, and specification of neural substrates—the outline presented gives clear and promising pointers of how to proceed.

The Problem

Our capacity to recognize faces has two aspects—first, a productive ability to encode new faces, to form some representation in memory of a previously unfamiliar face; second, the ability to recognize that face subsequently. Both are prodigious. Bahrick, Bahrick, and Wittlinger (1975) asked subjects to pick the familiar face from among five taken from high school yearbooks. Only one face of the five came from the subject's own yearbook; the rest were from other yearbooks of the same period. Recognition rates not only were over 90 percent, they were independent of class size (from 90 to 800) and of time elapsed between graduation and test (from 3 months to 35 years). In a 3- or 4-year period, and without conscious effort, high school students can make 800 faces familiar as easily as they can make 90 faces familiar. Even more astoundingly, they can recognize those faces years later as well as they can a few months later, indicating that learning new faces does not interfere with the representations of those already in memory. The limits of this enormous but everyday capacity, if any, have not been found.

Our impressive capacity to encode new faces has been confirmed, on a modest scale, in experimental studies. If subjects are allowed to inspect photographs of unfamiliar people for 3 to 5 seconds each and later must indicate which of two photographs were in the series, they perform at about a 90 percent level for set sizes ranging from 8 to 144 [Yin (1969), Hochberg and Galper (1967), Carey and Diamond (unpublished data)].

Although these studies tell us that the representations of faces stored in memory are highly effective for recognizing the same faces later, they tell us nothing about the nature of the representation itself. In terms of what kinds of features is a face stored? We know that the representations of familiar faces must be sufficiently abstract to support recognition in spite of changes in clothing, facial expression, hairstyles, glasses, mustaches, and even of the changes produced by many years of aging or by radical weight gain or loss. On the other hand, some stimulus transformations interfere markedly with the process of

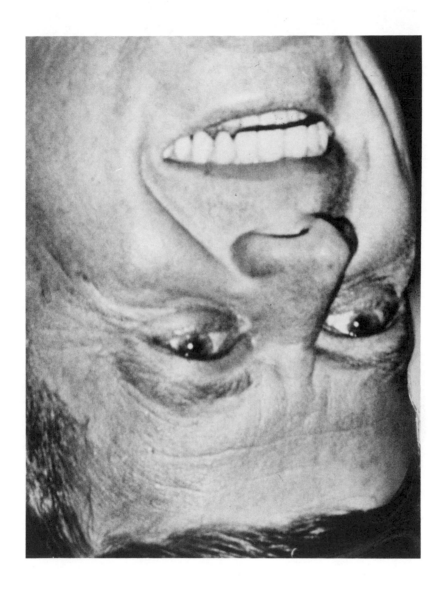

Figure 1 Recognizing inverted faces (see page 182)
(Courtesy The Boston Herald American)

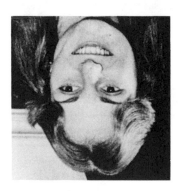

*Try to identify the upside down pictures of famous people shown here
and on page 181. Figure 1: John F. Kennedy. Figure 2: Mary Tyler
Moore, Billy Graham, Betty Ford, Patty Hearst and Jimmy Conners.
(Courtesy The Boston Herald American)*

matching current input of a face with the stored representation of that face. Inverted photographs of familiar people are recognized only half as efficiently as upright photographs [Rock (1974), Goldstein (1975)]. See Figures 1 and 2. Similarly, photographic negative/positive reversal makes familiar faces extremely difficult to recognize. The latter results place some limits on how abstract the mental representation of a familiar face can be: it must preserve at least some of the pictorial properties of orientation and normal lighting. Furthermore, the results suggest that the processes of matching input with stored representations cannot easily compensate for a mismatch involving such pictorial properties.

These same transformations, photographic negative/positive reversal and spatial inversion, interfere with the encoding of an unfamiliar face as well as with the recognition of a familiar face. That is, if a series of photographic negatives of unfamiliar faces is presented and subsequently tested for recognition (still as negatives), performance is markedly lower (30 percent) than if the photographs are all positives [Galper (1970)]. A similar decrement in performance is found with both initial presentation and subsequent recognition involving upside-down faces [Hochberg and Galper (1967), Yin (1969), Yarmey (1971)]. These studies involve no mismatch between the mental representation formed during inspection and that formed from the input during recognition. Thus such transformations must interfere with encoding those aspects of the mental representation by which faces are differentiated.

Both photographic negativity and spatial inversion interfere with the interpretation of shadow cues to depth, and indeed the effect of photographic negativity is not found when stimuli are line drawings of faces, suggesting that depth cues (not present in line drawings) play a role in making negative photographs difficult. In contrast, the effect of spatial inversion is almost the same when the stimuli are line drawings and full photographs [Yin (1969), Bradshaw and Wallace (1971)], suggesting that the inversion effect is not primarily dependent on depth cues.

The effect of spatial orientation on the encoding of faces is greater than its effect on any other class of stimuli yet examined. For houses, bridges, airplanes, costumes, and stick figures of men in motion, which also are customarily seen in only one orientation, the average advantage of upright presentation is only 10 to 15 percent [Yin (1969)]. The effects of inverting a face (30 percent) are significantly greater. Yin's results have been extended to other buildings and to dogs [Yarmey (1971), Scapinello and Yarmey (1970)] as well as to landscapes [Fish (1976)]. Although in all cases the stimuli are recognized worse when presented upside down, the decrement produced by inversion is significantly smaller than that for faces.

Finally, subjects are more proficient in tasks involving faces from their own racial group than those from different racial groups. Shepherd, Deregowski, and Ellis (1974) showed that black Rhodesians encode unfamiliar blacks better than unfamiliar whites. When the same stimuli were presented to white Britishers, these subjects did correspondingly better with the unfamiliar whites.

In summary, normal adults reveal an impressive productive capacity for making new faces familiar, a capacity which derives in part from their experience with faces (recognition is more efficient for faces from familiar racial groups). Furthermore, stimuli which are upside-down or in photographic negative do not fully engage this capacity. The ability to encode new faces is more vulnerable to transformations of orientation than is the ability to encode other classes of stimuli. Theories of the competence and psychological processes underlying face recognition will be constrained (weakly) by these characteristics of the capacity. As we shall see, attempts to discover the anatomical basis and developmental course of the capacity for face recognition add further constraints.

The Biological Basis:
Crude Localization

Unfamiliar faces   Patients with damage to the right cerebral hemisphere are impaired on tasks which include matching photographs showing the same face among several with different clothing, different angles of view, or different lighting [e.g., Benton and Van Allen (1968)], as well as those requiring inspection of unfamiliar faces and subsequent recognition of them [e.g., Yin (1970)]. Both types of tasks involve the encoding of unfamiliar faces. Thus that the right cerebral hemisphere appears to play a critical role in face recognition can be inferred from studies of patients with focal brain injury (Chapters 2 and 3 in this report discuss the logic and methodology of such inference).

Since faces are complex visual patterns and the right hemisphere has been implicated in the encoding of visual-spatial input other than faces, its involvement in face processing might simply reflect the general involvement of the right hemisphere in processing any complex visual stimulus. However, Yin (1970) showed that the encoding of upright and inverted faces, which must be equally complex as visual stimuli, are functionally dissociable. (That is, a lesion which affects one does not affect the other.) Patients with loss of tissue in the right posterior sector of the brain do not differ from normals in recognizing inverted faces, but they are deficient in recognizing upright faces. Clearly, the patients lost a capacity specific to the encoding of upright faces.

If the right and left hemispheres are differentially involved in processing faces, tachistoscopic presentation of face stimuli to the two lateral hemifields should reveal a left visual field (i.e., right hemisphere) advantage. In fact, a robust left visual field advantage has been demonstrated both in discriminative reaction-time tasks [Rizzolatti, Umilta and Berlucchi (1971), Geffen, Bradshaw, and Wallace (1971)] and in measures of accuracy [Hillard (1973), Klein, Moscovitch, and Vigna (1976), Ellis and Shepherd (1975)]. Left visual field advantages also have appeared in studies involving not faces but random Attneave patterns [Fontenot (1973)] or the location of elements in a matrix [e.g., Robertshaw and Sheldon (1976), Gross (1972), Kimura (1969)]. Thus the left visual field advantage for faces may reflect the involvement of the right hemisphere in processing visual patterns in general, rather than the presence in the right hemisphere of a processor specific to faces.

Comparing the sizes of the left visual field advantages for upright and inverted faces should decide the issue. If the right hemisphere is involved in processing both upright and inverted faces only as visual patterns, then the same left visual field advantage should be found for both. But if the right hemisphere is involved in processing not only visual patterns in general, but upright faces in particular, there should be a greater left visual field advantage for upright faces. Just that interaction is found. [See Figure 3; Leehey, Carey, Diamond, and Cahn (in press).] The difference between the results for left and right visual fields is much greater for upright faces than for inverted faces. This study supports the existence in the right hemisphere of a processor that is differentially involved in the encoding and recognition of upright unfamiliar faces.

We noted above that the encoding of houses, bridges, landscapes, etc., is less affected by orientation than the encoding of faces. Yin (1970) showed that the dissociability of upright and inverted faces with respect to the right hemisphere does not extend to houses. Patients with lesions of the right posterior cortex perform as normals do on both upright and inverted houses. These results suggest that faces are a special class of stimuli for which there is a processor in the right hemisphere. This processor is involved in the encoding of unfamiliar members, and requires normally oriented input. Of course, there may be other classes of stimuli with such associated processors; not many alternative classes have yet been investigated.

The attempts to localize the neural mechanisms of face recognition in the brain have yielded further constraints on correct performance and competence models for face recognition. From results on normals alone, we knew only that the encoding of faces was particularly vulnerable to inversion. Now we know that the advantage upright faces enjoy normally requires an intact right posterior hemisphere. The explanation of the advantage thus will involve an account of how the representation of upright faces differs (in information-processing terms) from that of inverted faces, as well as from that of both upright and inverted houses. Furthermore, this account must be consistent with what is known about the specialization of the right posterior cortex.

Characterizing the capacity: Speculation I. How the repre-

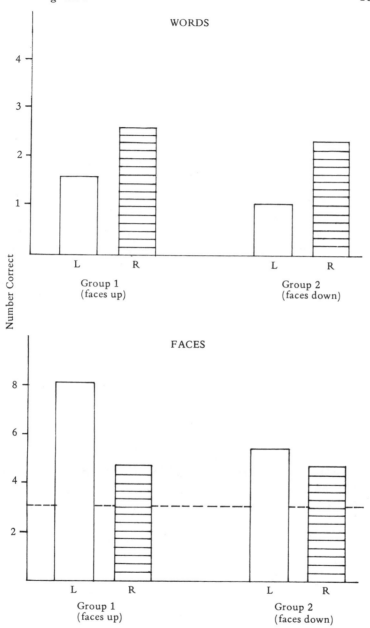

Figure 3. Performance levels in left visual field (L) and right visual field (R)
on words and faces

sentation of upright faces differs from inverted faces, and from both upright and inverted faces.

The encoded representation of an individual face probably includes such idiosyncratic features as scars, hairline, odd-sized features, and distinctive eyeglasses, but it appears unlikely that a list of such distinguishing features comprises our entire internal representation of a face. Some such features do not survive the transformations by time or fashion which recognition so readily survives: high school friends may look different, but they still are recognizable. The rest of these features probably do not sufficiently individuate the hundreds (thousands?) of faces each of us can recognize: how many people have big noses or dark eyes or glasses? Furthermore, individual faces present a more unique distinguishing feature — the spatial relations among their parts. For instance, "the ratio of the distance the hairline is above the chin to the distance the bridge of the nose is above the center of the upper lip" could be a distinctive feature which might serve to individuate faces. Represented by a number of such spatial relations, each face forms a Gestalt as unique as a snowflake. The speculation to be entertained here is that while both upright and inverted faces are encoded in terms of relatively isolated, piecemeal features, only upright faces can be encoded in terms of their configuration of features.

Why should the two representations be affected differently by inversion? Let us presume that in both kinds of encoding some reference is made to a canonical face, itself represented in normal orientation. To notice that a particular face has especially bushy eyebrows, the appropriate visual contours must be located and identified as eyebrows, and their density noted as greater than average. To the extent that canonical spatial location, e.g., "above the eyes," is used in the process of identifying the eyebrows, stimulus inversion would be detrimental even to the encoding of such piecemeal information. Thus we would expect some decrement in performance on face-recognition tasks and indeed on any such visual recognition task. But in an encoding based on the ratio of "the distance the hairline is above the chin" to the "distance the bridge of the nose is above the center of the upper lip," the sheer number of points to be located (and the precision with which the location must be specified) is undoubtedly greater than in the encoding of isolated features such as "bushy eyebrows." Furthermore, in specifying such configurational features some reference must be made to the range of ratios of distances given by the canonical face for such a ratio to serve to individuate a face. Therefore, as the canonical face is undoubtedly represented upright, the complex comparison of a particular face to the canonical ranges of potentially distinctive ratios is made very difficult by stimulus inversion. Thus we would expect a greater decrement to be produced by inverting faces than by inverting, say, houses.

An inverted face presents as much configurational information, of course, as an upright face. The difference must arise from our ability to exploit that information. By hypothesis, the processor for normally oriented faces located in the right hemisphere is specialized for the encoding of configurational distinctive features from upright faces. This reliance on subtle differences in spatial configurations is consistent with what is thought to be one of the main specializations of the right hemisphere [e.g., Kimura (1963)].

Apparently, we do not employ such a canonical representation of configurational features to encode normally oriented houses, since patients with right posterior lesions are not impaired in recognizing them. In fact, Yin's normal adults report remembering the houses in terms of such piecemeal, isolated, distinguishing features as a particularly distinctive porch, Greek columns, or a black chimney the length of the side. Asked how they remembered faces, they reported "looking at the whole face."

Familiar faces So far we have discussed encoding and recognizing previously unfamiliar faces. Another aspect of the capacity for face recognition—the ability to recognize as familiar people for whom a representation exists in memory— appears to have a slightly different anatomical base. The patients with unilateral right hemisphere lesions, who are impaired at encoding new faces, do not have difficulty recognizing highly familiar people. Apparently the representation of a familiar face remains intact after such lesions, as do whatever processes match current input against that representation. In contrast, there is a syndrome, prosapagnosia, marked by severe difficulty in recognizing highly familiar faces such as those of colleagues and immediate family. This rare syndrome typically is associated with bilateral lesions in left and right posterior cortex [see Meadows (1974) for a review of postmortem anatomical findings on prosapagnosia]. Patients with prosapagnosia often report that they attempt to recognize their friends and family members from their clothes or from such idiosyncratic features as a bow in the hair, a mustache, or a bald head. Except in the restricted contexts where particular people can be expected to appear, such devices are often ineffective (i.e., someone else can wear a hat like one's mother's or can be bald like one's father).

Paradoxically, such patients are not impaired on several of the paradigms used to diagnose the unilateral lesions which interfere with the encoding of a new face [Benton and Van Allen (1973)]. Some investigators have gone so far as to claim that prosapagnosics are unimpaired at encoding and recognizing unfamiliar faces. This is, of course, logically impossible, for if a patient were truly unimpaired at encoding unfamiliar faces, the encoding process would make that face familiar; but being a prosapagnosiac, the patient then would be unable to recognize the now familiar face. In fact, prosapagnosiac patients do not recognize people encountered after their injury any better than those encountered before. Nonetheless, their ability to cope with the tests of face recognition failed by patients with unilateral right posterior lesions is puzzling and unexplained.

The Development of Face Recognition

Since experience with a wide range of exemplars from the relevant populations of faces is required for forming a canonical representation of the normal (uninformative) range of con-figurational features, a protracted course of development of the processor for encoding unfamiliar faces is expected. Indeed, a wide range of converging evidence suggests that the processor remains not fully developed until the end of the first decade of life.

Six- and eight-year-old children recognize inverted faces almost as well as upright faces in tests using the Yin paradigm. Further, inversion does not affect faces more than houses. However, the normal adult advantage in recognizing upright faces has emerged by the time the subjects are 9 or 10 years old [Cary, Diamond, and Woods (in press)]. The significant effect of orientation on the encoding of faces which is present by age 10 results entirely from improvement in the encoding of upright faces. During the entire age range sampled (ages 6, 8, 10, 12, 14, and 16) the performance on inverted faces does not change and matches that of both normal adults and patients with right posterior cortical lesions (around 65 percent).

There is direct evidence that children under 10 represent unfamiliar faces in terms of relatively isolated features. When young children are asked to judge which two of four snapshots of a person are most alike, they base their choice on the paraphernalia common to the snapshots. See Figure 4.

Figure 4

*Different expressions
and paraphernalia*

Older children base similarity on the facial expression in the snapshots—a transition in the basis of resemblance which occurs at about age 10 [Levy-Schoen (1964)].

Such judgments of resemblance do not bear directly on the question of how individual faces are identified. Therefore, we presented three snapshots of two different people in different garb and with different expressions, asking, "Which are the same person?" Because expression and paraphernalia are confounded cues in some of our items (see Figure 5), relying exclusively on either will lead to the corresponding pattern of errors. These patterns provide direct evidence

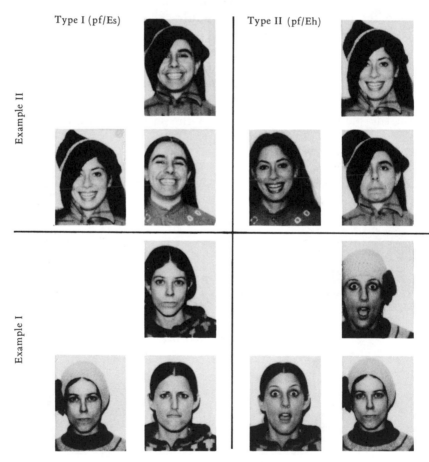

Figure 5 Conflicting expressions and parphernalia.

whether the child bases judgments of identity on isolated features, because we manipulated identity of expression and paraphernalia independently from the identity of the faces pictured. When photographs of two different persons wearing the same paraphernalia (Types I and II, see figure) were shown to 6- and 8-year-old children, they tended to judge that the photographs showed the same person. By age 10 this tendency was less frequent, and by age 12 it had disappeared. At no age was expression used as a basis for identity [Diamond and Carey (in preparation)].

From such evidence we conclude that 10-year-olds base their

Type III (ps/Ef)

Type IV (ph/Ef)

judgments on some properties of the faces which are veridical for identification. These properties could, of course, be isolated features such as eyebrow shape or a mole which were not confounded in our materials. That is, the older children might have a better theory of which features serve recognition than do the younger children. But since such features are apparent on inverted faces, inversion should not affect performance on faces at age 10, as it did. The effects observed in the two experiments converge on about 10 years as the age at which a change in the way of representing faces occurs.

Our analysis of the patterns of errors children produce argues that the shift by age 10 is from piecemeal to configurational encoding. As argued in the previous section, the loss of configurational encoding capacity is associated with right posterior lesions. This similarity in information-processing terms does not necessarily require common neural mechanisms. It is possible that the children's performance is mediated by the development of neural structures other than those that mediate the adults' ability. The first step in understanding the relationship between the developmental shift and the shift as a consequence of right posterior brain damage is to discover whether the involvement of the right hemisphere in the encoding of unfamiliar faces fails to occur before age 10. The

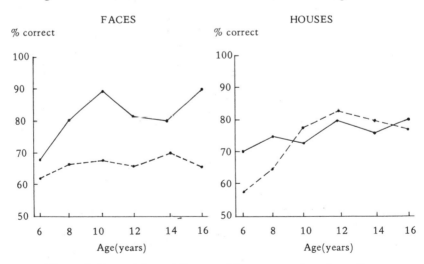

Figure 6   Reconition of faces and houses as a function of age

answer to this question seems to be "yes." In two different experiments Leehey (1976) found that the left visual field advantage for tachistoscopic encoding of unfamiliar faces is not present until age 9. The difference between the two half-fields, which emerges at age 9, is due to recognition of faces presented to the left visual field, that is, to an improvement in performance on faces processed by the right hemisphere. There is no change between ages 8 and 12 in the level of performance on faces presented to the right visual field (left hemisphere). In other words, the change in encoding efficiency for unfamiliar faces which occurs by around age 10 is mirrored by the emergence, at that age, of an advantage in processing unfamiliar faces by the right hemisphere.

We have summarized several respects in which the adult capacity for encoding unfamiliar faces is developed by age 9 or 10. Is there no further change after that age? Surprisingly, in several of the paradigms discussed so far, a reliable *reversal* from the adult pattern of results is obtained at ages 12 and 14. This was first noticed in the Yin paradigm (see Figure 6) in which the level of recognition for upright faces is diminished at ages 12 and 14, the difference between upright and inverted faces not even reaching significance at age 14. This pattern was confirmed (Figure 7) recently in a large study involving 20

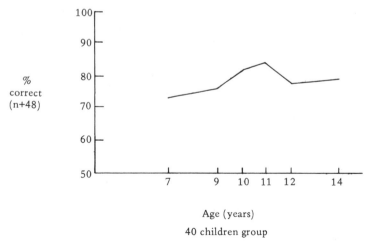

Age (years)

40 children group

Figure 7   Ability to recognize faces as a function of age

children each at ages 7, 9, 10, 11, 12, and 14; and 48 faces to encode and subsequently recognize. And finally, the left visual field advantage for the tachistoscopic encoding of unfamiliar faces, present at age 10, is lost at ages 12 and 14 for girls, and at age 14 for boys [Leehey (1976)]. Clearly, the development of the capacity to encode unfamiliar faces is not complete by age 10.

So far we have discussed the development of the capacity for encoding previously unfamiliar faces and concluded that the ability to form a configurational representation of a new face from just a few seconds' exposure to a still photograph is not present until age 10. We have yet to discuss two other aspects of the capacity for face recognition—the nature of the representation of highly familiar faces and the processes involved in recognizing as familiar those people for whom a representation exists in memory. In these domains, a quite different developmental picture emerges: children much younger than 10 perform like adults.

If the stimuli are photographs of the children's classmates, subjects as young as 5 years old easily ignore confounding paraphernalia and make almost no errors [Diamond and Carey (in press)]. And children at least as young as 8 show the normal left visual field (right hemisphere) advantage if the stimuli are photographs of familiar faces [Leehey (1976)]. Finally, the developmental course for the recognition of inverted photographs of familiar faces is totally different from the developmental course of the ability to encode inverted faces [compare Figure 6 with Figure 8; Goldstein (1975)]. Four-year-old children behave as adults do in being unable to recognize inverted photographs of people they can easily recognize when upright. This sensitivity to inversion of familiar faces decreases until age 14 and then increases to the adult level by college age. It is likely that the similarity between 4-year-olds and adults is mediated by different processes; 4-year-olds may have difficulty performing mental inversions of parts of faces or of salient distinctive features, while adults may have ceased to represent such salient isolated features of familiar faces altogether.

Discussion

In this section we shall characterize R(0), R(1), R(2), and R(3) (See Introduction) with respect to the biology of face recognition. The motivations for each characterization have been given in preceding sections of this chapter. As stated in our introduction, each is only crudely constrained by the present state of knowledge. But we contend that placing the work in this framework will help guide future research toward productive goals.

R(O): The competence Underlying a normal adult's competence for encoding unfamiliar faces is a canonical representation of the potential faces he/she might encounter. Included in this representation are the expected ranges of values for both isolated features and configuration features (ratios among parts). Particular features of an individual's face are distinctive when compared with these expected ranges of values, and thus form the basis of the stored representation of that individual's face.

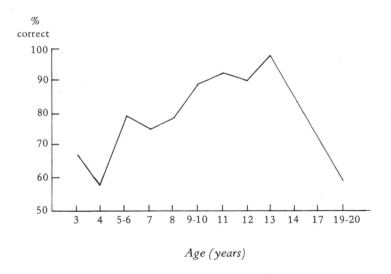

Figure 8 Ability to recognize and name faces of classmates as a function of age. [After Goldstein (1975).]

Future research: A top priority for future research is to characterize the nature of both configurational and piecemeal features precisely. No significant progress to this end has yet been made, although some rough attempts have been made by research in artificial intelligence [e.g., Duda and Hart (1973)]. A second top priority for future research is to discover whether there are canonical representations of the configurational features for other classes of stimuli. If not, why not? Is the competence to form such representations limited genetically to faces, or are the members of no other class of stimuli important enough and similar enough to require that they be encoded on the basis of subtle configurational features?

R(1): Processing mechanisms   We must discover the processes of identifying the distinguishing features of an unfamiliar face. Presumably some comparison with the canonical face is involved. What is the time course of these processes? Are isolated features picked out before configurations when time is a premium? Obviously, no real progress on these questions can be made until further progress has been made on $R(0)$.

R(2): The neurological basis   Again, until further progress is made on $R(0)$, it will be difficult to go beyond the rather gross localization of face recognition in the right hemisphere. Further work on the dissociation of the neural mechanisms underlying processes involved in encoding unfamiliar faces and those involved in recognizing familiar ones is needed.

R(3): The developmental course, maturation and plasticity   We know that the development of the capacity to encode a new face in configurational terms from relatively impoverished input is accomplished by around age 10. We know also that this development is accompanied by the emergence, at the same age, of right hemisphere specialization for this capacity. This parallel, by itself, does not implicate a maturational component to the develop-canonical representation of configurational features of faces depends merely on much experience with a wide range of faces. Suppose further that it is not until age 10 or so that the child has had enough of that experience. Suppose also that the right hemisphere is specialized for configurational representations of faces much earlier than age 10, but that it is only until the canonical schema for encoding new faces in such terms is developed that unfamiliar faces engage the right hemisphere processes. If all these assumptions were plausible, and there is no reason to rule them out, then there might be no maturational component to the development of the adult schema for representation of unfamiliar faces by age 10. On the other hand, it is also possible that the maturational state of the right posterior hemisphere places an upper limit on the power of the developing schema for unfamiliar faces, and that the emergence of the adult pattern by age 10 reflects the completion of some genetically determined maturational process. Consistent with this hypothesis is the fact that the posterior cortex, the parietal and temporal lobes, are the latest-maturing parts of the brain with respect to myelinization, which is completed around age 10. Also, it is hard to see why, if development depended entirely on experiential factors, there should be a dip in performance at ages 12 and 14, apparently associated with the onset of puberty.

A major research effort should be to develop techniques to decide the issue of whether the emergence, by age 10, of the adult face schema for encoding unfamiliar faces involves a maturational component. One fruitful line of research would be to study sex differences in the dips at age 12 and 14, in order to determine whether the temporary disruption of the capacity is correlated with the hormonal changes which accompany puberty.

Another fruitful line of research is the comparison between the developmental course of the capacity for face recognition and that of other right hemisphere capacities. A preliminary search of the literature reveals that over a wide range of right hemisphere functions, a landmark in the development of the right cerebral hemisphere appears to be reached between ages 10 and 12. Such regularity would support the maturational view of the developmental course of face recognition. Some examples supporting this regularity are provided in the work of Kohn and Dennis (1974), Rudel (1974), and Woods and Teuber (in preparation). Kohn and Dennis studied patients who had undergone right hemidecortication for infantile hemiplegia. With only their left hemisphere intact these patients perform adequately a number of visual and spatial tasks on which persons who sustain right hemisphere injury as adults are markedly deficient. Sparing is limited to those tasks on which normal children succeed before age 10. Thus, at or soon after age 10, the right hemisphere assumes certain functions that the left hemisphere cannot assume. A second example concerns the Braille alphabet. Readers of Braille perform better with their left than their right hands, presumably because the tactual configurations of the Braille alphabet are best mediated by the right hemisphere. Rudel (1974) has shown that young sighted children who are taught to discriminate the letters of Braille do not show this pattern. Superiority for the left hand first appears at age 11 for boys and age 12 for girls, probably reflecting a sex difference in the age at which the relevant right hemisphere specialization occurs. This result is analogous to Leehey's discovery that the left visual field advantage for upright faces is not present until around age 10. Finally, recovery from aphasia is more rapid and complete if injury to the left hemisphere is sustained before ages 10 to 12 (see Woods and Teuber for a critical review). This might be due to commitment of the right hemisphere to some of its visual-spatial functions around age 10, reducing its availability for participation in language.

Although the above studies are consistent with placing the faces results in the context of general right hemisphere maturation, many studies show right hemisphere specializations considerably before age 10. For instance, Kimura demonstrated left ear (right hemisphere) advantages for environmental sounds as early as age 4. Clearly, further analysis is needed to distinguish those right hemisphere functions for which age 10 seems privileged and those for which it is not.

Suppose that there is a maturational component in the achievement, at age 10, of the adult capacity for encoding and subsequently recognizing unfamiliar faces. What animal model of plasticity, if any, might apply to this development? It may prove fruitful to look for developmental asymmetries between the left and right posterior cortex of the sort described by

Goldman in the case of orbital and dorsolateral frontal cortex in monkeys. Possibly the right posterior cortex reaches functional maturity later than the left and can assume some normally left hemisphere functions in cases of left hemisphere injury. Consistent with this application of Goldman's model are two sets of facts:

1. Certain right hemisphere functions (like face recognition) are developed rather late (age 10). No known left hemisphere capacities (or left hemisphere cerebral specializations) are achieved so late.
2. As mentioned above, plasticity for left hemisphere linguistic capacities exists up until age 10, diminishing thereafter. Recent work by Woods and Teuber suggests there is no comparable plasticity for right hemisphere functions, perhaps because the earlier commitment of the left hemisphere prevents it from being available for the assumption of normally right hemisphere capacities.

One direct prediction from Goldman's model to the present case could be tested. If the right posterior cortex matures functionally later than the left, children younger than 10 years who sustain right posterior lesions shold not *appear* deficient on those tasks compared with normals of the same age. The deficiency should appear at age 10, the age at which the right hemisphere would have assumed that function in normals.

5

Current Studies of Animal Communication as
Paradigms for the Biology of Language

EDWARD WALKER

A number of chimpanzees have been taught to use hand gestures or geometric symbols, the hope being that their acquisition and use of symbol systems could be profitably compared to the development and use of language. So far, little effort in these studies has been devoted to understanding what underlying capacity the chimpanzees' symbol manipulation manifests. Those examples of behavior which have been taken as similar to language can be described by any of several other rule systems. Consequently, there is little use debating whether chimpanzees have the capacity to use language, some formal system equivalent to language, or some capacity irrelevant to language until some information is at hand regarding which rules actually govern the chimpanzees' performance.

If the chimpanzees' symbol systems and language were as similar as the behavior of speakers of different languages, or if they eventually developed full language ability, as normal children do, we might safely assume that their capacity is like ours and pursue the comparison. But there is every reason to suppose that chimpanzees, unlike children or speakers of different languages, are not developing or using language. Therefore, making any comparisons must depend on understanding not only the capacity to use language but also the chimpanzees' capacity, whatever it may be, whether or not the behavioral manifestations of these capacities are similar.

Several attempts have been made to examine functional components of language capacity as they occur in other species. Recently it has been suggested that the development and neural mechanisms of birdsong can be profitably compared with human vocalization. The similarities between birdsong and speech which have so far been pointed out are either those which apply to innately specified capacities in general or those which have little to do with the use of speech as a medium for language. Consequently, the comparison of birdsong and speech, as currently pursued, has little application to the study of human language capacity.

A good deal of research is based on the assumption that studies of normal animals or of animals whose experience or physical integrity has been systematically manipulated eventually will be applicable to the explanation of some human capacity. How useful or fruitful comparisons between human beings and other animals will be depends on whether the physical and behavioral mechanisms that give rise to similarities between species actually correspond. Birds, bees, bats, and people fly, but to infer correspondences between these species just because they all engage in "flying" would be to confuse quite different acts which have the same name.

A similar confusion has arisen about the significance of claims that chimpanzees can talk, read, and gesture in American Sign Language; or that birdsong and speech are comparable. If such claims use "language" merely to allude to "some system that can be used to communicate," then obviously chimpanzees and birds do use language, and so do many other species. On the other hand, if the term is taken in its ordinary sense to refer to the spoken or written language that human beings use, then neither chimpanzees nor birds nor any other beast uses language.

Since the superficial resemblance of chimpanzee symbol systems, birdsong, and language is either trivial or nonexistent, the term "language" must allude to similarities or identities in those capacities which underlie the use of language by human beings, the use of symbol systems by chimpanzees, and the use of song by birds. If so, then some characterization of each animal's capacity is a prerequisite for comparing the behaviors.

Yet it is exactly the characterization of what capacity a behavior manifests that is most often ignored when animal communication and language are compared. Because of this oversight, very little can be learned about how chimpanzees' symbol systems relate to language. Similarly, the failure to consider what human language capacity entails has obscured the content of comparisons between speech and birdsong.

Teaching Chimpanzees Language (Viki)

The most obvious difference between chimpanzees' and human beings' language capacity is that human beings develop and use language spontaneously, while chimpanzees do not. Even if they are given painstaking training and almost continuous exposure to human vocalization, chimpanzees exhibit almost no capacity to learn to speak, although they do learn to respond appropriately to 50 to 100 words and to spoken commands such as "show me the bow-wow."

The experience of Viki, a chimpanzee who was adopted into a human home shortly after her birth, is typical of attempts to teach chimpanzees language directly. Viki was raised, as nearly as possible, as a human child. By the time she died at age seven, she spoke only seven words, four of them "human" and three of them her own standardized vocalizations.

Language training and testing were only part of a general survey of Viki's cognitive capacity and development, relative to that of human beings. The ingenuity and resemblance to human beings that Viki (and several other chimpanzees) have displayed in performing nonlinguistic tasks should impart more skepticism than they have to claims of a "breakthrough" in reports of chimpanzee "language" projects.

Viki demonstrated her ability to communicate spontaneously by such behavior as presenting a picture of a glass of tea to her trainer, uttering 'cup' (one of her human words) and pulling the trainer to the refrigerator in order to indicate that she wanted a drink. She also selected appropriate pictures when asked "show me" after uttering both 'cup' and her own word for cigarettes, and she presented a picture of a lipstick as a ticket to the bathroom, where her toiletries and cosmetics were kept. This use of pictures deteriorated almost completely when her trainers attempted to add a picture of a comb to her repertoire. Even after a recess of several months, Viki refused to use any pictures communicatively except those of cars, with which she continued to indicate that she wanted a car ride.

Viki enjoyed car rides, and showing a picture of a car was only one of many ways she asked for a car ride. She also gestured toward the car, touched or led her trainers to the drawer containing the key to the front door, brought a purse to her trainer, or chattered her teeth in her characteristic vocalization of this request. While such behavior does show imagination in generalizing across modalities and symbols, it unfortunately characterizes all Viki's communicative efforts, which were minimal and never went beyond her expressing her immediate wants and requesting that they be satisfied. In this respect, Viki's behavior resembles that of the family dog, who barks, fetches his leash, scratches the door, or otherwise signals his desire to go out.

Even though Viki showed considerable accomplishment at expressing her wants and responding to simple instructions, her trainers commented that the difficulty of communicating was the greatest hindrance they encountered in assessing her abilities and their development, and they have not suggested that Viki learned to use language.

Nonvocal Substitutes for
Language (Washoe, Sarah, and Lana)

There are arguments against taking Viki's failure to speak as a demonstration that chimpanzees cannot learn to use language. Although chimpanzees do produce a considerable variety of vocalization, their vocalizations resist modification by training, and wild chimpanzees do not appear to use them effectively for communicating. On the other hand, both wild and captive chimpanzees exhibit a natural skill at using stylized gestures, of which the familiar begging gesture is an example. This propensity suggests that the chimpanzees might more readily learn language via some nonvocal medium, and a number of active research projects are pursuing that possibility.

In one of these, a chimpanzee named Washoe has been taught to use a symbol system based on American Sign Language, which relies on symbolic gesturing as a medium of communication. Several chimpanzees have been or are being taught sign language. Washoe's recent experiences, and those of several of her colony mates, are described in Fleming (1974) and Linden (1974). Signing is used by a large community of deaf people and is, in fact, the first language learned by some of these. [Human sign language is discussed in Bellugi and Klima (1975).] Thus using a symbol system based on American Sign Language not only employs a nonvocal medium but also somewhat reduces the difficulty of finding or creating a suitable language.

Primarily by having her hands guided into the desired shapes, Washoe learned to make approximately 160 signs; and she combined these signs in spontaneously produced sequences up to five symbols long. There is no evidence either that the sequencing of the gestures is rule-governed or that sequences occur in circumstances which do not considerably constrain the selection of gestures. [Washoe's and Sarah's symbol systems and language are contrasted pessimistically in Brown (1970, 1973), Bever, Fodor, and Garrett (1974), and Limber (1976).] Furthermore, it is difficult to determine whether Washoe appreciated even the temporal arrangement of the signs themselves, and there is little evidence that she either observed syntactically based relational constraints or used her knowledge of sequence structure to produce novel sequences of her own (but see below).

In a project whose primary feature is its strict control of the stock of symbols and the circumstances under which sequences can be generated, another chimpanzee named Sarah was trained to manipulate a symbol system consisting of strings of geometric shapes placed on a magnetic board. [Sarah's accomplishments and those of several similarly trained chimpanzees are discussed in Premack (1976).] Unlike Washoe's evanescent gestures, Sarah's plastic chips and their configuration are semi-permanent, and her trainer allows Sarah to use only the chips he chooses. Thus the kind and number of symbols and sequences used in a learning or test session is subject to more systematic constraint than is possible with Washoe. Of course, the variety of symbol sequences which Sarah can create is somewhat reduced by these constraints.

Sarah learned to assign arbitrary referents to about 120 chips, and she can insert single chips which refer to objects and actions and to the concepts same and different, negation, question, name of, color of, shape of, and size of appropriately into sequences of chips. Furthermore, she has learned to observe the consequences of a conditional relation between two strings and to recognize that a single occurrence of a chip can apply to two partial sequences of chips.

Unfortunately, the conditions of the training and testing sessions prohibited Sarah from demonstrating, either by producing her own novel sequences or by making instructive errors, which rules of form she was observing. While her training indicated that she had considerable facility at recognizing the consequences of the rules applied by the trainer to the form of sequences, we have no way of knowing the basis of her performance. She might be demonstrating the competence at recognizing and using rules of form which is ascribed to her, but she could also observe the trainer's constraints on sequences by following any of several strategies, including some which bear little or no relation to the symbol sequences themselves [see Brown (1973)].

A chimpanzee named Lana had a somewhat greater chance than Sarah to demonstrate her capacity to manipulate symbols. Lana was free to generate and respond to sequences of symbols by using a computer-controlled keyboard. She pressed keys with geometric symbols on them in standard sequences in order to obtain food, toys, music, a look out the window, or some other inducement of the good life. By projecting the symbols on screens, Lana's trainers could pose sequence-completion problems to her. She learned to use about 75 symbols to generate or complete partial sequences of the very simple type shown below, and she rejected the incorrect sequences (indicated by an asterisk) when they were presented to her.

	juice	
please machine give	banana	period
	*music	

	window open	
please machine make	music	period
	*banana	

What Do the Chimpanzees Learn?

Lana's trainers called what she did "sentence completion." Discovering what Lana was doing is as hard as discovering what we might do in the circumstances. We might fill in such blanks by selecting one of a set of symbols that we know can follow 'give' or 'make.' On the other hand, we might complete the sequence by choosing from a set containing symbols for things that can be 'given' or 'made'; yet again we might choose a symbol that completes a compound symbol (e.g., basketball or football, but not shoulderball). We might even select a symbol which completes a well-formed sequence of symbols. Any of these strategies (as well as many others) would allow us to perform as Lana does.

One way to discover how we do fill in such blanks (aside from asking) is to give us new blanks or new symbols and determine from our performance in these novel circumstances which strategies were used to complete the familiar sequences. A common example of this procedure was used to discover the basis on which Viki separated nails, bolts, brads, and stapleback metal buttons from plastic, glass, and bone buttons during a test session. In a subsequent test, she separated coins and stapleback metal buttons from plastic, glass, and bone buttons, as well as from metal buttons with holes. The results of the second test suggest that Viki's sorting strategy may have been based on the presence of holes, rather than on material, as it seemed at first. Without a test including metal buttons with holes, Viki's trainers might have assumed that she was sorting objects according to material in both tests. The point is a simple one: the capacity that a chimpanzee displays in performing a task may not be the one that its trainer sought to inculcate or reveal by posing the task. In other words, one cannot assume that Washoe, Sarah, or Lana actually had the capacity ascribed to her just because she performed a task "correctly." For that one needs evidence that the capacity itself is the basis of correct performance.

In both children and adults, the capacity for language demonstrates itself in the comprehension or production of novel well-formed utterances, or by the kinds of systematic "mistakes" in comprehension or production which indicate an inappropriate or unusual appreciation of some structural distinction (or lack of it). In addition, adults or children may be able to produce related forms of a sentence or identify as ungrammatical attempts to do so. A human being might use one strategy to complete Lana's sequences as follows:

	juice	
	banana	
	two juices	
please machine give	a different juice	period
	red juice	
	anything but juice	
	at the office	
	me the strength to persevere	
	up	

In other words, human beings perform as if they knew not only the properties of the set of symbols which can be inserted but also the properties that govern which sets of symbols can be used to complete the sequence. And they display their knowledge of such properties by being able to extend them to new symbols and new sequences.

There is little evidence that chimpanzees extend their symbol systems productively. In fairness to the animals, it must be noted that their trainers and the environment of the experiments conspire to prevent them from applying their symbol systems in new situations. Sarah had numerous symbols which she might have used productively if she had been allowed. She could use 'color of' to make up a new sequence such as 'X is the color of Y' (book is the color of apple), but she was allowed only to choose one of two chips to complete a sequence already presented or to make up previously trained sequences. Apparently she had no access to the plastic chips of her language during off-hours and so could show no interest in manipulating them outside the test sessions. In fact, even if she were to produce novel sequences, the criteria of the experiment would require that any such novel sequences be scored as errors.

The most optimistic estimate of Sarah's appreciation of sequence structure is that she understood that 'insert' applies to both subsequences 'banana pail' and 'apple dish' in the sequence below.

Sarah insert banana pail apple dish

It may be true that she did so, but her successful performance itself was not sufficient evidence that she used this (or any other) structural dependency as the basis of that performance. Although she performed correctly when tested with such sequences, she learned to do so by learning to criterion the step-by-step reductions of the full sequence indicated by the insertion of X's in the sequences below.

Sarah insert banana pail Sarah insert apple dish
Sarah insert banana pail   X   insert apple dish
Sarah insert banana pail   X   X   apple dish

Consequently we have no evidence that she understood anything beyond the functional synonymy of full and reduced sequences.

Since Washoe's signs were her own, and she could use them spontaneously and freely, the possibility that she would create novel sequences did exist. However she took little advantage of it. A few tantalizing anecdotes suggest her creative use of the signs themselves (making the signs 'water' and 'bird' on seeing a duck for the first time; signing 'dirty' and 'monkey' to name a fearsome colony mate; signing to another chimpanzee 'go' and 'drink' while competing with it for fruit). But Washoe's novel gesture sequences are so heavily constrained by her surroundings that in themselves they give us no idea what structure they might have, so far as Washoe was concerned.

The shortcomings of Lana's "sentence completions" were

outlined above. Presumably the computer which recognized Lana's symbol sequences and acted appropriately on them would boggle at a novel sequence from her and did not present her with novel sequences of its own. Consequently, the possibility that Lana either produced or recognized novel sequences is remote.

This brief discussion reveals how little about what the chimpanzees have learned can be determined from the project reports of their performance. Finding out whether what the chimpanzees do resembles language in any respect depends on understanding systematically and completely what capacity underlies their behavior. To claim that studying the chimpanzees' capacity to use symbol systems is a useful paradigm for research in the biology of language is therefore premature. More importantly, attempting to make such claims obscures what interest these projects may have as inquiries into primate behavior: the obsession to characterize the symbol systems as "language" prevents them from being used to explore or explain any chimpanzee capacity in its own right.

Why Call the Chimpanzees' Behavior Language?

In calling the chimpanzees' symbol systems "language," their trainers apparently assume that human language capacity is present in rudimentary form in chimpanzees. In this view, the chimpanzees, or their behavior, may provide a simpler or more primitive version of language which, although it may differ in degree, does not differ in kind from human language. If other animals could be taught to use language, the species specificity of language supposedly would have been trivialized, and the assumption that experimental results can be generalized across species supported. Incidentally, a population of nonhuman language users would have been created which could then be subjected to the kinds of environmental and anatomical abuse by which the critical experiential and anatomical features on which language depends might be isolated.

There is, however, a great deal of evidence (see Chapter 1)

which supports the claim that the human capacity to develop
and use language is not just more of the same kind of capacity
found in other species, but a qualitatively different capacity
arising from a genetic endowment which only human beings
possess and exercise. This claim means nothing more or less
than that the cognitive capacity and associated neural
mechanisms by which language develops and is used occur in
only one species, man. Such a claim implies that some behavioral capacities vary nontrivially across species and that the
capacity of a chimpanzee to use a symbol system may be
irrelevant to the study of human language (see below).

Studies of Nonprimate Animal Communication

It is not necessary to dispute whether language is species-
specific in order to argue that comparing animal and human
behavior and anatomy may provide useful paradigms for
studying various aspects of language. We are animals, and
language is one of our behaviors. From this point of view,
studies of bees dancing, ants marking trails, wolves posturing
their social status, birds vocalizing, and human beings talking all
may provide data which will influence general theories of
animal communication. (The relation of general and particular
theories being what it is, it would be wise to note that such
suggestions may be more facile than useful.) Furthermore, the
functional components of language capacity may be studied
separately in other species.

For example, infants apparently have an innate capacity to
discriminate among various speech sounds. One aspect of this
capacity depends on the ability of the infant's perceptual
mechanisms to categorize as similar acoustically different
instances of the same stop consonant before different vowels.
This ability appears to rely on the auditory system's capacity to
detect the latency of the onset of voicing after the opening of
the vocal-tract closure which characterizes a stop consonant. If
the ability does rely on some capacity of the auditory system,
possibly other animals with similar auditory systems make
similar categorizations. And indeed it appears that chinchillas,

whose auditory system resembles that of human beings, can learn to recognize similar distinctions in speech sounds.

It is important to notice that the nature of the resemblance between human beings and chinchillas is posited from (partial) theories of human speech perception and of the auditory systems of chinchillas and human beings. All too often co-incidental resemblances in the behavior, anatomy, or development of animals have given rise to comparisons (along whatever lines the resemblances suggest) in the absence of any formal understanding of what is being compared and what the comparison involves.

The observation that dolphins communicate by vocal-auditory means and display such "human" behavior as helping their fellows in distress led to a considerable effort to establish communication with them. [Most of this research is reported in Lilly (1961, 1967). At first Washoe's sign-language project was also characterized as an attempt to establish two-way communication with another species.] More recently, it has been suggested that human and bird vocalization can profitably be compared. Although the existence of some relation between birds' vocalization and speech cannot be excluded, explaining any such relation will depend on more than asserting that it exists and observing gross similarities in the two behaviors or in the neural mechanisms on which they rely.

These are the facts reported. [Several workers' findings are summarized by Nottebohm (1974) and Marler (1975). The critical remarks here are not made against the intrinsic interest or desirability of doing research on the development, neural mechanisms, or biological utilities of birdsong itself but are directed against the claim that birdsong and human speech may be profitably compared.] Some birds sing songs unique to their species. Of these, some will develop the normal song of their species even if they are deafened before they hear any birdsong at all. Other species do not develop their song unless they hear another bird singing (not necessarily one of their own species), and still other species do not develop their song fully unless they hear their own species' song before puberty. From these facts it is argued that at least some features of birdsong must be innately specified but that, at least in some species, the normal development of song depends on some interaction between environmental stimuli or models and an innately specified "auditory template" during a critical period in maturation.

In addition to these developmental phenomena, it has been observed that cutting the left hypoglossal nerve of mature birds of some species appears to destroy more of the song sequence than does cutting the right. Furthermore, if either nerve is cut before the development of singing, the intact nerve appears able to subsume some of the function of the cut one.

It is these features—an innately specified song pattern, the influence of environment on the development of full song, the critical period for learning, and the "lateralization of function" in the hypoglossal nerves—together with alleged similarities in the stages of language acquisition and the development of birdsong from fledgling cries to full song—that have led to the suggestion that the two forms of vocalization, their neural specification, and their development ought to be compared.

Since birdsong appears to rely on the time-varying properties of sound for significance, and such aspects of sound serve in the exchange of signs by human beings, it is not unlikely that some features of the two animals' behavior, or even of the organs supporting it, are similar. But as we have noted earlier, making sense of this similarity will depend on understanding which mechanisms are involved and what their function is in each animal.

The function of birdsong appears to be species and individual identification, localization, warning, and assembly. While human vocalization can, and does, serve many of these functions, speech is distinct from mere vocalization in that it also conveys linguistic constructs. That is to say, whatever the similarities may be between bird and human vocalization, they are not necessarily similarities between birdsong and language.

The observation that some behaviors are innately specified and that the full development of some of these behaviors requires interaction with the environment during a "critical period" is not novel. In human beings, behaviors such as talking, walking, and carrying infants seem to develop spontaneously and, to greater or lesser extent, are characteristically modified by environmental influences during their development. And, as

which give rise to the behavior in which such similarities occur may differ markedly or not at all, regardless of the similarities noted.

That human beings develop language spontaneously in a normal environment is an often ignored aspect of its species specificity. If other species could learn to use language, in the human sense, we might have to concede that with explicit training, guidance, change of medium, and so forth, some other animal can be taught to use language. But there is no reason to suppose that the capacity developed by the other species through training and that developed spontaneously by human beings are the same. Apparently, even human beings who learn second languages do not acquire the same capacity as they do in learning their native tongue.

This is a biological version of the classic simulation problem. Solutions which produce the same answer to a problem may not be related in any other way. Potentially, at least, many rule systems can specify a solution: there is more than one way to skin a cat. Comparing another species' capacity with human language capacity involves nothing less than solving the problem of the biology of language for both species.

Appendix

*Some Neurological Techniques for
Assessing Localization of Function*

DAVID ROSENFIELD

Most neurological techniques involve simple tests of such ordinary language functions as reading aloud, naming objects, or memorizing lists of words. These tests are administered both to patients suffering from loss of some function and to normal or control subjects, who serve as a standard of comparison for the neurological population. The performance or response of the patients and that of the normal subjects are correlated in order to establish which functions have been lost or impaired and, conversely, which brain structures are likely to support those functions.

Although the tests usually involve relatively passive and noninvasive procedures which can be employed with both patients and normal subjects, the patients themselves suffer from either temporary or permanent changes in the bio-chemical, electrical, or anatomical character of their brains. Consequently, generalizations about the localization of language function based on their performance are always subject to the proviso that they are derived from the behavior of abnormal brains and hence may reflect abnormal function.

For example, the corpus callosum, a bundle of nerve fibers connecting the hemispheres, is sometimes cut in order to control the spread of severe epileptic seizures. Because the operation partially disconnects the hemispheres, it permits studying the capacities of one hemisphere without the possibility of a direct contribution by the other (see below). But some caution must accompany extensions from the performance of commissurectomy patients to the explanation of normal brain function. The hemispheres of a normal brain are not disconnected (at least anatomically), and such surgery is performed only on patients with a neurological disorder severe enough to warrant drastic intervention, a disorder which may or may not affect brain function before or after the operation.

This caution applies generally to explanations of findings from preoperative diagnosis or postoperative or posttraumatic assessment of the nature and extent of the loss of some capacity. In addition, formulating theories about the localization of function based on such studies, or explaining their results, inevitably will depend on understanding normal function: one can characterize a loss of function only so far as one can characterize the function. Because of these constraints, neurological methods themselves are unlikely to provide direct insight into the mechanisms underlying normal language capacity for some time to come.

Nevertheless testing of neurological patients offers extraordinary opportunities for establishing which neural structures support the capacity for language, and for studying at least partially isolated neural components of the brain mechanisms involved in language use. Moreover, as the characterization of normal language capacity becomes more complete, neurological methods for assessing or predicting loss of that capacity by injury or disease will become more precise. In this sense, interdisciplinary research in the biology of language is an important prerequisite to the development and sophistication of neurological procedures. The brief survey below compares the ability of right and left hemispheres to perform verbal tasks, reviews techniques for inducing transient loss and recovery of language function, and discusses methods for assessing which neural structures are involved in processing speech sounds. The conclusions reached are necessarily tentative, but they suggest important areas in which neurological techniques can be applied to assess localization of function.

Commissurectomy and Hemispherectomy

The extent to which the capacity for language is innately specified, and the particular nature of this capacity relative to other cognitive structures, is a topic of central concern in the biology of language. In most adults, the capacity for language clearly resides in the left hemisphere. A variety of neurological tests and findings suggest that neural specialization for this capacity is innate. Furthermore, specialized areas of the left hemisphere involved in language function have been isolated and discussed extensively (see Chapters 2 and 3). However, the degree to which the right hemisphere has, or can develop, any capacity to perform verbal tasks remains an open question. Two distinct classes of neurological patients, those whose hemispheres are disconnected and those who have had one hemisphere removed or damaged extensively in early life, offer unique opportunities to study and compare the capacities of right and left hemispheres.

Cutting the corpus callosum severs cortical communication between the hemispheres. This commissurectomy effectively isolates each hemisphere from the other at the cortical level. Auditory stimuli still reach both hemispheres via subcortical pathways from each cochlea, but visual input can be restricted to one hemisphere by presenting the stimulus to only one visual field (see Chapter 5). Similarly, the hemisphere implicated in making a response can be manipulated by specifying which hand must execute the response. Thus some capacities of each hemisphere can be tested separately by controlling the presentation of visual input and requiring one hand to make response.

The results of tests applied to commissurectomy patients accord generally with the observation that language capacity normally resides in the left hemisphere. Responses made by the right hand to stimulation which reaches only the left hemisphere demonstrate an apparently intact language capacity. Using only their left hemisphere, the patients can recognize and name objects, produce verbal responses, and respond appropriately and naturally to verbal commands. On the other hand, they are unable to name objects placed in their left hand or presented visually to only their right hemisphere. The patients are also unable to make appropriate verbal responses to stimulation received by only the right hemisphere.

Indeed, when they are restricted to using their right hemisphere, the commissurectomy patients seem virtually mute. However, the right hemisphere is not entirely unable to accomplish linguistic tasks. When a word is presented visually to the right hemisphere, patients can use their left hand to select the object referred to from among several. Similarly, they can respond to a verbal instruction to select a particular object, again using their left hand. It even appears that patients are able to write left-handed responses to simple written instructions shown to only the right hemisphere. But despite their considerable ability to use their right hemispheres to recognize or select objects referred to by concrete nouns and perform simple tasks, commissurectomy patients identify the actions described by verbs or derived nouns only poorly, and they display only such basic syntactic capacities as recognizing the tense or voice of an utterance.

Evidence that the right hemisphere possesses even a restricted verbal capacity is intriguing, but the contribution of the previously connected and intact left hemisphere to the development (or lack of development) of language function in the right hemisphere of these patients is virtually impossible to assess. In addition, it is difficult to judge the extent to which the patients' performance indicates the presence of a true language ability in the right hemisphere, rather than an adventitious ability to perform verbal tasks based on some essentially nonlanguage capacity. Finally, there are obvious limits to the subtlety with which the verbal ability of the right hemisphere can be tested by nonverbal means.

Some of the technical difficulties in assessing right hemisphere capacities are mitigated in patients who have sustained damage to their left hemisphere early in life. A major insult to the left hemisphere of a normal adult is devastating to language capacity, but the same overwhelming loss of language function does not occur when the damage is incurred in infancy or early childhood. Such patients appear to develop much greater capacity to communicate than that displayed by commissurectomy patients relying on their right hemisphere. Basser (1962) concluded from examining patients who had suffered early left or right hemisphere lesions that speech does develop in the intact hemisphere, regardless of which hemisphere is damaged. In other words, the right (nondominant) hemisphere evidently can develop at least some language function, and the contribution of the left hemisphere to this function, or its development, is certainly minimal at least among those whose lesions occurred in infancy.

The greater ability of the patients to communicate makes more comprehensive testing possible. Dennis and Whitaker (1976) found that the language skills developed in the remaining left or right hemisphere after a hemispherectomy differ markedly: while "phonetic" and "semantic" abilities develop similarly, regardless of which hemisphere remains, "syntactic" competence is deficient in patients without a left hemisphere. These patients are particularly deficient at such tasks as detecting and correcting errors of sentence structure, repeating stylistic variants of sentences, producing tag questions, determining sentence implication, replacing missing pronouns, and judging interrelationships of words.

Thus it appears that the right hemisphere has some capacity to use linguistic form, or at least sufficient plasticity to develop a capacity to do so. However, the language functions so far discovered in the right hemisphere differ markedly from those in the left. In particular, restrictions on the right hemisphere's apparent incapacity to perform tasks relying on the form of sentences argue that the potential for full language function resides only in the left hemisphere. Further comparisons of the right and left hemispheres' capacities to perform language-related tasks will undoubtedly reveal more clearly both the extent of the right hemisphere's capacity and the precise character of the innate specification for language in the left.

Amytal Injection, Electroconvulsive Therapy,
Cortical Stimulation

Several neurological procedures result in transient suppression or recovery of language function. While these techniques have been applied primarily to locate and map brain function before surgery, they also offer a unique means for studying language capacity, along a continuum from "normal" language function to aphasia. Furthermore, when they are applied unilaterally, they offer yet another opportunity to compare the language functions of right and left hemispheres.

An injection of sodium amobarbitol (amytal) temporarily depresses brain function, and when the injection is to the carotid artery supplying the dominant hemisphere (Wada test), the patient gradually (and temporarily) becomes aphasic and paralyzed on the right side of the body. Somewhat para-doxically, the intravenous administration of amytal to aphasic patients temporarily improves their language performance [see Linn (1947)], presumably by suppressing inhibition. Carotid injections have also been used to study the role of the right hemisphere in the production of aphasic speech. Kinsbourne (1971) inferred from observing the performance of aphasics following intercarotid injection of amytal that some aspects of aphasic speech might be programmed in the nondominant hemisphere. Exactly which aspects of speech are, or can be, controlled by the nondominant hemisphere remains to be established.

Like an injection of amytal, electroconvulsive therapy (ECT) transiently compromises brain function. The recovery of function following ECT occurs over a period ranging from a few hours to several days. The course of this treatment and recovery provide a second opportunity to study the temporary loss of language function, as well as stages in its recovery. Furthermore, the depressive patients to whom the treatment is generally administered represent a distinct population from the neuro-logical patients who receive amytal injections. The results so far obtained from examining ECT patients during their recovery from therapy support the major findings of other techniques for determining localization of function (when the therapy is administered unilaterally), and suggest that more detailed study of the language capacity present during stages in recovery is warranted.

Amytal injection or electroconvulsive shock eliminates the

function of an entire hemisphere, whether gradually or suddenly. The gross effects produced by these procedures make interpreting results difficult at best. The suppression or excitation of language performance caused by direct cortical stimulation is less general and can be described more precisely. Penfield and Roberts (1959) discovered that when a small electric current is applied to the surface of the cortex, speech is either stimulated or interfered with. This technique affects cortical functions less generally than either amytal or ECT. Current applied to the motor areas of either hemisphere stimulates vocalization or results in a disorder of the motor control of speech. Similarly, various alterations of speech—arrest, hesitation, slurring, repetition and distortion, confusion of numbers while counting, inability to name, misnaming, perseveration, difficulty in reading or writing, and so forth—can be induced by current. To a certain extent, mapping of specific functions onto areas of cortical surface has been possible, and once again theories about the gross localization of language functions have been corroborated. Although much remains to be determined about how the application of current interferes with normal function, the technique offers interesting possibilities for temporarily compromising specific cortical functions.

Electrodiagnosis

In addition to using electric current to stimulate or suppress cortical function, it is also possible to record the electrical activity produced in the cortex by natural stimulation or by the effort to make some response. Acoustic or visual stimuli evoke specific responses which occur at a fairly constant delay following stimulation, and which can be recorded from electrodes placed over the cortical area appropriate to the modality, laterality, and type of stimulation.

For example, Cohn (1971) noted that mechanical clicking noises produce a greater initial electrical response over the right hemisphere, and verbal stimuli such as *cat* or *bar* produce equal or even larger responses over the left hemisphere. Morrell and

Balamy, (1971) observed that the cortical-evoked responses to natural speech stimuli are larger over the left hemisphere, particularly over the left temporal-parietal area. And Matsumiya et al. (1972) reached the still more specific conclusion that the largest auditory evoked response to verbal stimuli occurs over Wernicke's area about 100 milliseconds after stimulation.

These broad findings agree with the common localization of receptive function gained from using other techniques. Moreover, the asymmetry of hemispheric function apparently does not depend on extensive linguistic experience. Molfese (1972) recorded markedly different responses to linguistic and non-linguistic stimuli from groups of subjects representing all ages. The evoked response in not only adults and children but also infants shows greater left hemisphere activity after they hear syllables and words, and greater right hemisphere activity after such nonlinguistic sounds as piano chords and noise bursts, the largest asymmetries of all being produced by infants.

The electrical activity produced by voluntary vocalization displays similar speech/nonspeech asymmetries. McAdam and Whitaker (1971) recorded slow negative potentials from electrodes placed over Broca's area when subjects spontaneously produced polysyllabic words, and they observed equal potentials from both hemispheres when subjects produced nonspeech vocalizations.

The methodology of recording auditory evoked potentials in response to speech is still being developed, but the findings so far produced again corroborate localizations of language function in Broca's and Wernicke's areas. Widespread application of the method to populations of neurological patients remains to be accomplished. But once the basic parameters of the auditory evoked response are established, the most obvious step is systematically to manipulate the character of the stimuli used to evoke responses.

Dichotic Listening

Systematically manipulating the acoustic parameters of stimuli is the hallmark of dichotic listening studies. In this paradigm, a different stimulus is presented to each ear. Although each cochlea is connected neurally to both hemispheres, listeners consistently report hearing only the stimulus in one ear when similar stimuli (e.g., two speech sounds) are presented simultaneously. Which stimulus is reported depends on both the type of stimulus and the ear to which it was presented. A left-ear advantage has been demonstrated for melodies, chords, and environmental sounds, while a right-ear advantage commonly occurs with such speech sounds as nonsense syllables, tape-recorded speech played backward, and synthetic consonant-vowel syllables. Apparently stimuli are processed most effectively in the hemisphere contralateral to the ear in which they are presented; thus a right-ear advantage for speech sounds indicates that speech is processed primarily in the left hemisphere.

Trading on an ear advantage, the acoustic character of the competing stimuli, their temporal arrangement, or other aspects of their acoustic makeup can be manipulated in order to determine which components of the stimulation are critical to that ear advantage. As aspects of normal performance are isolated by these methods, tests of them can be applied to neurological patients with damage to the neural structures in which such processing is accomplished. For example, a lesion of the auditory cortex should reduce or eliminate any contralateral advantage for sounds presented dichotically. In fact, Berlin et al. (1972a) found that after either right or left temporal lobectomy, contralateral dichotic stimuli are reported poorly. Similarly, normal subjects report the trailing stimulus better as the temporal separation of dichotic stimuli increases. However, the temporal lobes are also implicated in short-term memory, and lobectomy patients predictably show no improvement as the temporal separation of stimuli increases. Furthermore, when noise or an ipsilateral stimulus which is below threshold is used as the competing stimulus, the contralateral ear of the patient performs at nearly 100 percent, indicating that ipsilateral pathways are intact. However, the contralateral scores drop markedly as the intelligibility of the competing ipsilateral stimulus increases, suggesting that in noncompetitive situations the undamaged lobe performs normally.

Consonant-vowel (CV) syllables are intelligible when presented monaurally to either ear of normal subjects or to patients with temporal-lobe lesions sparing the primary auditory and speech areas. However, the weak ear of lobectomy patients performs very poorly on dichotic tasks using such stimuli, even when the CV presented to the strong ear is up to 20 decibels less intense than that presented to the weak ear. A competing CV stimulus suppresses performance most strongly, but vowels or signals with acoustic features similar to a CV suppress performance as well, even when they are 20 to 40 decibels less intense than the competing CV stimulus.

When dichotic listening tasks are applied to patients with hemispherectomies, the strong ear performs far better than that of normal subjects, suggesting that the ear advantage in normals depends at least in part on competitive suppression of ipsilateral input, as well as on a left hemisphere processing advantage for contralateral input. This conclusion is supported by results from dichotic tests of commissurectomy patients, whose strong (right) ear shows very little left-ear interference in speech tasks.

By now dichotic listening studies of normal subjects have developed considerable subtlety at manipulating and contrasting acoustic features of the dichotic stimuli. Ear advantages for pitch and tone, as well as several classes of segmental speech sounds, have been examined at length. However, like most of the techniques discussed above, these refinements are just beginning to find application in a neurological context. Applying dichotic listening tasks to neurological patients with sufficiently restricted lesions affords a chance to study components of the brain mechanisms underlying speech perception. While they are in their preliminary stages at best, the neurological techniques surveyed here lend themselves particularly well to neuropsychologically and linguistically well-founded investigations of the localization of language function.

References

Introduction

Bromberger, S. (1963) A theory about the theory of theory and about the theory of theories. In Bernard Baumrin (ed.), *Philosophy of Science: The Delaware Seminar,* vol. II. New York: John Wiley & Sons, Inc.

Chomsky, N. (1975) *Reflections on Language.* New York: Pantheon Books.

Lenneberg, E. (1964) A biological perspective of language. In E. Lenneberg (ed.), *New Directions in the Study of Language.* Cambridge, Mass.: MIT Press.

Lenneberg, E. (1967) *Biological Foundations of Language.* New York: John Wiley & Sons, Inc.

Luria, S.E. (1973) *Life: The Unfinished Experiment.* New York: Charles Scribner's Sons.

Marx, O. (1967) The history of the biological basis of language. In Lenneberg (1967).

Skinner, B.F. (1950) Are theories of learning necessary? *Psychological Review,* 57, 193-216.

Chapter 1

Atkinson R.C., and J.F. Juola (1974) Search and decision processes in recognition memory. In D.H. Krantz, R.C. Atkinson, R.D. Luce, and P. Suppes (eds.), *Contemporary Developments in Mathematical Psychology.* San Francisco: Freeman.

Atkinson, R.C., D.J. Herrmann, and K.T. Wescourt (1974b) Search processes in recognition memory. In R.L. Solso (ed.), *Theories in Cognitive Psychology: The Loyola Symposium.* New York: John Wiley & Sons, Inc.

Bartram, D.J. (1973) The role of comprehension in remembering sentences, *Cognitive Psychology*, 4, 229-254.

Bartram, D.J. (1973) The effects of familiarity and practice on naming pictures of objects, *Memory and Cognition*, 1, 101-105.

Bartram, D.J. (1974) The role of visual and semantic codes in object naming, *Cognitive Psychology*, 6, 325-356.

Carpenter, P.A., and M.A. Just (1975) Sentence comprehension: A psycholinguistic processing model of verification, *Psychological Review*, 82, 45-73.

Collins, A.M., and E.F. Loftus (1975) A spreading activation theory of semantic processing, *Psychological Review*, 82, 407-428.

Cummins, R. (1975) Functional analysis, *The Journal of Philosophy*, 72, no. 20, Nov. 20.

Garrett, M. (1975) The analysis of sentence production. In G. Bower (ed.), *The Psychology of Learning and Motivation: Advances in Research and Theory* vol. 9. New York: Academic Press, Inc.

Geschwind, N. (1969) Anatomy and the higher functions of the brain. In Robert S. Cohen and Marx W. Wartofsky (eds.), *Boston Studies in the Philosophy of Science*, vol. 4. Dordrecht, Holland: D. Reidel.

Geschwind, N., and E. Kaplan (1962) A human cerebral deconnection syndrome, *Neurology*, 12, 675-685.

Gibson, E.J., and H. Levin (1975) *The Psychology of Reading*. Cambridge, Mass.: MIT Press.

Griffin, D.P. (1962) *Animal Structure and Function*. New York: Holt, Rinehart and Winston, Inc.

Harmon, G. (1973) *Thought*. Princeton, N.J.: Princeton University Press.

Head, H. (1963) *Aphasia and Kindred Disorders of Speech*, vol. 1. New York: Hafner Publishing Company, Inc.

Hempel, C. (1965) The logic of functional analysis. In *Aspects of Scientific Explanation*. New York: The Free Press.

Kahneman, D. (1973) *Attention and Effort*. Englewood Cliffs, N.J.: Prentice-Hall, Inc.

Lachman, R. (1973) Uncertainty effects on time to access the internal lexicon, *Journal of Experimental Psychology*, 99, 199-208.

Lachman, R., J.P. Shaffer, and D. Hennrikus (1974) Language and cognition: effects of stimulus codability, name-word frequency, and age of acquisition on lexical reaction time, *Journal of Verbal Learning and Verbal Behavior*, 13, 613-625.

Luria, A.R. (1970) The functional organization of the brain, *Scientific American*, 222, March.

Nelson, K. (1974) Concept, word, and sentence: interrelations in acquisition and development, *Psychological Review*, 81, 267-285.

Potter, M.C., and B.A. Faulconer (1975) Time to understand pictures and words, *Nature*, 253, 437-438.

Potter, M.C., V.V. Valian and B.A. Faulconer (1977) Representation of a sentence and its pragmatic implications. Verbal, imagistic, or abstract? *Journal of Verbal Learning and Verbal Behavior* 16, 1-12.

Seymour, P.H.K. (1973) A model for reading, naming and comparison, *British Journal of Psychology*, 64, 35-49.

Wernicke, C. (1908) The symptom complex of aphasia: a psychological study on an anatomical basis. In A. Church (ed.), *Diseases of the Nervous System*. New York: Appleton Century Crofts.

Wimsatt, W.C. (1972) Teleology and the logical structure of function statements, *Studies in the History of Philosophy of Science*, 3: no. 1.

Chapter 2

Alajouanine, T. (1956) Verbal realization in aphasia, *Brain*, 79.

Alajouanine, T., A. Ombredane, and M. Durand (1939) *Le syndrome de la desintegration phonetique dans l'aphasie*. Paris: Masson et Cie.

Alajouanine, T., and F. Lhermitte, (1964) Aphasia and the physiology of speech. In Rioch and Weinstein (1964).

Arnoff, M.H. (1977) *Word-Structure*. Cambridge, Mass. M.I.T. Press.

Baker, A.B., and L.H. Baker (1971) *Clinical Neurology*. New York: Harper & Row, Publishers, Incorporated.

Bastian, H.C. (1887) On different kinds of aphasia, *British Medical Journal*, 2.

Bastian, H.C. (1898) *A Treatise on Aphasia and other Speech Defects*: London: Lewis.

Bay, E. (1964) Principles of classification and their influence on our concepts of aphasia. In de Reuck and O'Connor (eds.), *Disorders of Language*, Boston: Little, Brown and Co.

Benson, D.F. (1967) Fluency in aphasia: Correlation with Radioactive scan localization, *Cortex*, 3.

Benson D.F., and N. Geschwind (1971) The aphasias and related disturbances. In Baker and Baker (1971).

Bernard (1885) *De l'Aphasie et de ses Diverses Formes*, Paris: A. Delahaye and E. Lecrosnier.

Bever, T., and W. Weksel (eds.) (In press) *The Structure and Psychology of Language*. The Hague: Mouton.

Bloomfield, L. (1933) *Language*. New York: Holt, Rinehart and Winston, Inc.

Blumstein, S. (1968) Phonological aspects of aphasic speech. In Gribble (1968).

Blumstein, S. (1970) *Phonological Implications of Aphasic Speech*, unpublished Ph.D. thesis, Harvard.

Blumstein, S. (1973a) *A Phonological Investigation of Aphasic Speech*, The Hague: Mouton.

Blumstein, S. (1973b) Some phonological implications of aphasic speech. In Goodglass and Blumstein (1973).

Blumstein, S., W. Cooper, E. Zurif, and A Caramazza (1977) The perception and production of VOT in aphasia, *Neuropsychologia*. 115, 371-83.

Boller, F. (1968) Latent aphasia: Right and left "nonaphasic" brain-damaged patients compared, *Cortex,* 4.

Boller, F., and L.A. Vignolo (1966) Latent sensory aphasia in hemisphere-damaged patients: an experimental study on the token test, *Brain,* 89.

Bradley, D. (1976) What derivational complexity won't buy you, Unpublished Ms., MIT.

Brain, R. *(1961) Speech Disorders.* Washington: Butterworth.

Bresnan, J.W. (1973) Sentence stress and syntactic transformations. In Hintikka, Moravcsik and Suppes (eds.) *Approaches to Natural Language.*

Broca, P. (1861) Remarques sur le siège de la faculté du langage articulé, suivis d'une observation d'aphémie, *Bulletin de la Societe Anatomique de Paris.*

Brown, R. W. (1970) *Psycholinguistics.* New York: The Free Press.

Carterette, E.C. (ed) (1966) *Brain Function, vol. III,* Berkeley: University of California Press.

Chase, R.A. (1967) Ictal speech automatisms and swearing, *Journal of Nervous and Mental Diseases,* 144.

Chomsky, N. (1959) Review of Skinner's *Verbal Behavior, Language,* 35.

Chomsky, N. (1965), *Aspects of the Theory of Sybtax,* Cambridge Mass.: MIT Press.

Chomsky, N. (1968*b) Language and Mind.* New York: Harcourt Brace, Jovanovich, Inc. Extended edition, 1972.

Chomsky, N. (1975) Knowledge of language. In Gunderson and Maxwell (1975).

Chomsky, N. (1976) *Reflections on Language.* New York: Pantheon Books.

Chomsky, N., and M. Halle (1968) *The Sound Pattern of English.* New York: Harper & Row, Publishers, Incorporated.

Chomsky, N., and J.J. Katz (1975) On Innateness: a reply to Cooper, *Philosophical Review,* vol. LXXXIV.

Cohen, R.S., and M. Wartofsky (eds.) (1968) *Boston Studies in the Philosophy of Science, vol. III,* Dordrecht, Holland: D. Reidel.

Conrad, K. (1954) New problems of aphasia, *Brain,* 77.

Cooper, W.E. (1976) *Syntactic Control of Timing in Speech Production,* unpublished Ph.D. thesis, MIT.

Critchley, M. (1967) Aphasiological nomenclature and definitions. *Cortex,* 3.

Critchley, M. (1973) Articulatory defects in aphasia: the problem of Broca's aphemia. In Goodglass and Blumstein (1973).

Dejerine, J. (1914) *Séméiologie des Affections du Systè me Nerveux.* Paris: Masson et Cie.

De Renzi, E., and L.A. Vignolo (1962) The token test: a sensitive test to detect disturbances in aphasics, *Brain,* 85.

Dingwall, W.O. (ed.) (1971) *A Survey of Linguistic Science*. College Park, Md.: University of Maryland.

Evarts, E.V. (1967) The output side of information processing. In Millikan and Darley (1967).

Fillenbaum, S., L.V. Jones and J.M. Wepman (1961) Some linguistic features of speech from aphasic patients, *Language and Speech*.

Flores d'Arcais, G.B., and W.J.M. Levelt (eds.) (1971) *Advances in Psycholinguistics*. Amsterdam: North-Holland Publishing Company.

Foder, J.A. (1975) *The Language of Thought*. New York: Thomas Y. Crowell Company.

Fodor, J.A., and T.G. Bever (1965) The psychological reality of linguistic segments, *Journal of Verbal Learning and Verbal Behavior*, 4.

Fodor, J.A., T.G. Bever, and M.F. Garrett (1974) *The Psychology of Language*. New York: McGraw-Hill Book Company.

Fromkin, V. (1971) The nonanomolous nature of anomolous utterances, *Language*, 47, 27-52.

Fromkin, V. (ed.) (1973) *Speech Errors as Linguistic Evidence*. The Hague: Mouton.

Fry, H. (1959) Phonemic substitution in aphasic patients, *Language and Speech*, 2.

Garrett, M.F. (1975) The analysis of sentence production. In G. Bower (ed.), *The Psychology of Learning and Motivation: Advances in Research and Theory*, vol. 9, New York: Academic Press, Inc.

Garrett, M.F. (1976) Syntactic processes in sentence production. In Walker and Wales (eds.) *New Approaches to Language Mechanisms*. Amsterdam: North-Holland Publishing Company.

Geschwind, N. (1964) Development of the brain and evolution of language. *Georgetown Monograph Series on Language and Linguistics*, 17, Washington, D.C.: Georgetown University Press.

Geschwind, N. (1965) Disconnexion syndromes in animals and man, *Brain*, 88. Reprinted in Geschwind (1974a).

Geschwind, N. (1966) Carl Wernicke, the Breslau School, and the history of aphasia. In Carterette (1966).

Geschwind, N. (1967) Brain mechanisms suggested by studies of hemispheric connections. In Millikan and Darley (1967).

Geschwind, N. (1970) The organization of language in the brain, *Science*, 170.

Geschwind, N. (1974a) *Selected Papers on Language and the Brain*, Dordrecht, Holland, D. Reidel.

Geschwind, N. (1974b) Wernicke's contribution to the Study of Aphasia. In Geschwind (1974a).

Geschwind, N. (1974c) Problems in the anatomical understanding of aphasias. In Geschwind (1974a).

Geschwind, N. (1974d) A review: *Traumatic Aphasia* by A.R. Luria. In Geschwind (1974a).

Geschwind, N., F.A. Quadfasel, and J. Segarra (1968) Isolation of the speech area, *Neuropsychologia*, 6.

Gleason, J.B., H. Goodglass, E. Green, N. Ackerman, and M. Hyde (1975) The retrieval of syntax in Broca's aphasia. *Brain and Language*, 2.

Goldstein, K. (1917) *Die transkortikalen Aphasien.* Jena: Gustav Fischer Verlag.

Goldstein, K. (1948) *Language and Language Disturbances.* New York: Grune & Stratton, Inc.

Goodenough, C., E.B. Zurif, and E. J. Weintraub (1977). The comprehension of definite and indefinite reference. *Language and Speech.* 20, 11-19.

Goodglass, H. (1973) Studies on the grammar of aphasics. In Goodglass and Blumstein (1973).

Goodlass, H., and J. Mayer (1958) Agrammatism in aphasia, *Journal of Speech and Hearing Disorders*, 23.

Goodglass, H., and J. Hunt (1958) Grammatical complexity and aphasic speech, *Word,* 14.

Goodglass, H., and J. Berko (1960) Aphasia and inflectional Morphology in English, *Speech and Hearing Research,* 3.

Goodglass, H., C. Quadfasel, and W.H. Timberlake (1964) Phrase length and the type and severity of aphasic disturbances, *Cortex,* 3.

Goodglass, H., I.G. Fodor, and C. Schulhoff (1967) Prosodic features in grammar-evidence from aphasia, *Speech and Hearing Research,* 10.

Goodglass, H., and M. Hunter (1970) A linguistic comparison of speech and writing in two types of aphasia, *Communications Disorders*, 3.

Goodglass, H., J.B. Gleason, N.A. Bernholz, and M.R. Hyde (1972) Some linguistic structures in the speech of a Broca's aphasic, *Cortex,* 8.

Goodglass, H., and E. Kaplan (1972) *The Assessment of Aphasia and Related Disorders.* Philadelphia: Lea & Febiger.

Goodglass, H., and S. Blumstein (eds.) (1973) *Psycholinguistics and Aphasia.* Baltimore: The Johns Hopkins Press.

Green, E. (1969) Psycholinguistic approaches to aphasia, *Linguistics,* 53.

Green, E. (1970) On the contribution of studies of aphasia to psycholinguistics, *Cortex,* 6.

Green, J.B., and W.J. Hamilton (1975) Is anosognosia for hemiplegia a disconnection syndrome? Paper presented at the 27th annual meeting of the American Academy of Neurology.

Gribble, C. (ed.) (1968) *Studies Presented to Professor R. Jakobson by His Students.* Cambridge, Mass.: Slavica.

Gunderson, K., and G. Maxwell (eds.) (1975) *Minnesota Studies in Philosophy of Science,* vol. VI.

Gutman, E. (1942) Aphasia in children, *Brain,* 65.

Halle, M. (1959) *The Sound Pattern of Russian.* The Hague: Mouton.

Halle, M., and S. J. Keyser (1975) Sur les bases théoreques de la poésie métrique. In J.P. Faye (ed.) *Change de Forme, 1,* Collection 10-18, Union generale d'editions, Paris.

Hankamer, J., and J. Aissen (1974) The sonority hierarchy, Chicago Linguistics Society, 10.

Head, H. (1963) *Aphasia and Kindred Disorders of Speech,* vols. I and II. New York: Hafner Publishing Company, Inc.

Hécaen, H., and R. Angelegues (1965) *Pathologie du Langage.* Paris: Librairie Larousse.

Hécaen, H., and S. Consoli (1973) Analyse des troubles du langage au cours des lesions de l'aire de broca, *Neuropsychologia,* 11.

Hintikka, J., J.M.E. Moravcsik, and P. Suppes (eds.) (1973) *Approaches to Natural Language,* Dordrecht: Reidel Publishing Co.

Howes, D. (1964) Applications of the word frequency concept to aphasia. In de Reuck and O'Connor (1964).

Howes, D., and N. Geschwind (1964) Quantitative studies of aphasic language. In Rioch and Weinstein (1964).

Jackson, J.H. (1958) *Selected Writings,* vol. II., J. Taylor (ed.) New York: Basic Books.

Jakobson, R. (1964) Towards a linguistic typology of aphasic impairments. In de Reuck and O'Connor (1964).

Jakobson, R. (1966) Linguistic types of aphasia. In Carterette (1966).

Jakobson, R. (1968) *Child Language, Aphasia, and Phonological Universals,* A.R. Keiler, trans. The Hague: Mouton.

Jakobson, R. (1973) Towards a linguistic classification of aphasic impairments. In Goodglass and Blumstein (1973).

Jakobson, R., and M. Halle (1956) *Fundamentals of Language.* The Hague: Mouton.

Jeffress, L.A. (ed.) (1951) *Cerebral Mechanisms in Behavior.* New York: John Wiley & Sons, Inc.

Joynt, R. (1964) Paul Pierre Broca: his contribution to the knowledge of aphasia, *Cortex,* 1.

Kehoe, W.J., and H.A. Whitaker (1973) Lexical Structure Disruption in Aphasia. In Goodglass and Blumstein (1973).

Kerschenteiner, M., K. Poeck, and E. Brunner (1972) The fluency-nonfluency dimension in aphasia, *Cortex,* 8.

Lashley, K.S. (1951) The problem of serial order in behavior. In Jeffress (1951).

Lecours, A.R. and F. Lhermitte (1969) Phonemic paraphasias: linguistic structures and tentative hypotheses, *Cortex,* 5. Reprinted in Goodglass and Blumstein (1973).

Lenneberg, E. (1967) *Biological Foundations of Language.* New York: John Wiley & Sons, Inc.

Lesser, R. (1974) Verbal comprehension in aphasia: an English version of three Italian tests, *Cortex,* 10.

Lhermitte, F., A.R. Lecours, B. Ducarne, and R. Escourolle (1973) Unexpected anatomical findings in a case of fluent jargon aphasia, *Cortex*, 9.

Locke, S., D. Caplan, and M. Kellar (1973) *A Study in Neurolinguistics*, Springfield, Ill.: Charles C. Thomas, Publisher.

Luria, A.R. (1958) Brain disorders and language analysis, *Language and Speech*, 1.

Luria, A.R. (1966) Neuropsychology in the local diagnosis of brain damage, *Cortex*, 1.

Luria, A.R. (1966) *Higher Cortical Functions in Man*. New York: Basic Books.

Luria, A.R. (1966) *Human Brain and Psychological Processes*. New York: Harper & Row, Publishers, Incorporated.

Luria, A.R. (1970) *Traumatic Aphasia*. The Hague: Mouton.

Marie, P. (1906) La troisième circonvolution frontale gauche ne joue aucun role special dans la fonction du language, *Sem Méd Par*, 26.

Meyer, A. (1974) Frontal lobe syndromes, the aphasias and related conditions, *Brain*, 97.

Meyerson, R., and H. Goodglass (1972) Transformational grammar of three agrammatic patients, *Language and Speech*, 15.

Millikan, C.H., and F.L. Darley (eds.) (1967) *Brain Mechanisms Underlying Speech and Language*. New York: Grune & Stratton, Inc.

Mohr, J.P. (1975) Broca's Area and Broca's Aphasia. In Whitaker and Whitaker (eds.) *Studies in Neurolinguistics*.

Nielson, J.M. (1936) *Agnosia, Apraxia and Aphasia*. New York: Paul B. Hoeber, Inc.

Noll, J.D., and W. Berry (1969) Some thoughts on the Token Test, *Indiana Speech and Hearing Associations* 27.

Orgass, B., and K. Poeck (1966) Clinical evaluation of a new test for aphasia: an experimental study on the Token Test, *Cortex*, 2.

Osgood, C.E., and M.S. Miron (eds.) (1963) *Approaches to the Study of Aphasia*. Urbana: University of Illinois.

Parisi, D., and L. Pizzamiglio (1970) Syntactic comprehension in aphasia, *Cortex*, 6.

Penfield, W., and L. Roberts (1959) *Speech and Brain Mechanisms*, Princeton, N.J.: Princeton University Press.

Pick, A. (1913) *Die agrammatischen Sprachstörungen*. Berlin: Springer-Verlag OHG.

Pizzamiglio, L., and D. Parisi (1970) Studies on verbal comprehension in aphasia. In G.B. Flores D'Arcais and W.J.M. Levelt (1971).

Pizzamiglio, L., and A. Appicciafuoco (1967) Test a scelta multipla per la valutazione dei disturbi di comprehensione negli afasici. *Archivio Psicologia Neurologia Psichiatria*, 6.

Poeck, J., M. Kerochenstuner, and W. Hargje (1972) A quantitative study on language understanding in fluent and nonfluent aphasia, *Cortex*, 8.

de Reuck, A.V.S., and M. O'Connor (eds.) (1964) *Disorders of Language*. London: Churchill.

Rioch, D.M., and E.A. Weinstein (eds.) (1964) *Disorders of Communication,* Baltimore: The Williams & Wilkins Company.

Roberts, L. (1966) Central brain mechanisms in speech. In Carterette (1966).

Russell, W.R., and M.L.E. Espir (1961) *Traumatic Aphasia.* London: Oxford University Press.

Sasanuma, S., and O. Fujimura (1971) Selective impairment of processing phonetic and non-phonetic transcriptions of words in aphasic patients: kana and kanji in visual recognition and writing, *Cortex,* 7, 196-218.

Sasanuma, S., and O. Fujimura (1972) An analysis of writing errors in Japanese aphasic patients: kanji versus kana words, *Cortex,* 8, 265-282.

de Saussure, F. (1966) *Course in General Linguistics.* New York: McGraw-Hill Book Company.

Schnitzer, M. (1972) *Generative Phonology—Evidence from Aphasia.* State College, Pa.: Pennsylvania State University.

Schnitzer, M. (1974) Aphasiological evidence for five linguistic hypotheses, *Language,* 50.

Schuell, H., J.J. Jenkins and E. Jimenez-Pabon (1964) *Aphasia in Adults* New York: Harper & Row, Publishers, Incorporated.

Selkirk, E.O. (1972) *The Phrase Phonology of English and French,* unpublished Ph.D. thesis, MIT.

Shankweiler, D., and K.S. Harris (1973) An experimental approach to the problem of articulation in aphasia. In Goodglass and Blumstein (1973).

Shewan, C.M., and G.J. Canter (1971) Effects of vocabulary, syntax, and sentence length on auditory comprehension in aphasic patients, *Cortex,* 7.

Swisher, L.P., and M.T. Sarno (1969) Token Test scores of three matched patient groups: left brain-damaged with aphasia, right brain-damaged without aphasia, non-brain-damaged, *Cortex,* 5.

Vignolo, L. (1964) Evolution of aphasia and language rehabilitation: a retrospective exploratory study, *Cortex,* 1.

von Stockert, T.R. (1972) Recognition of syntactic structure in aphasic patients, *Cortex,* 8.

de Villiers, J. (1974) Quantitative aspects of agrammatism in aphasia, *Cortex,* 10.

Wagenaar, E., C. Snow, and R. Prins (1975) Spontaneous speech of aphasic patients: a psycholinguistic analysis, *Brain and Language,* 2.

Weigl, E., and M. Bierwisch (1970) Neuropsychology and linguistics: topics of common research, *Foundations of Language,* 6.

Weisenberg, T.S. and K.L. McBride (1964) *Aphasia.* New York: Hafner Publishing Company, Inc.

Wepman, J.M., and L.V. Jones (1964) Five aphasics: a commentary on aphasia as a regressive linguistic phenomenon. In Rioch and Weinstein (1964).

Wernicke, C. (1874) *Der aphasiche Symptomencomplex: Eine psycho-logische Studie auf anatomischer Basis.* Breslau: Cohen & Weigert.

Wernicke, C. (1881) *Lehrbuch der Gehirnkrankheiten.* Berlin: Fischer.

Whitaker, H.A. (1970) Linguistic competence: evidence from aphasia, *Glossa,* 4.

Whitaker, H.A. (1971) *On the Representation of Language in the Human Mind.* Edmonton: Linguistic Research.

Whitaker, H.A. (1971) Neurolinguistics. In Dingwall (1971).

Whitaker, H.A., and J.D. Noll (1972) Some linguistic parameters of the token test, *Neuropsychologia,* 10.

Whitaker, H., and H.A. Whitaker (eds.) (1976) *Studies in Neuro-linguistics.* New York: Academic Press, Inc.

Zurif, E., and S. Blumstein (1976) Language and the brain: evidence from aphasia. Paper presented at the Convocation on Communication in celebration of the Centennial of the Telephone, MIT.

Zurif, E., A. Caramazza, and R. Meyerson (1972) Grammatical judgments of agrammatic aphasics, *Neuropsychologia,* 10.

Zurif, E., and A. Caramazza (1976) Psycholinguistic structures in aphasia: studies in syntax and semantics. In Whitaker and Whitaker (eds.) *Studies in Neurolinguistcs.*

Chapter 3

Amey, T.J. (1973) Perceptual factors in word recognition, unpublished thesis, Psychology Department, Monash University.

Bednall, E.S. (1976) The interaction of frequency and semantic related-ness in lexical access, unpublished paper, Monash University.

Bower, T.G.R. (1970) Reading by eye, in H. Levin and J.P. Williams (eds.) *Basic Studies on Reading.* New York: Basic Books.

Bradley, D. (1976) Lexical representations of related word forms, un-published paper, Massachusetts Institute of Technology.

Bradshaw, J.L. (1975) Three interrelated problems in reading: a review, *Memory and Cognition,* 3, 123-134.

Brown, J.W. (1972) *Aphasia, Apraxia and Agnosia: Clinical and Theoretical Aspects.* Springfield, Ill.: Charles C. Thomas, Publisher.

Brown, R.W., and D. McNeill (1966) The tip of the tongue phonomenon, *Journal of Verbal Learning and Verbal Behavior,* 5, 325-327.

Chambers, S.M. (1974) Word similarity and interference in lexical decision tasks, paper read at the First Experimental Psychology Conference, Monash University.

Chambers, S.M., and K.I. Forster (1975) Evidence for lexical access in a simultaneous matching task, *Memory and Cognition,* 3, 549-559.

Chomsky, N. (1970) Remarks on nominalization in R.A. Jacobs and P.S. Rosenbaum (eds.) *Readings in English Transformational Grammar.* Boston: Ginn and Company.

Coltheart, M., E. Davelaar, J.T. Jonasson, and D. Besner (1976) Access to the internal lexicon, paper presented at Attention and Performance VI, Stockholm.

Fay, D., and A. Cutler (1976) Malapropisms and the structure of the mental lexicon. *Linguistic Inquiry.* 8, 505-520.

Forster, K.I. (1976) Accessing the mental lexicon. In Walker and Wales (eds.) (1976).

Forster, K.I., and E.S. Bednall (1976) Terminating and exhaustive search in lexical access, *Memory and Cognition,* 4, 53-61.

Forster, K.I., and S.M. Chambers (1973) Lexical access and naming time. *Journal of Verbal Learning and Verbal Behavior,* 12, 627-635.

Frederichson, J.R., and J.F. Kroll (1974) Phonemic recoding and lexical search in the perception of letter arrays, paper presented at Psychonomic Society, Boston.

Garrett, M.F. (1976) Syntactic processes in sentence production. In Walker and Wales (1976).

Marshall, J.C., and F. Newcombe (1966) Syntactic and semantic errors in paralexia. *Neuropsychologia,* 4, 169-176.

Meyer, D.E., and R.W. Schvaneveldt (1971) Facilitation in recognizing pairs of words: evidence of a dependence between retrieval operations, *Journal of Experimental Psychology,* 90, 227-234.

Meyer, D.E., and R.W. Schvaneveldt (1976) Meaning, memory, structures, and mental processes, *Science,* 192, 27-33.

Morton, J. (1970) A functional model of human memory. In D.A. Norman (ed.) *Models of Human Memory.* New York: Academic Press, Inc.

Novik, N. (1974) Parallel processing in a word-nonword classification task, *Journal of Experimental Psychology,* 102, no. 6, 1015-1020.

O'Connor, R.E. (1975) An investigation into the word frequency effect, unpublished honors thesis, Monash University.

Oldfield, R.C., and A. Wingfield (1965) Response latencies in naming objects, *Quarterly Journal of Experimental Psychology,* 17, 273-281.

Potter, M.C. (in preparation) Mental comparison: images and meanings.

Potter, M.C., and B.A. Faulconer (1975) Time to understand and words, *Nature,* 253, 437-438.

Rinnert, C. and H.A. Whitaker (1973) Semantic Confusions by aphasic patients, *Cortex,* 9, 56-81.

Rubenstein, H., L. Garfield, and J.A. Millikan (1970) Homographic entries in the internal lexicon, *Journal of Verbal Learning and Verbal Behavior,* 9, 487-492.

Rubenstein, H., S.S. Lewis, and M.A. Rubenstein (1971) Evidence for phonemic recoding in visual word recognition. *Journal of Verbal Learning and Verbal Behavior,* 10, 645-757.

Selfridge, O.G., and U. Neisser (1960) Pattern recognition by machine, *Scientific American,* 203, 60-68.

Stanners, R.F., and G.B. Forbach (1973) Analysis of letter strings in word recognition, *Journal of Experimental Psychology,* 98, 31-35.

Taft, M. (1973) Detecting homophony of misspelled words, unpublished paper, Monash University.

Taft, M., and K.I. Forster (1975) Lexical storage and retrieval of prefixed words, *Journal of Verbal Learning and Verbal Behavior,* 14, 638-647.

Taft, M., and K.I. Forster (1975) Lexical storage and retrieval of polymorphemic and polysyllabic words, *Journal of Verbal Learning and Verbal Behavior.* 14, 638-647.

Walker, E., and R. Wales (eds.) (1976) *New Approaches to Language Mechanisms.* Amsterdam: North-Holland Publishing Company.

Weigl, E., and M. Bierwisch (1970) Neuropsychology and linguistics: topics of common research, *Foundations of Language,* 6, 1-18.

Chapter 4

Bahrick, H.P., P.O. Bahrick, and R.P. Wittlinger (1975) Fifty years of memory for names and faces: A cross-sectional approach, *Journal of Experimental Psychology,* 104, 54-75.

Benton, A., and M.W. Van Allen (1968) Impairment in facial recognition in patients with cerebral disease, *Cortex,* 4, 344-358.

Benton, A.L., and M.W. Van Allen (1973) *Manual: Test of Racial Recognition.* Iowa City, Iowa: Department of Neurology, University Hospitals.

Bower, G.H., and M.B. Karlin (1974) Depth of processing pictures of faces and recognition memory. *Journal of Experimental Psychology,* 103, 751-757.

Bradshaw, J.L., and G. Wallace (1971) Models for the processing and identification of faces, *Perception and Psychophysics,* 9, 443-447.

Carey, S., R. Diamond, and B. Woods (in press) The development of face perception—a maturational component? *Neuropsychologia.*

Duda, R.O., and P.E. Hart (1973) *Pattern Classification and Scene Analysis.* New York: John Wiley & Sons, Inc.

Ellis, H.E., and J.W. Shepherd (1975) Recognition of upright and inverted faces presented in the left and right visual fields, *Cortex,* 11, 3-7.

Fish, D. (1976) Faces and landscapes: right-side up and upsidedown, Working paper, MIT.

Fontenot, D.J. (1973) Visual field differences in the recognition of verbal and nonverbal stimuli in man, *Journal of Comparative and Physiological Psychology,* 85, 564-569.

Gaffen, G., J.L. Bradshaw, and G. Wallace (1971) Interhemispheric effects on reaction times to verbal and non-verbal stimuli, *Journal of Experimental Psychology,* 87, 415-422.

Galper, R.E. (1970) Recognition of faces in photographic negative, *Psychonomic Science*, 19, 207-208.

Goldman, P.S. (1972) Developmental determinants of cortical plasticity, *Acta Neurobiologiae Experimentalis*, 32, 495-511.

Goldman, P.S., H.T. Crawford, L.P. Stokes, T. Galhin, and H.E. Rosvold (1974) Sex-dependent behavioral effects of cerebral cortical lesions in the developing Rhesus monkey, *Science*, 186, 540-542.

Goldstein, A.G. (1975) Recognition of inverted photographs of faces by children and adults, *Journal of Genetic Psychology*, 127, 109-123.

Gross, M.M. (1972) Hemispheric specialization for processing of visually presented verbal and spatial stimuli, *Perception and Psychophysics*, 12, 357-363.

Hilliard, R.D. (1973) Hemispheric laterality effects on a facial recognition task in normal subjects, *Cortex*, 9, 246-258.

Hochberg, J., and R.E. Galper (1967) Recognition of faces: an exploratory study, *Psychonomic Science*, 9, 619-620.

Hubel, D.H., and T.N. Wiesel (1962) Receptive fields, binocular interaction, and functional architecture in the cat's visual cortex, *Journal of Physiology*, 160, 106-154.

Hubel, D.H., and T.N. Wiesel (1970) The period of susceptibility to the physiological effects of unilateral eye closure in kittens, *Journal of Physiology*, 206, 419-436.

Kimura, D. (1963) Right temporal lobe damage, *Archives of Neurology*, 8, 264-271.

Kimura, D. (1969) Spatial localization in left and right visual fields, *Canadian Journal of Psychology*, 23, 445-458.

Klein, D., M. Moscovitch, and C. Vigna (1976) Perceptual asymmetrics and attentional mechanisms in tachistoscopic recognition of words and faces, *Neuropsychologia*, 14, 44-66.

Kohn, B., and M. Dennis (1974) Selective impairments of visuospatial abilities in infantile hemiplegics after right cerebral hemidecortication, *Neuropsychologia*, 12, 505-512.

Leehey, S. (1976) Face recognition in children: Evidence for the development of right hemisphere specialization, unpublished doctoral dissertation, MIT.

Leehey, S., S. Carey, R. Diamond, and A. Cahn (in press) Upright and inverted faces: The right hemisphere knows the difference, *Cortex*.

Lévy-Schoen, A. (1964) L'Image d'Autrui chez L'Enfant, Publications de la Faculté des lettres et Sciences Humaines de Paris. Série. Recherches, tome XXIII. Paris: Presses Universitaires de France.

Meadows, J.C. (1974) The anatomical basis of prosopagnosia, *Journal of Neurology, Neurosurgery and Psychiatry*, 37, 489-501.

Rizzolatti, G., C. Umilta, and G. Berlucchi (1971) Opposite superiorities of the right and left cerebral hemispheres in discriminative reaction time to physiognomic and alphabetical material, *Brain*, 94, 431-442.

Robertshaw, S., and M. Sheldon (1976) Laterality effects in judgment of the identity and position of letters: a signal detection analysis *Quarterly Journal of Experimental Psychology,* 28, 115-121.

Rock, I. (1974) The perception of disoriented figures, *Scientific American,* 230, 78-85.

Rudel, R.G., M.B. Denckla, and E. Spalten (1974) The functional asymmetry of Braille letter learning in normal, sighted children, *Neurology,* 24, 733-738.

Scapinello, K.F., and A.D. Yarmey (1970) The role of familiarity and orientation in immediate and delayed recognition of pictorial stimuli, *Psychonomic Science* 21(6), 329-331.

Schneider, G.E. (1973) Early lesions of superior colliculus: factors affecting the formation of abnormal retinal projections, *Brain, Behavior and Evolution,* 8, 73-109.

Shepherd, J.W., J.B. Deregowski and H.D. Ellis (1974) A cross-cultural study of recognition memory for faces, *International Journal of Psychology,* 9, 205-212.

Spencer, M.A., R.F. Thompson, and D.R. Neilson, Jr. (1966) Alternations in responsiveness of ascending and reflex pathways activated by iterated cutaneous afferent volleys, *Journal of Neurophysiology,* 29, 240-252.

Wall, P.D. (1975) Signs of plasticity and reconnection in spinal cord damage. In CIBA Foundation Symposium 34 (new series) *Outcome of Severe Damage to the Central Nervous System,* New York: Elsevier, pp. 54-64.

Woods, B.T., and H.L. Teuber (1973) Early onset of specialization of cerebral hemispheres in man, *Transactions of the American Neurological Association,* 98, 113-115.

Woods, B., and H.L. Teuber (in preparation) Changing patterns of childhood aphasia.

Yarmey, A.D. (1971) Recognition memory for familiar "public" faces: effects of orientation and delay, *Psychonomic Science,* 24, 286-288.

Yin, R.K. (1969) Looking at upside-down faces, *Journal of Experimental Psychology,* 81, 141-145.

Yin, R. (1970) Face recognition by brain injured patients: a dissociable ability? *Neuropsychologia,* 8, 395-402.

Chapter 5

Alison, J. (1972) *The Evolution of Primate Behavior.* New York: The Macmillian Company.

Bellugi, U., and E. Klima (1975) Aspects of sign language and its structure. In Kavanagh and Cutting (1975).

Brown, R. (1970) The first sentence of child and chimpanzee, *Psycholinguistics,* Cambridge Mass: The Free Press

Brown, R. (1973) *A First Language: The Early Stages.* Cambridge, Mass.: Harvard University Press.

Burdick, C., and J. Miller (1975) Speech perception by the Chinchilla: discrimination of sustained /a/ and /i/, *Journal of the Acoustical Society of America,* 58, no. 2.

Chase, R.A. (1966) Evolutionary aspects of language development and function. In Smith and Miller, *The Genesis of Language.*

Darley, F.L. (ed.) (1967) *Brain Mechanisms Underlying Speech and Language.* New York: Grune & Stratton, Inc.

Evans, W.F. (1968) *Communication in the Animal World.* New York: Thomas Y. Crowell Company.

Fleming, J.D. (1974) Field report: the state of the apes, *Psychology Today,* 7, no. 8.

Fleming, J.D. (1974) The Lucy and Roger talk show, *Psychology Today,* 7, no. 8.

Fodor, J.A., T. Bever, and M. Garrett (1974) *The Psychology of Language.* New York: McGraw-Hill Book Company.

Fodor, J.A., M. Garrett, and S. Brill (1975) Pi-ka-pu: the perception of speech sounds by prelinguistic infants, *Perception and Psychophysics,* 18, no. 2.

Frings, H., and M. Frings (1964) *Animal Communication.* New York: Blaisdell Publishing Company.

Gardner, B., and R.A. Gardner (1971) Two-way communication with an infant chimpanzee. In Schrier and Stollnitz, *Behavior of Nonhuman Primates.*

Gardner, R.A., and B. Gardner (1969) Teaching sign language to a chimpanzee, *Science,* 165, 664-672.

Glass, A.V., M.S. Gazzaniga, and D. Premack (1973) Artificial language training in global aphasics, *Neuropsychologia,* 11, 95-103.

Hayes, K., and C. Nissen (1971) Higher mental functions of a home-raised chimpanzee. In Schrier and Stollnitz, *Behavior of Nonhuman Primates.*

Kalmus, H. (1966) Ontogenetic, genetical, and phylogenetic parallels between animal communication and prelinguistic child behavior. In Smith and Miller, *The Genesis of Language.*

Kavanagh, J., and J. Cutting (1975) *The Role of Speech in Language.* Cambridge, Mass.: MIT Press.

Kuhl, P., and J. Miller (1975) Speech perception by the Chinchilla: voiced-voiceless distinction in alveolar plosive consonants, *Science,* 190, 69-72.

Lenneberg, E.H. (1966) The natural history of language. In Smith and Miller, *The Genesis of Language.*

Lenneberg, E. (1967) *Biological Foundations of Language.* New York: John Wiley & Sons, Inc.

Lenneberg, E. (1968) Language in the light of evolution. In Sebeok, *Animal Communication.*

Lenneberg, E. (ed.) (1974) Language and Brain: Developmental Aspects, *Neurosciences Research Program Bulletin*, 12, no. 4.

Lilly, J.C. (1961) *Man and Dolphin: Adventures on a New Scientific Frontier.* New York: Doubleday & Company, Inc.

Lilly, J.C. (1967) *The Mind of the Dolphin.* New York: Doubleday & Company, Inc.

Limber, J. (1977) Language in child and chimp. *American Psychologist,* 32.4, 280-294.

Linden, E. (1974) *Apes, Men, and Language.* Baltimore: Penguin Books, Inc.

Marler, P. (1975) On the origin of speech from animal sounds. In Kavanagh and Cutting (1975).

Ploog, D., and T. Melnechuk (1969) Primate communication, *Neurosciences Research Program Bulletin,* 7, no. 5.

Ploog, D., and T. Melnechuk (1971) Are apes capable of language? *Neurosciences Research Program Bulletin,* Vol. 9, no. 5.

Premack, A.J. (1976) *Why Chimps Can Read,* New York: Harper & Row.

Premack, A., and D. Premack (1972) Teaching language to an ape. *Scientific American,* vol. 227, no. 4, pp. 92-99.

Premack, D. (1971) On the assessment of language competence in the chimpanzee. In Schrier and Stollnitz, *Behavior in Nonhuman Primates.*

Premack, D. (1972) Language in chimpanzee? *Science,* vol. 172, pp. 808-822, May 21, 1971.

Premack, D. (1975) Symbols inside and outside of language. In Kavanagh and Cutting, *The Role of Speech in Language.*

Premack, D., and A. Schwartz (1966) Preparations for discussing behaviorism with chimpanzee. In Smith and Miller, *The Genesis of Language.*

Rumbaugh, D., and T. Gill (1973) Reading and sentence completion by a chimpanzee (Pan). *Science,* vol. 182, pp. 731-33.

Rumbaugh, Duane M. (1974) Lana learns language. *Yerkes Newsletter,* vol. 11, no. 1, Yerkes Regional Primate Research Center.

Schrier, A., and F. Stollnitz (eds.) (1971) *Behavior of Non-Human Primates: Research Trends,* vol. 4, New York: Academic Press.

Sebeok, T. (ed.) (1968) *Animal Communication: Techniques of Study and Results of Research,* Indiana University.

Smith, F., and G. Miller (eds.) (1966) *The Genesis of Language,* Cambridge, Mass.: MIT Press.

Wilson, E.O. (1971) *The Insect Societies,* Harvard University.

Worden, F.G., and R. Gamambos (1972) Auditory processing of biologically significant sounds. *Neurosciences Research Program Bulletin,* vol. 10, no. 1.

Appendix

Basser, L.S. (1962) Hemiplegia of each onset and the faculty of speech with special reference to the effect of hemispherectomy, *Brain*, 85, 427-460.

Bergman, P.S., and M. Crech (1951) Aphasia: effect of intravenous sodium amytal, *Neurology*, 1, 471-475, November—December.

Berlin, C., S.S. Lowe-Bell, J.K. Cullen, C.L. Thompson, and M.R. Stafford (1972*a*) Is speech "special"? Perhaps the temporal lobectomy patient can tell us, *Journal of the Acoustical Society of America*, 52:2:2, 702-705.

Berlin, C., S.S. Lowe-Bell, P.J. Jannetta, and D.G. Kline (1972*b*) Central auditory deficits after temporal lobectomy, *Archives of Otolaryngology*, 96, 4-10.

Berlin, C.I., J.K. Cullen, S.S. Lowe-Bell, and H.L. Berlin (1974) Speech Perception after Hemispherectomy and Temporal Lobectomy. Speech Communication Seminar, Stockholm, Aug. 1-3.

Blumstein, S., and W.E. Cooper (1974) Hemispheric processing of intonation contours, *Cortex*, 10, no. 2, 146-158.

Cohen, B.D., C.D. Noblin, and A.J. Silverman (1968) Functional asymmetry of the human brain, *Science*, 162, 475-477.

Cohn, Robert (1971) Differential cerebral processing of noise and verbal stimuli, *Science*, 172, 599-601.

Cullen, J.K., Jr., C.L. Thompson, L.F. Hughes, C.I. Berlin and D.S. Samson (1974) The effects of varied acoustic parameters on performance in dichotic speech perception tasks, *Brain and Language*, 1, 307-322.

Curry, Frederick (1967) A comparison of left-handed and right-handed subjects on verbal and non-verbal dichotic listening tasks, *Cortex*, 3, 343-352.

Cutting, J.E. (1974) Different speech-processing mechanisms can be reflected in the results of discrimination and dichotic listening tasks, *Brain and Language*, 1, 363-374.

Dennis, M., and H.A. Whitaker (1976) Language acquisition following hemidecorticates: linguistic superiority of the left over the right hemisphere, *Brain and Language*, 3, no. 3.

Gardner, W., L.J. Karnosh, C. McClure, and A.K. Gardner (1965) Residual function following hemispherectomy for tumor and for infantile hemiplegia, *Brain*, 78, 487-502.

Gazzaniga, M.S. (1970) *The Bisected Brain*. New York: Appleton Century Crofts.

Geschwind, Norman (1965) Disconnection syndromes in animals and man (part I), *Brain*, 88, part II, 237-294.

Godfrey, J.J. (1974) Perceptual difficulty and the right ear advantage for vowels, *Brain and Language*, 1, 323-336.

Gordon, Harold (1970) Hemispheric asymmetries in the perception of musical chords, *Cortex,* 6.4, 387-398.

Haggard, Mark, and A. Parkinson (1971) Stimulus and task factors as determinants of ear advantage, *Quarterly Journal of Experimental Psychology,* 23, 168-177.

Kiloh, L.G., A.J. McCumas, J.W. Osselton (1972) *Clinical Electroencephalography.* London: Appleton Century Crofts.

Kimura, Doreen (1961a) Cerebral dominance and the perception of verbal stimuli, *Canadian Journal of Psychology,* 15.3, 166-171.

Kimura, Doreen (1961b) Some effects of temporal-lobe damage on auditory perception, *Canadian Journal of Psychology,* 15, 156-165.

Kimura, Doreen (1964) Left-right differences in the perception of melodies, *Quarterly Journal of Experimental Psychology,* 17, 355-358.

King, F.L., and Doreen Kimura (1972) Left-ear superiority in dichotic perception of nonverbal sounds, *Canadian Journal of Psychology,* 26.2, 111-116.

Kinsbourne, Marcel (1971) The minor cerebral hemisphere as a source of aphasic speech, *Archives of Neurology,* 25, 302-306.

Linn, L. (1947) Sodium amytal in treatment of aphasia, *Archives of Neurology and Psychology,* 58, 357-358.

McAdam, D.W., and H.A. Whitaker (1971) Language production: Electroencephalographic localization in the normal human brain, *Science,* 172, 499-502.

Matsumiya, Y., et al. (1972) Auditory evoked response: Meaningfulness of stimuli and interhemispheric asymmetry, *Science,* 175, 790-792.

Milner, B., S. Taylor, and R.W. Sperry (1968) Lateralized supression of dichotically presented digits after commissural section in man, *Science,* 161, 184-185.

Molfese, D.L. (1972) Cerebral Asymmetry in Infants, Children, and Adults: Auditory Evoked Responses to Speech and Noise Stimuli. An Abstract of a Psychology Thesis. Pennsylvania State University.

Morrell, L.K., and D.A. Huntington (1971) Electrocortial localization of language production, *Science,* 174, 1359-1360.

Morrell, L.K., and J.G. Balamy (1971) Hemispheric asymmetry of electrocortical responses to speech stimuli, *Science,* 174, 164-166.

Oscar-Berman, M., E.B. Zurif, and S. Blumstein (1975) Effects of unilateral brain damage on the processing of speech sounds, *Brain and Language,* 2, 345-355.

Penfield, W., and L. Roberts (1959) *Speech and Brain Mechanisms.* Princeton, N.J.: Princeton University Press.

Smith, Aaron (1966) Speech and other functions after left (dominant) hemispherectomy, *Journal of Neurology, Neurosurgery, and Psychiatry,* 29, 467-471.

Library of Congress Cataloging in Publication Data

Massachusetts Institute of Technology Work Group in
   the Biology of Language.
   Explorations in the biology of language.

   (Series in higher mental processes)
   Bibliography: p.
   1. Biolinguistics.   2. Brain—Localization of functions.
3. Aphasia. I. Walker, Edward, 1942-II. Title. III. Title:
The biology of language. IV. Series.
P132.M3 1978
ISBN 0-89706-000-8   410   78-18532

Designed by Mary Mendell

Typeset by A & B Typesetters, Inc., Concord, New Hampshire
Printed and bound by Alpine Press, Inc., South Braintree, Massachusetts
Artwork by Laura Maine, Deering, New Hampshire

Smith, Aaron (1972)   Dominant and nondominant hemispherectomy. In W.L. Smith (ed.) *Drugs, Development and Cerebral Function.* Springfield, Ill.: Charles C Thomas.
Sparks, Robert, and Norman Geschwind (1968)   Dichotic listening in man after section of neocortical commissures, *Cortex,* 4, 3-16.
Sparks, Robert, Harold Goodglass, and B. Nickel (1970)   Ipsilateral versus contralateral extinction in dichotic listening resulting from hemispheric lesions, *Cortex,* 6, 249-260.
Sperry, R.W. (1961)   Cerebral organization and behavior, *Science,* 133, 1749.
Sperry, R.W. (1968)   Hemisphere disconnection and unity in conscious awareness, *American Psychologist,* 23, 723-733.
Studdert-Kennedy, M., and D.P. Shankweiler (1970)   Hemispheric specialization for speech perception, *Journal of the Acoustical Society of America,* 48, 579-594.
Wada, J., and T. Rasmussen (1960)   Intracarotid injection of sodium amytal for the lateralization of cerebral speech dominance: Experimental and clinical observations, *Journal of Neurosurgery* 17, 266-282.
Weigel, R., and M. Bierwisch (1970)   Neuropsychology and Linguistics: topics of common research, *Foundations of Language,* 6, 1-18.
Weiss, M.S., and A.S. House (1973)   Perception of dichotically presented vowels, *Journal of the Acoustical Society of America,* 53, 51-58.
Wood, C.C., W.R. Goff, and R.S. Day (1971)   Auditory evoked potentials during speech perception, *Science,* 173, 1248-1251.
Zaidel, E. (1975)   The right hemisphere has something to say after all, *Psychology Today,* 21.
Zurif, E.B., and P.E. Sait (1970)   The role of syntax in dichotic listening, *Neuropsychologia,* 8, 239-344.
Zurif, E.B. (1974) Auditory-lateralization: prosodic and syntactic factors, *Brain and Language,* 1, 391-404.